Gerald M. Costello

WITHOUT FEAR OR FAVOR

George Higgins on the Record

TWENTY-THIRD PUBLICATIONS
Mystic, Connecticut

DEDICATION

To three teachers who were special to me:

The late Frank O'Malley of the University
of Notre Dame, Father Joseph Fitzpatrick,
S.J., and the late Edward A.Walsh, both of
Fordham University. . .

And to all those men and women who make
a positive change in the lives of the students
they teach.

LK 11-21-86

FOREWORD

GERALD M. COSTELLO'S EXCELLENT BIOGRAPHY OF A REMARKABLE priest, Msgr. George C. Higgins, calls to mind an old Jewish legend. The legend traces back to the prophet Isaiah, revealing that in every age there are thirty-six truly just people in the world. According to this tradition, if just one of them is lacking, human suffering multiplies.

If it seems strange that a review of a book about a Catholic cleric begins with a Jewish legend, it should be recalled (as the author recounts) that Msgr. Higgins has been an ecumenical priest long before ecumenism became a popular word and policy.

Father Higgins's lifetime career, in the service of God and humanity, proves the essential truth of this legend. Absent Msgr. Higgins and his outstanding contributions from a just society and the sufferings of humankind would, indeed, multiply.

Mr. Costello recounts in absorbing detail how Father Higgins, from the time of his ordination, has been a champion against the evils that afflict humanity: discrimination, abridgement of the rights of wage earners, poverty, anti-Semitism, intolerance, violation of human rights, and war. He has confronted these monstrous injustices forthrightly with the humility that should be, but not always is, the earmark of a devout minister of religion, of whatever persuasion.

Mr. Costello's biography demonstrates that Father Higgins is cast in the same mold as Pope John and Cardinal Bea, of blessed memory. There can be no greater or more deserving praise.

Despite his good works and deeds, Msgr. Higgins was not elevated to higher office, and suffered humiliation by the Church, which ordered his early retirement—an order, after protests, happily rescinded by an outstanding prelate, Archbishop John Quinn of San Francisco. It is not for me, a non-Catholic, to question why Msgr. Higgins was cavalierly dismissed from a post he so competently filled by the Church he so loyally served. The author, a Catholic, is to be commended for dealing with this obviously sensitive subject.

Mr. Costello's book establishes that Father Higgins throughout his ministry has conducted his crusade against injustice within the framework of the Church. He is not a militant departing from doctrine, but neither is he fearful of challenging, by action as well as words, outmoded concepts lacking in theological support. One of the many outstanding aspects of Mr. Costello's biography is his portrayal of Father Higgins as a person, with or without his Roman collar.

This is not easy to do. Although Msgr. Higgins is a confidant of labor leaders and working people, of presidents and cabinet officers, of cardinals and priests, of clerical colleagues of other faiths, of lay persons, Catholic and non-Catholic, and of intellectuals who read his informative newsletter with avidity, he has retained throughout the spiritual serenity of a pastor. Father Higgins is a man of this world, but always a deeply religious man, steeped in the doctrine of his Church and its teachings.

My family has treasured Father Higgins's friendship for more than thirty-five years. He has shared both our triumphs and tribulations. Although we are of different faiths, he is, for us, an outstanding example of the role and mission of a spiritual leader. Mr. Costello explains why this is so, for us and countless others.

In his biography, the author documents Msgr. Higgins's capacity for friendship, love, understanding, compassion and spiritual commitment. He also establishes that Father Higgins is not just a priest of good will to all people—a sort of "knee jerk" liberal cleric. The Father can be "tough" and "stiff necked" when the occasion warrants. But, in the many years of our friendship, I have never heard him "bad mouth" any person.

Mr. Costello's biography is not an idolatrous portrayal of a minister of the Gospel. Rather it is an excellent and readable account of an extraordinary, truly committed priest and a man for all seasons, Msgr. George G. Higgins.

Arthur J. Goldberg*

*Former Associate Justice of the Supreme Court of the United States, Ambassador to the United Nations, and Ambassador-at-Large and Chairman of the American Delegation to the Helsinki Review Conference at Belgrade, 1977-78. On Mr. Goldberg's appointment, Msgr. Higgins was a member of the American delegation.

PREFACE

Msgr. George Higgins has played a unique role in the ongoing story of the Catholic Church in the United States. He is the Church's best-known spokesman in the field of organized labor and in matters dealing with relations between Catholics and Jews. His efforts on behalf of farm workers led Cesar Chavez to call him "the best friend we have," and his untiring work for civil rights legislation helped to change the lives of millions of men and women. Steeped in the gospel tradition and schooled by the great social encyclicals of the popes, he is an uncompromising champion of the rights of the poor.

As the Church's leading voice in matters dealing with social action, he follows in the footsteps of his one-time mentor, Msgr. John A. Ryan.

Msgr. Higgins has brought the social message to his fellow Catholics—and to all men and women of good will—through his talks and articles, and in personal encounters beyond number at labor conventions, Church-related meetings, and late-night social gatherings, where the conversation, no matter how spirited, never strayed far from his main agenda.

Most of all, he has reached his audience through The Yardstick, the weekly Catholic press column that he began writing, as a newly-ordained priest, in 1945. The Yardstick—that collection of nearly 2,000 weekly columns that concentrate on the Church's social teaching, and in the process touch subjects that range from McCarthyism to labor union mergers to the Second Vatican Council—is at the heart of this book.

A friend considered that eclectic approach as we discussed The Yardstick. "You'll never get George shooting off his mouth on something he doesn't know anything about," he said. "But there aren't many things he doesn't know something about."

In *Without Fear or Favor* I have attempted to provide a journalist's study of Higgins and the great issues the Church has faced in his time—of what he has had to say, of how he has said it, and of the role he has played as the events of those years unfolded.

The book will serve, I hope, to provide in capsule form a summary of the positions Msgr. Higgins has so precisely staked out, week after week, over so many years—in a phrase, George Higgins on the record. I hope it serves another purpose as well: to lead readers to a deeper appreciation of the importance of the great social action pioneers who have served the American Church, and of how much they enrich the lives of all of us today.

Gerald M. Costello

ACKNOWLEDGMENTS

REV. FREDERICK MCGUIRE, C.M., GOT THIS BOOK STARTED FOUR years ago when he asked me to give some thought to compiling the best columns of Msgr. George G. Higgins and publishing them in book form.

When Father McGuire died in May 1983, the Church in the United States lost an outstanding priest and a great friend of the missions, and many of the rest of us simply lost a great friend. I'm deeply sorry he's not here to see his project through to completion—in somewhat altered form, to be sure—but his name is the first to come to mind when I think of those who must be thanked.

Another friend of George Higgins who has been supportive from the beginning is William Kircher, retired director of organizing for the AFL-CIO. I am grateful to Bill Kircher not only for his friendship and his encouragement, but also because he was instrumental in arranging a travel grant that made possible the personal interviews and other research essential to this story.

The grant came from the Hotel and Restaurant Employees International Union, AFL-CIO. To that organization and its general president, Edward T. Hanley, I offer a special word of thanks for their interest, so generously demonstrated, in the production of a book about Msgr. Higgins.

When this project began I was editor of *The Beacon,* the weekly newspaper of the Paterson (N.J.) Diocese; at its conclusion I am editor of *Catholic New York,* weekly publication of the Archdiocese of New York. I owe an expression of thanks to my two bishop-publishers, Bishop Frank J. Rodimer of Paterson and the late Cardinal Terence Cooke of New York, for their encouragement, and to co-workers at both publications—especially Victor F. Winkler at *The Beacon* and Anne Buckley at *Catholic New York*—for assistance in any number of ways.

Most of those who have been associated with George Higgins are busy people with demanding schedules. That is all the more reason why I am appreciative of the time provided by the men and women who were interviewed for this book. That is especially so in the case of the late Nevila McCaig, who was Msgr. Higgins's secretary for more than 25 years. She provided a wealth of information about him, and leads that proved to be invaluable. As Msgr. Higgins put it, she ran his office when he was out of town—and when he was there as well.

It is difficult to know where to begin in thanking Eileen Riley for her contributions to the book. My former secretary and now special assistant to the secretary for communications, U.S. Catholic Conference, Eileen transcribed long hours of tape-recorded interviews and typed the final version of the manuscript. She accomplished these tasks with thoroughgoing professional skill and—a blessing as deadlines neared—a fine sense of humor. I am grateful to her for making this task an easier one, and a better one as well.

That holds true for my family—especially my wife, Jane, who was patient with all the travel the book required

Finally, a word of special gratitude to George Higgins himself, for his cooperation with the project, for introductions within the labor community, for hours and hours spent in interviews from one coast to another, and at points in-between.

I am grateful to these and all others who have provided me with a marvelous opportunity, the chance to tell the story of what George Higgins has meant to the Church, and to all the men and women whose lives he has touched.

November 1983
New York

CONTENTS

CHAPTER ONE

YOUNG GEORGE HIGGINS

C.V. HIGGINS WAS THE WAY HE SIGNED HIS NAME, AND HE affixed it with authority to thousands of letters in his lifetime. Most of them were letters to the editor—to the editors of Chicago daily newspapers, to *America* and *Commonweal,* the national Catholic weeklies, and to *The New World,* as Chicago's archdiocesan newspaper was known then.

C.V. Higgins had opinions worth expressing, on everything from the League of Nations to the living wage. Express them he did, and it was a rare reader of that time and place—the Chicago area, mostly, a generation or two ago—to whom the signature of C.V. Higgins was not known.

When he was not writing, C.V. Higgins was reading, and when failing eyesight curtailed that consuming passion—even before

1

that time, as if in preparation for its coming—he had his son George read to him. George was his father's delight, clearly someone who was destined for good things. He was a bright and friendly boy, and his parents were right about his future. His priestly career, as the American Church's best-known spokesman in the field of labor and social justice, would one day put him in regular contact with popes and presidents. But George's mother and sister remember him still, home at noontime from his parish school classroom, standing at the kitchen table, reading aloud from the small columns of type in *America* or *Commonweal,* with C.V. Higgins nodding in approval.

Mr. Higgins was not a wealthy man, and not an educated man in the classic sense, but he passed along to George and to his other children the strong sense of value he placed on education. He had a memorable way of expressing it to George. "The investment I've made in your education," he said, "will be worthwhile—if you're impatient whenever *Commonweal* or *America* is late in the mail."

Charles Vincent Higgins dominated the early years of his son George. He was a formidable and yet loving presence who sensed the potential for greatness in the serious young boy, and wanted to encourage its development as best he could.

"My father had an obsession in getting me interested in serious things," George Higgins said, recalling his boyhood in the Twenties. "And when I look back on it, he did it with some sacrifice, because he was dirt poor. He never missed an important lecture in Chicago. Chesterton would come to town, Belloc would come to town. He used to go to hear them, and he'd take me with him. I remember him taking me to hear Chesterton when I was about 10 years old. There we were, sitting up in the gallery of Orchestra Hall, and it didn't mean a damn thing to me. But he said, 'He's a great man; you should see him. Later on you'll appreciate it that you did.' It probably cost him three or four bucks, which was a lot of money in those days, especially for him. I remember in 1928—I would have been 12 years old then—Al Smith came to Chicago. He spoke at a public park, which one I don't recall. We spent the whole day there, and I can still remember the streetcar ride. It probably took us two hours to get there; it seemed like forever to me. But I know this: I remember it today."

George Higgins's friends remember his father today, too.

"Everybody knew C.V. Higgins," said Msgr. John Egan, a long-time social activist who followed George by three years through the Chicago seminary system. "Mr. Higgins kept up on the pros and cons of the serious questions of the day, the controversies, the matters of interest. None of them was trivial. It seems to me that he had, as George has, objectivity, that ability to stand and look at a situation objectively without becoming personally involved in it. A letter from C.V. Higgins would give an honest opinion on a particular matter without invective, without accusation, without going into personalities. He'd let you know where he stood, and why. And none of that was lost on George as he was growing up."

Charles V. Higgins never went beyond the eighth grade. He was a railroad man whose family came from Springfield, Illinois, where his brothers shared his union interests, but not his intellectual pursuits. He met his bride in Springfield, a petite young woman named Anna Rethinger, whose German-speaking father had immigrated to the United States from Alsace-Lorraine. They were married in 1912 and later moved to Chicago, where George was born January 21, 1916. (George's middle name of Gilmary, an old Irish name suggested by his father, was an acquisition at confirmation.) Four other children were born to the couple: Anna in 1914; Bridget Elizabeth, or Betty, in 1918, and Eugene, in 1920. Another sister, Mary Catherine, died in 1926 at the age of three.

By that time C.V. Higgins had left railroading to work as a postal clerk, and when George was five the growing family moved to LaGrange, an easy commute on the Burlington line, whose tracks were only a half-block away from the comfortable new Higgins family homestead.

George Higgins has said that his mother is a woman of special intelligence. His boyhood friends recall her as a strong woman who tolerated with good humor the two great intellects in her home, all the while making life pleasant and delightful. But it was C.V. who was clearly in charge of family discussions, his constant reading providing him with more than enough conversation material.

"I don't know where his passion for reading came from," George said, "but he was probably the best-read man I ever met in my life. He was a great devotee of the theater, art museums, and the lecture circuit, but he was mainly a reader. Even when his eyesight began to fail, he insisted on reading at least two hours a day. I was always astounded by it—a man with an eighth-grade education who read every issue that *Commonweal* ever published, every issue of *America,* all of Maritain, all of Christopher Dawson. He didn't even have enough money to subscribe to *Commonweal;* somebody gave it to him for Christmas. Or he'd go down to the library. But he was the most persistent reader I've ever come across.''

George Higgins spent a happy boyhood in the home at 32 North Kensington, where his front bedroom window provided a view of the small town, past the Dutch elm branches that formed a bridge over the quiet street.

    .   La Grange was a placid community of about 10,000 people at the time, overwhelmingly Protestant—"a Wasp-ish kind of place,'' George recalled. There was one Catholic parish, St. Francis Xavier, in among some 15 Protestant congregations, and it was to the parish school that C.V. Higgins—a Mass-going Catholic, but not particularly pious—decided George should get his grammar school education. ("Dad was loyal and never anticlerical,'' the son recalls, "but I remember that one time we got a pastor whose social views were quiet different from his. The pastor had been a seminary dean, and people thought he was quite intellectual. He said in a sermon one time that the only two books you'd ever need to read were the Bible and the *Imitation of Christ.* My father went along with that to a degree. 'Maybe,' he said, 'but I wish he'd keep his mouth shut about political problems.' '')

    George's friends were mostly his fellow students at St. Francis Xavier, but as he grew older he spent more and more time in the adult world. Each noontime he'd make his hurried trip home, two blocks away, to read to his father (who worked the night shift in Chicago's main post office). His after-school hours were taken up increasingly in the library of St. Francis Xavier's pastor, a one-time Shakespearean actor from Massachusetts named John Henry Nawn. Soft-spoken, cultured, he made a memorable impression on young Higgins.

    "Nawn never got over his acting days,'' Higgins recalled. "One of the highlights of my school memories is the way he'd come in to relieve the nuns every now and then and read to us . . . a Father Brown detective story, perhaps, and he'd dramatize it. We were spellbound.''

Father Nawn was well read by the standards of the day, and had what was considered a good library. He shared it with both C.V. Higgins, a good friend, and young George, whose intellectual promise he quickly recognized. He encouraged the boy to take out books whenever he wanted, and spent a great deal of free time with him, even to the point of teaching him how to drive. The priest exerted no particular pressure about a vocation, but the subject was discussed openly, at home and in the rectory library. It was an easy decision, finally, and not long after he had been graduated from the eighth grade, George Higgins became a seminarian for the Archdiocese of Chicago.

Going off to Chicago was an exhilarating experience for young George Higgins. He didn't know that much about the city, despite the cultural excursions he'd made with his father, and he reveled in the sense of independence his daily trips provided him. He remembers going off on the train each day, and the thrill of walking down Michigan Boulevard, feeling quite grown-up in the midst of throngs of commuters and shoppers.

"It was great exposure," he said. "If I'd gone to school in LaGrange, I would've missed all of it."

Quigley Preparatory Seminary on the city's Near North Side was filled with young students who hoped to be priests, its enrollment well over a thousand at the time. On his first day there, George Higgins didn't know a single one of them. Large city parishes, usually Irish or Polish, would have 30, 40, or even 50 students in Quigley at one time, and all of them, Higgins recalls, seemed to know one another. But if he knew no one at first, he wasted little time in making friends. There was an appealing quality about the serious newcomer from LaGrange, his fellow seminarians discovered—a special intelligence, to be sure, and a rare knowledge of world and national events, but also a genuine interest in others, and a matter-of-fact, open kind of friendship. From the beginning, his classmates liked him and respected him.

Looking back at it now, Higgins enjoyed his Quigley years immensely, although he felt the institution was deficient from an academic standpoint. All of the students were commuters, and the attrition rate was high. ("In those days," he laughed, "they'd fire you for looking out the window.") He especially liked the diversity, the mix of people that Quigley provided, and by the time he and his remaining classmates were ready to move on to St. Mary's, the archdiocesan major seminary at Mundelein, he was sure that in the priesthood he had found the life he wanted.

Mundelein was a monument to its founder, Cardinal George Mundelein, the archbishop of Chicago from 1915 until his death in 1939. A princely figure who was nevertheless thought of as one of the leading social progressives of the day (he was a close friend, and frequent defender, of President Franklin D. Roosevelt), he encouraged his priests to personal growth, setting the stage for much of the prominence that Chicago's people and programs would attain in subsequent years.

He was intensely interested as well in seminaries and seminarians. He not only knew most of his students by name, but kept informed about their progress and their family life ("I remember him telling me where my father worked," Higgins said). The major seminary he built (on a 2,500-acre tract in Area, Illinois, a postal designation subsequently changed to Mundelein) contained 12 separate buildings and was a facility unsurpassed in any other American diocese. Higgins's original Quigley class had numbered some 250 or 300; that group had been whittled down to about 50 by the time they started Mundelein. Higgins's high academic standing and his ability to get along with his classmates made him a natural leader, and his years there saw him taking on added responsibilities.

In large measure, the story of St. Mary of the Lake Seminary in those days was the story of its rector, Msgr. Reynold Hillenbrand, a remarkable figure ranked by Church historians among the outstanding American priests of the twentieth century.

"Reiny" Hillenbrand, born in 1905 to a comfortable German-American family in Chicago, went through the archdiocesan seminary system before going to Rome after his ordination in 1930 for postgraduate studies. After teaching at Quigley for a few years, he was named rector of St. Mary of the Lake in 1936, an unusual appointment for someone so recently ordained. In Higgins's words, he "turned things upside down."

Taking to heart a forward-looking document on seminary education issued the previous year by Pope Pius XI, Hillenbrand supplemented the curriculum with an emphasis on the social teaching of the Church. He gave particular attention also to new developments in the field of liturgical reform and the lay apostolate.

Higgins took to him almost on sight. For one thing, he was an avid reader, and urged his students to follow suit. With the head start he received from his own father and Father Nawn, Higgins needed no encouragement. "He was a kind of a breath of fresh air when he came into the seminary," Higgins said. "When he first came back from Rome, he taught us English. He was a good teacher because he took the kids seriously and got them reading. He'd come in every day with his briefcase full of books and throw it on his desk. Whoever wanted the books could take them along and bring them back whenever they were finished."

"He was just a phenomenal influence," said Msgr. John S. Quinn, a classmate and close friend of George Higgins. "The priests of the diocese regarded him as a kind of saint. He was in the middle of all the great movements. And he recognized George's potential, too. He had a special regard for him."

The feeling was more than mutual. Writing in 1979, not long after Msgr. Hillenbrand's death, Higgins said the former rector had a more profound influence on the Archdiocese of Chicago than any other individual priest or bishop in recent generations. His example went beyond the classroom setting, Higgins continued; Hillenbrand would use his limited spare time to promote the cause of social and interracial justice, the lay apostolate and liturgical reform.

"I must leave it to others to assess his influence as an innovative leader in developing the Young Catholic Workers, Young Catholic Students, Catholic Family Movement and other specialized lay apostolate movements, since I did not observe his work in those areas at close range," Higgins wrote. "But I am certain that no American priest during the past 50 years has made such a lasting contribution as he did in the field of the lay apostolate."

Progressively-oriented priests of the archdiocese—Father Daniel Cantwell among them—became fulltime seminary teachers with Hillenbrand's encouragement, and the emphasis on the social question which began to permeate seminary life found no more attentive a student than Higgins.

"Those were exciting days," said Msgr. Egan, whose friendship with Higgins had begun to grow at the time. "We had not only the influence of Hillenbrand at the seminary, but so many things happening outside: Msgr. John Ryan in Washington, Dorothy Day and the Catholic Worker movement, all of the things that were going on with organized labor and the New Deal. The papers were full of this, day after day: the Wagner Act, the NRA, the sit-down strikes. These were the things that George was already versed in, thanks to his father, so he just naturally followed up on them.

"There was a certain conscience that George had already developed through his years in the minor seminary, because of his dad's influence, but it didn't emerge fully until he was in the major seminary. Then through his studying, his reading, his conversations, he began to develop this overwhelming interest in the social teachings of the Church, in economics, in laws governing everything from wages to working conditions.

"I remember walking around the lake at the seminary talking with George about elements of justice, the whole question of labor organization, the race question, of poverty, of parliamentary law. George was a walking encyclopedia."

Classmates and faculty recognized Higgins's special abilities. As his ordination approached, in 1940, he stood high in the class of 28 (as he had at Quigley, and at St. Francis Xavier). A mock "declaration" written on the jacket of his graduation photo by four classmates (Raymond J. Sullivan, Hubert Hoffman, Donald Masterson and John M. Kelly) called attention to the 23 offices or titles he held, including head prefect ("ruler of the entire student body") and reviewer-censor of all seminary movies ("N.B.—Rather strict!"). The inscription went on: "The class of 1940 considers only one difficulty between George Gilmary Higgins and the episcopate, and that is the matter of his age. We testify that we all realize that when George becomes of canonical age, he will immediately assume the purple and will thereafter be known as His Excellency."

By the time the class was ordained, its members had a new archbishop. Samuel Stritch, the former archbishop of Milwaukee (and one time bishop of Toledo, an appointment he was given when he was only 34), succeeded Cardinal Mundelein in 1940 and seemed destined to follow the broad liberal practices established by his predecessor. Higgins found him an appealing figure, and years later, asked to name some of the country's outstanding bishops, quickly put Stritch's name at the top of the list.

"Stritch was a very impressive man," he said. "He was permissive, for one thing. Chicago rightly or wrongly had a reputation for movements getting started, and that couldn't have happened without Stritch. You never knew whether he fully agreed or not, but he encouraged things, very much as Mundelein had done. Along with Cardinal [Edward] Mooney of Detroit, he had an international point of view which is now taken for granted by the bishops' conference. Up until the time of the Second Vatican Council, the general feeling was that Rome didn't want national hierarchies getting themselves involved in international matters. Despite that impression, Stritch and Mooney did. Stritch set up the U.S. bishops' committee on peace, and established an office in the United Nations. Today it looks mild, but in those days that kind of international interest was something rare.''

Stritch's decision (made at Hillenbrand's recommendation) to send Higgins and several of his classmates to The Catholic University of America in Washington, D.C. for further studies caused a mild sensation on the campus. Mundelein had had a long-standing policy of not sending his priests to Catholic University or to the North American College in Rome (because, according to the clerical gossip mill, as a student himself at Rome's Propaganda College he had been snubbed by the American college people) and the school was pleasantly surprised to have to find room for 12 Chicagoans.

They studied in a variety of fields, apparently because Hillenbrand was looking ahead to building up his seminary faculty. Higgins's major subject was economics (with a first minor in political science and a second in sociology), and he plunged into his work with zest. He enjoyed the Washington setting a great deal. Not only were there many fellow Chicagoans for company; he had a chance to meet people like Msgr. Ryan and his associate in the social action department of the old National Catholic Welfare Conference, Father Raymond McGowan. Father John Hayes, whom Higgins knew from his social action work in Chicago, was still another staff member.

His letters home not only reflected the enjoyment he found in his assignment; they were extensions of his kitchen-table dialogues with his father about the topics of the times. Other young priests in Washington might be writing home about the weather or the people they happened to see at the Capitol, but George Higgins had meatier matters to discuss with his father—as he did in this typical letter, from early in 1944: "I have written a letter to the editor of *America* in mild opposition to the Godfrey Schmidt article in

America of January 9. . . . I am positive that he went too far in condemning the trend toward the nationalization of labor legislation. I cannot help but think that a reactionary could and would say the same things about the Wagner Act and a half-dozen other laws which I, for one, think that we could discard only at our peril.''

Increasingly, as his days at Catholic University were drawing to a close, Higgins wondered in his letters home about his future assignment. On March 30, 1944 he told his parents that Archbishop Stritch wanted him to stay on at C.U. until September, as a faculty member, and that Hillenbrand was "angling" to get him back to Mundelein to teach. "I would prefer that," he said, "to teaching down here."

His doctoral dissertation was titled "Voluntarism in Organized Labor in the U.S., 1930-1940." In it, Higgins asserted that the change from labor voluntarism to a greater reliance on state regulatory activity had been accepted grudgingly by the American Federation of Labor, but encouraged by the Congress of Industrial Organizations (the two labor groups being separate entities at the time). Creation of the National Labor Relations Board had led to government interference with the collective bargaining process to some degree, he said; as a result unions were being forced increasingly into political action in order to guard the gains they had made.

Higgins breezed through his oral exams, sounding uncharacteristically cocky about the experience as he wrote home: "I had a little fun antagonizing two of the examiners who are admittedly antilabor," he said. "I am certain that I was as calm as I've ever been in my life."

An illness intervened at that point, one which was to change the course of Higgins's life. It was not his own sickness, but rather that of Father Hayes—a case of tuberculosis, forcing Hayes to move to the Southwest and away from his social action post in Washington.

Father McGowan approached Higgins on April 8, 1944 and discussed the matter with him: "You're just about finished with school now; why don't you come and spend the summer with us?" On that same day, he wrote home to LaGrange with the news, adding that since Stritch was coming to Washington soon for a visit, he expected a decision then. He added: "Say a prayer that God's will be done in the matter, and that if I am chosen for the job I may do a good piece of work."

Stritch never made a formal decision on it, simply allowing the move to take place without commenting on it (or without assigning Higgins anywhere else). There was an unwritten understanding between all parties—Higgins, Ryan, McGowan, and, presumably, Stritch—that when Higgins joined the conference, it was on a temporary basis. As things turned out, he didn't leave until September 1, Labor Day, 36 years later. That was the day he retired.

CHAPTER TWO

THE CONFERENCE

"IT WAS LIKE A FAMILY, REALLY, BEFORE BUREAUCRACY inevitably and inexorably set in," George Higgins said. "We couldn't have had more than 75 people in the whole building, and everybody there knew everybody else. The conference was much less structured than it is today. It was smaller, and poorer, of course, but there was a quality about the place then. . . ."

Higgins felt at home, immediately and completely, at the National Catholic Welfare Conference — NCWC, as it was most often referred to in Church circles, or "the conference," as the staff itself called it. His letters home at the time reflected some of the informal atmosphere of the old days at 1312 Massachusetts Avenue. "Old Msgr. Ryan provides a little entertainment two or three times a day," he wrote in 1944, not long after he joined, however unofficially, the NCWC organization. "He wanders in his shuffling way from an adjoining office to make some comment on something he has just written."

His more recent recollections about the conference reflect the same kind of down-home memories: "Frank Hall was here then, and if you want to talk about characters in the old building, you could start with him. He was the director of NC News Service, a newspaperman of the old school. He and McGowan were great friends, a couple of small-town Missourians who loved nothing better than getting together, putting their feet up on the desk and just gabbing away. Everybody loved to kid Hall. I stopped him in the corridor one day and said, 'Frank, that was a great story you had on such-and-such,' and he just stuttered and stammered. Had no idea at all of what I was talking about. 'Don't worry, Frank,' I said, 'all you're supposed to do is put the stuff out. You don't have to read it.' "

The organization to which Higgins so quickly adapted, the NCWC, traced its roots to the years of World War I, when, at the initiative of a remarkable Paulist priest named John J. Burke, the Catholic Church in the U.S. became intensely involved in the American war effort. Burke had been inspired by the work of another notable priest, Father William Kerby, who taught at Catholic University for 40 years and founded in 1910 the National Conference of Catholic Charities. Kerby taught Burke and, according to Burke's biographer, Father John B. Sheerin, C.S.P., led him to an abiding interest in the whole field of social action and social reform.

Only days after the U.S. entered the war in April 1917, Burke organized the Chaplains' Aid Association. That work, in turn, moved him to a broader vision. According to Sheerin, he developed "a scheme for some sort of ecclesiastical organization through which Catholic action might be provided" during the war. With the approval of the country's three cardinals—Gibbons of Baltimore, O'Connell of Boston, and Farley of New York—he convened a meeting (at Catholic University, August 11-12, 1917) of 115 delegates, clergy and lay, representing 68 dioceses and assorted national Catholic organizations. The National Catholic War Council, formed as a result of the meeting, elected Burke as its president, endorsed the wartime efforts already begun by the Knights of Columbus, and determined to "study, coordinate, unify, and put in operation all Catholic activities incidental to the war." The original administrative committee proved unwieldy, however, and in November 1917, the archbishops who headed U.S. ecclesiastical provinces restructured the NCWC, placing its administration in the hands of four bishops: Patrick J. Hayes of New York (later New York's cardinal-archbishop), William T. Russell of Charleston, Joseph Schrembs of Toledo (later bishop of Cleveland), and Peter J. Muldoon of Rockford, Illinois. Burke was named chairman of the Committee on Special War Activities, and according to the historian Aaron I. Abell, was "zealous and businesslike" and "mobilized millions of Catholics through subcommittees on finance, men's activities, women's activities, chaplains' aid, Catholic interests, historical records, reconstruction and after-war activities." His efforts were instrumental in helping the War Council record an unusual degree of success in its fund-raising, social, and educational work during the war.

In February 1919, not long after the war ended, 77 American bishops gathered in Washington to celebrate the golden jubilee of Cardinal Gibbons's episcopacy. Moved by the success of the War Council—and by a plea from Pope Benedict XV (delivered through his representative, Archbishop Bonaventura Cerretti) that they join him in working through a permanent organization for peace through education and social justice—the bishops determined to hold annual meetings, a decision endorsed by the Holy Father several weeks later.

There had been no full meeting of the American hierarchy since Baltimore's Plenary Council of 1884 (although the metropolitans, the archbishops who headed major dioceses, had been holding informal, off-the-record gatherings since 1890) when 92 of the 101 bishops in charge of the dioceses met in Washington on September 24-25, 1919. They voted the establishment of the National Catholic Welfare Council—a direct successor of, although differently structured from, the National Catholic War Council—and set up a seven-member administrative committee to direct it. Voting in secret ballot, they elected Archbishop Edward J. Hanna of San Francisco as chairman. When that committee met three months later, it formed seven major committees and chose an "executive secretary," soon thereafter designated general secretary, to head a Washington-based department which would coordinate NCWC activities and its day-to-day business. The man they chose was Father Burke, and he turned to the task with an unusually high degree of organizational skill.

Msgr. Higgins knew Burke only indirectly, through the memories of Father Raymond McGowan. "I often heard him say," Higgins wrote in 1975, "that Msgr. Burke, for whom he had genuine affection, was one of the few men he had ever known who had a touch of genius about him." Burke's biographer, Father Sheerin, said his subject was "pre-eminently an organizing genius."

Organization was precisely what was required, since the National Catholic Welfare Council was to be decidedly different from its predecessor, the National Catholic War Council (which co-existed for a time with the newer NCWC as wartime activities were phased out). Bishops Muldoon, Schrembs (now of Cleveland) and Russell were on the administrative committee, as were Archbishops Dennis Dougherty of Philadelphia and Austin Dowling of St. Paul, and Bishop J.F. Regis Canevin of Pittsburgh, in addition to Archbishop Hanna. Burke set out to work with them as best he could, but confessed to misgivings about the assignment in a letter written to his secretary in 1920:

"I don't want the Welfare Council work. I'm not fitted for it. I never went into the priesthood for it. I don't think I'm called in any way to direct the national work of the Catholic Church in the United States. It's a pain and just now little short of an agony to accept it. . . ."

The first major challenge that Burke had to weather involved the very existence of the Council. Some American bishops were worried about its effect on their personal authority within their own dioceses, and in Rome there were Curia officials who feared the Council for what it might attempt to accomplish if it viewed itself as a permanent canonical body. The strength of these two influential forces was enough to result in a decree of supression of the National Catholic Welfare Council, prepared while Pope Benedict XV was still alive but actually issued, on February 25, 1922, under the hand of the new Holy Father, Pius XI. The decree noted that some American bishops felt the NCWC was "no longer needful or useful," and in addition to disbanding the organization, forbade the continuation of the American hierarchy's annual meetings.

Father Burke was present when the NCWC's administrative committee held an emergency meeting at Bishop Schrembs's home in Cleveland which resulted in Schrembs being sent to Rome, armed with a letter of support signed by 81 American bishops, to fight the decree. In a letter sent home to Burke, Schrembs blamed a combination of Vatican political infighting and the complaints of two U.S. cardinals—Dougherty of Philadelphia (although he had been a member of the original administrative committee) and O'Connell of Boston—for the Vatican's ruling. By June, the on-the-scene work performed by Schrembs (who relied heavily on Burke for strategy and advice) resulted in a decree from the Consistorial Congregation allowing the NCWC to go forward, with two important provisos: its title was to be changed from National Catholic Welfare Council to National Catholic Welfare Conference (an indication of its deliberative, rather than juridical, nature) and its actions were to be viewed as nonbinding on individual dioceses. The decision was clearly a triumph for the NCWC, for Schrembs and the committee, and for Burke.

The Paulist priest acquitted himself as well in the other early crises faced by the fledgling organization. Bishop William E. McManus of Fort Wayne-South Bend, a long-time NCWC staff member and chronicler of its personnel and times, credited Burke with building a talented staff whose love of the Church surmounted particular academic interests. "I think Father Burke probably envisioned the national organization as being a center from which the best of Catholic scholarship, some of it readily available at Catholic University, could be thrust into the marketplace. . . . He was a holy, zealous, well-organized, prophetic kind of priest."

Writing 39 years after Burke's death, when Father Sheerin's biography of him appeared in 1975, Msgr. Higgins put the Burke role in perspective: "One shudders to think of what might have happened, what direction NCWC might have taken if its first general secretary—who, regardless of his background and his orientation, was inevitably destined to leave an indelible mark on the organization—had come from a more hide-bound or conservative theological and political tradition. . . . The Conference . . . got off to a basically progressive start under Msgr. Burke's far-sighted and resourceful leadership. We have good reason to honor him. . .He was undoubtedly one of the most influential figures in the history of twentieth-century Catholicism."

It was natural that much of the work of NCWC in the early years would have had such a marked social dimension. Emerging as it did from wartime activities, in which the Church's temporal responsibilities were emphasized, the council also determined in its earliest days to include a bureau of social service—"informative, directive, inspirational"—which would coordinate charitable activities and stimulate legislative reform. The office that grew from that decision was the Department of Social Action, which was to have two offices: one in Chicago, under the leadership of John A. Lapp, a layman, and the other in Washington, which would be chaired by John A. Ryan. Its original budget was far less than the $125,000 that its framers had suggested; indeed, it would remain below that figure for years to come. But its assets included the two towering figures of Ryan and Father Raymond McGowan. Their work and their presence gave the department a status which it would never lose, and which extended to the conference as a whole.

"I used to look at Ryan in awe," Higgins said at the time of his own retirement. "He was something of a legend. Rarely around the place, of course, but when he was, you paid attention to him. I had gotten to know him through Msgr. Harold Smith of New York, who had studied under Ryan and entertained him whenever he was in the city. He loved to go out and be entertained. I remember him as a loveable old guy, but also someone who was as tough as nails."

Higgins's acquaintance with his predecessor was brief, coming as it did at the end of Ryan's long and colorful career. A native Minnesotan, Ryan was, by general agreement, the foremost social reformer of American Catholicism in the first half of the twentieth century. A national figure whose reputation was established in 1906 with the publication of "A Living Wage" (an impassioned argument on behalf of legislated minimum-wage standards), he bolstered his ideas on social reform with a strong background in economics. To the public in later years, he was best known as the Church's most outspoken defender of Franklin D. Roosevelt's domestic policies (Francis L. Broderick's definitive biography of Ryan is subheaded "Right Reverend New Dealer"), but within church circles he was recognized as an eloquent spokesman for the rights of the common man, a priest who never backed off from a fight or declined a hand offered in friendship. His interests extended to rural concerns, labor matters, racial issues, religious freedom—the package a later generation would identify with "civil rights"—and he carried them out mainly through his books and articles and his teaching position at Catholic University.

At NCWC, Broderick says, "Ryan did little more than answer his mail, dictate a lecture or an article, or consult briefly with someone from another department." Broderick quotes Higgins as saying that much of what Msgr. Ryan did would have been done about as well and in much the same way if there had been no NCWC." But, the writer continues, "as Ryan shuttled from the university to his office at the NCWC, he worked with interacting authority," one position strengthening the impact of the other.

Whatever his most important base, his biographers make it clear that Ryan had a profound effect on the Church in his time, and even beyond. According to the historian David J. O'Brien:

"Ryan became the link between American Catholics and liberal, progressive groups, interpreting them to each other and helping lead his fellow Catholics to a more complete awareness not only of the Church's social teaching but of the necessity for reform in order to realize the ideals of their dual American and Catholic heritage."

The relationship between Ryan and his long-time deputy, Father McGowan, was a fascinating one. In his 1941 autobiography, *Doctrine in Action,* Ryan conceded that McGowan had been responsible for most of the planning and operations of the Social Action Department, but his praise of the younger priest had a stand-offish quality about it. In the book, as in life, he was not "Ray" or "Raymond," but "Father McGowan."

They had differences in approach, O'Brien points out. Ryan was more concerned with short-term goals, McGowan with long-range planning.

"Ryan interpreted and defended American reform in terms of Catholic thought," O'Brien writes. "McGowan reversed the process, rigorously measuring reform proposals against 'the yardstick' of papal teachings and seeking to develop an independent Catholic program based on the occupational group idea."

Higgins's own observations are more personal.

"McGowan really ran the department," he said in 1980. "Ryan was teaching; I don't think he ever came to the office before noon. Everything of a programatic nature always came from McGowan. He was a remarkable man, but very little is known about him today. Mention his name in the building, and there wouldn't be three people who'd know him or remember him. He was a very likeable man, but so unsystematic that he didn't leave good records.'' Higgins recalled McGowan as a man who had ''all the best qualities of a small-town upbringing,'' with good instincts and sound judgment. ''I never heard him say an uncharitable word about anybody, and God knows there were plenty of bishops he could've knifed,'' Higgins said. ''But he considered it beneath his dignity.'' McGowan managed to stay in the shadows, Higgins said, always deferring to Ryan, to whom he referred, directly and in the third person, as Doctor Ryan.

Together, Ryan and McGowan formed an unusually effective team, Ryan presenting the Catholic social program to the public and McGowan putting it to work from the inside. Their disagreements were few, and if Ryan ever felt compelled to treat McGowan as an underling, the treatment had a note of friendly needling about it. One fairly sore subject was McGowan's frequent absence from the NCWC building (often occasioned by fact-finding trips to Latin America). McGowan's one-word reply to a telegram from Ryan inquiring when he'd be home from one trip was a simple ''March.'' Not to be outdone, Ryan wired back: ''What year?''

If Higgins respected Ryan, as he assuredly did, he revered McGowan, with whom he had a much longer, and much more personal, contact. His eulogy at the Month's Mind Mass for McGowan in December 1962 (McGowan had died while Higgins was attending the first session of the Second Vatican Council), ranks among his best and most personal talks. He singled out four qualities of McGowan that had inspired him: imaginative vision, coupled with ''a rare degree of daring and initiative'': courage; cheerful and good-natured patience; and disinterested modesty and humility. He specifically cited McGowan's long-standing concern for Latin America: ''Father McGowan was one of the first Americans to sense the urgency of these problems and one of the first to try to do something about them. He had an instinctive feeling for the interdependence of the Americas and a genuine and deeply personal sympathy for our Latin American neighbors, a quality which won him their lasting admiration and affection.''

In the eulogy, Higgins also referred to the Ryan-McGowan relationship, an unusual kind of working arrangement which had kept McGowan hidden, to a large measure, from public view. ''Father McGowan literally worshiped the very ground that Msgr.

Ryan walked on, but, even at that, it required true greatness of soul
on his part to play second fiddle, so to speak, for so many years,
even to such an acknowledged giant in the field of Catholic social
action. He deliberately stayed in the background, doing all of the
tedious chores and runnning all the errands so that Msgr.
Ryan. . .might have the necessary leisure to pursue his chosen
apostolate of scholarly writing and lecturing in the field of Catholic
social theory.''

Father McGowan was a simple man, Higgins continued, a
humble priest ''without a trace of envy or duplicity in his entire
makeup.'' His sense of privacy made him ''allergic to flattery'' or
merited praise, Higgins said, still describing him as ''a man all of
us loved and revered for his simplicity and charity and contagiously
cheerful friendliness and whom we all admired for his selfless contribution to the cause of social justice.''

Higgins transmitted a copy of the eulogy to McGowan's sister
with a personal note that revealed even more directly the special place
which McGowan held in his life: ''Ray's death was a grievous loss
to me personally. . . . Everything I know about Catholic social theory
and Catholic social action I learned from him. He was a kind,
thoughtful, generous, and very patient teacher, always willing to be
helpful and always ready with a word of encouragement when the
going was rough. I owe him more than I can possibly calculate, and
I know that I don't have to tell you that my indebtedness to him
extends far beyond the field of Catholic social action. His priestly
qualities of mercy, kindness, and compassion and his almost child-
like confidence and trust in the Providence of God were an inspiration to me at all times as well as to countless other priests who were
privileged to know him intimately.''

The conference would remain George Higgins's home base
throughout his priestly career, until his retirement in 1980. The
organization was to undergo major changes, the most far-reaching
being its division in 1967 into the U.S. Catholic Conference and the
National Conference of Catholic Bishops. (The former was to serve
as the operational arm of the NCCB, an ecclesiastical body with
defined juridical authority over the American Church.) To intimates
such as Higgins, however, it remained ''the conference,'' and he
served it much as had his predecessors, Ryan and McGowan, pro-

viding it with an expertise on labor and economics that combined academic perceptions with practical, day-to-day knowledge in a way that few, if any, could equal.

The record shows that he served the conference with distinction, but beyond that his service possessed a quality of devotion, almost affection. He loved what he did, and he never gave the job anything less than his best effort. Looking back recently, he summed up his feelings about his career by quoting the British historian and social philosopher, R.H. Tawney: " 'If a man has important work and enough leisure and income to enable him to do it properly, he is in possession of as much happiness as is good for any of the children of Adam.' That's the way I feel about my years at the conference.''

As Ryan (and to a lesser-known extent, McGowan) had been, Higgins would become the conference's "labor man," the person to whom the bishops turned for guidance and, eventually, for leadership in dealing with matters connected with labor. And as Ryan did, Higgins used the position, in a positive framework, in a number of ways, most notably to advance causes and people he thought worthy of support—the issue of racial justice, for example, or the farm labor crusade of Cesar Chavez. He never based these actions on partisan motives, undertaking them instead because he was convinced that the interests they represented coincided with those of the conference, and of the Church—and more than anything else, because he was sure they were right.

He went beyond Ryan's "social action" interests, too, lending the prestige he gained as the years went by to areas of ecumenical interest, international peace, minority causes—all the fields that would be identified under the general heading of human rights.

"No one person did any more to bring the religious community into unity behind civil rights than George," said Joseph Rauh, long-time leader of Americans for Democratic Action, in 1980. His sentiments were echoed by Rabbi Marc Tanenbaum of the American Jewish Committee: "On every major issue of human welfare, George Higgins was always there."

What is as remarkable as anything else about the Higgins record is that it was achieved without any sign of a formal appointment to the conference.

"There's nothing in the files to show why I came here," he said in 1980. "It was one of those things. I came and I never left."

The appointment was much on George Higgins's mind in 1944. After having written to his parents on April 8 of that year that he had been asked to replace Father Hayes in the Social Action Department, and that he expected a decision "soon" from the then-Archbishop Stritch, he still had no answer two weeks later, after having seen Stritch. "The archbishop said nothing about it," he wrote home, "and I couldn't raise the question." The final reference to the matter in his letters to LaGrange came in October 1944, when he said there had been "no further news" about his appointment, and that he planned to "sit tight" until the bishops' meeting in November.

The matter was obviously resolved by default, but it continued to surface from time to time between Higgins and his ordinaries in Chicago.

"The only time Stritch ever referred to it was after I'd been here for a long time," Higgins said. "He was here for a bishops' meeting, and we went up to his room—he was a cardinal by this time—for a drink before dinner. He had a dinner appointment, and was almost out of the door, and said, 'Higgins, what diocese do you belong to?' This was after a very nice conversation, and I said, 'Well, I've been working on the assumption it was Chicago, and I was kind of hoping that you had the same assumption.' He said, 'Well, I'd think we'd see more of you; we never see you.' I answered, 'Well, I work here.' After that I went to see Msgr. Howard Carroll, who was our general secretary then, wondering what this was all about, and we decided that perhaps I ought to take a trip out to Chicago. So a few days later I flew out there and went to his office, and I said, 'Your Eminence, I was just passing through and I thought I'd say hello,' and he said, 'Yes, Father, come in any time; we're always glad to see you.' I walked out and that was the last time I ever was in the chancery office. I never even sat down, and I'd spent a hundred bucks to get out there."

Whatever the purpose of Stritch's twitting, it had obviously passed. His regard for Higgins was more than professional; as the years went by, Higgins (often accompanied by then-Father McManus, a fellow Chicagoan) was a regular guest at the cardinal's winter retreat in Florida.

Higgins's Washington career was similarly undisturbed by the seven-year term (1958-1965) of Stritch's successor, Cardinal Albert Meyer. Meyer was an unusually shy man, quiet to the point of being uncommunicative when he first came to Chicago. He had served as a seminary rector, bishop of Superior, and archbishop of Milwaukee. Highly respected by the priests of Chicago, he grew enormously in his role as archbishop, particularly during the Vatican Council years (aided in this regard, according to Higgins, by his then vicar general, Cletus O'Donnell, now bishop of Madison). To the end, however, he preferred to shun the spotlight of publicity. Higgins has always delighted in telling the story of Meyer's standoff with Msgr. Egan on the subject: "Jack, then as now, knew everything that was going on everywhere and was always after Meyer to get more press exposure. 'You're a leading church figure,' Jack told him. 'You ought to be in the papers more. You ought to be on television. You owe it to the people.' Well, Meyer had been though this sort of thing before with Jack, and he simply answered, 'Father Egan, you and I are like trains passing in the night. You don't seem to be getting my point. I will be happy if I die without ever seeing my name in the newspapers.' "

Higgins's relationship with Meyer was friendly, but for whatever reason the subject of his work at the conference never came up. It arose only once under Cardinal John Cody, shortly after his appointment to succeed Meyer as archbishop of Chicago. The two were on a flight home from Rome when Cody asked Higgins if he'd like to stay on in Washington. "I said yes," Higgins recalled, "and that was it."

In many respects, Higgins's early years in the conference served as an extension of the education he had begun when he came to Washington in 1940 to start formal studies at Catholic University. Some of the process carried over from the campus to Massachusetts Avenue. An avid pupil who forgot very little, he learned from people such as Father Hayes and Father Francis J. Haas just as he did from Ryan and McGowan.

Haas was a notable influence, first during Higgins's student days. Hired on by Father Burke as director of the National Catholic School of Social Service (replacing Father Karl J. Alter, who became bishop of Toledo and later archbishop of Cincinnati, as well as episcopal chairman of the Social Action Department and eventually head of the bishops' administrative committee), Haas had been, at one time, a student of Ryan's.

"Haas was very good to me," Higgins said. "He was active in things like labor arbitration, and he was wonderful in the way he'd bring me into things. He was always interested in his students—in those days, there were many more students in the social field than there are today—and for some reason he took a liking to me. I was just a young kid, standing on the sidelines, but he let me spend a lot of time with him. It was probably through him as much as anyone else that I got to know McGowan. After he became a bishop—which never should have happened; he never wanted to be a bishop and was never very good at it—he used to come back to Washington quite often, and I'd often look forward to seeing him." (One of their meetings took place in 1945, when Haas, by that time bishop of Grand Rapids, delivered the eulogy at Ryan's funeral.)

Higgins's letters home in the months following his de facto assignment to the conference were filled with details about his day-to-day activities. One of his tasks in the early years, inherited from John Hayes, was the preparation of Social Action Notes for Priests, a copy of which he sent home in June 1944. A mimeographed update on events and people in the Catholic social action field (the six-page sample copy he sent to LaGrange included notes about Ryan, McGowan, Jesuit Father Benjamin Masse, and a Connecticut labor priest named Joseph Donnelly, with whom he would spend long hours on the farm labor issue in years to come), Social Action Notes was no problem for Higgins. "There's nothing very heavy about it," he wrote. "It's a newsy letter sent out to about 800 priests to try to stir things up."

From the beginning, much of his time was spent traveling throughout the Northeast—later, throughout the country—to attend meetings in which he would participate or represent the bishops' conference. He described a typically crowded schedule in March 1945, reporting that he had been in New York the previous evening to attend a World Unity Conference sponsored by the CIO, where he found "more Communists than you could shake a stick at." He took the midnight train back to Washington, arriving at the office the next morning to go through the mail. He was leaving that evening to attend a priests' meeting in Columbus, and two days later would fly from Columbus to Richmond to take part in a "big interracial meeting."

NC News Service began to chronicle Higgins's activities in January 1945, noting that he was to speak at a "Religion in Life" week at the University of Georgia. The clippings came quickly after that. Here was Higgins delivering the opening prayer at a United Auto Workers convention in Atlantic City, urging support for striking telephone workers at a local ADA meeting in Washington, trading blows with the *Daily Worker,* the Communist Party newspaper, over the wisdom of the Industry Council Plan.

A lengthy interview with "young, aggressive Father George G. Higgins" appeared in September 1948, following his six-month stay in Germany to survey social action in the labor field for the religious affairs branch of the U.S. Military Government: "Out of the rubble and ruin inherited from World War II, Germany has uncovered a new day for its organized labor movement and the outlook is bright. 'The outlook for the Catholic social movement in Germany in the labor field is hopeful,' Father Higgins said. 'There is a great need, and the German leaders themselves recognize this, for more international contacts, especially with the labor and Catholic social action movements in the United States. They are working toward this goal and I think they will make it.' "

Higgins stepped up his book reviewing ("a bad habit which grows on you by geometric progression," he wrote to his parents). From time to time his letters home offered side comments on the news of the day, as on the day President Roosevelt died: "Say a prayer for the piano player from Kansas City. Jim Farley will answer on Judgment Day for his part in the scrapping of Henry Wallace."

More and more, he came in contact with important people in labor and politics. From an NCWC-sponsored meeting in Grand Rapids in 1947, he described an informative get-together with the CIO's president: "Phil Murray asked me to meet him in his room. He wanted to talk and let down his hair. I left at 5:15 AM, with my head full of knowledge of the CIO and the labor movement." There were chance meetings, too, of which Higgins took full advantage. Hospitalized for minor surgery in 1946, he discovered that Supreme Court Justice Frank Murphy was a fellow patient, under an assumed name, and sought him out. "He thinks the only thing that kept him from being president," he reported without comment, "was his Catholic religion."

All the while he was gaining in personal stature, in the Church and the labor community, George Higgins was deepening his appreciation of the conference, and the role it held in advancing the social action tradition of the Catholic Church in America. He helped see Ryan through his final days in 1945, even flying with him in a private plane to Minnesota, since the old priest had expressed a desire to die at home. (Before death finally overtook the "Right Reverend New Dealer" in September, he wrote his final article, flat on his back in bed. It was a posthumous salute to Roosevelt, in which he affirmed FDR's program as having "done more to promote social justice than all the other federal legislation enacted since the adoption of the Constitution.")

In 1946 Higgins helped welcome to the Social Action Department, then being chaired by McGowan, another priest who was destined to have a long and productive career in the conference. Sulpician Father John F. Cronin was already well known for his studies in economics and political science when he joined the staff as assistant director (the same title held by Higgins). Recruited by Archbishop Alter (with McGowan's knowledge, if not his enthusiastic approval) at a time when the Church and the country were becoming increasingly stirred by fears of communism, real and imagined, Cronin had as one of his first tasks the preparation of a major report for the bishops on the topic of communism in America. (His work on the report helped to solidify a friendship with Richard Nixon, then a young congressman from California. The friendship grew, and during Nixon's vice-presidential years Cronin served as one of his principal speechwriters.)

Cronin and McGowan were good friends but never completely compatible, partly because Cronin's interests at the time were almost entirely centered on communism and related issues. Higgins, on the other hand, was dealing in the same broad range of social questions with which McGowan had been concerned for years, and McGowan's respect for him grew as he saw the progress the younger priest was making.

Higgins loved the old man, not only for his personal qualities but for what he had accomplished in his chosen apostolate. Years later, in his Month's Mind eulogy, Higgins ticked off a list of important Church organizations associated with McGowan: the Catholic Conference on Industrial Problems, the Catholic Association for International Peace, the Bishops' Committee for the Spanish-Speaking, the Catholic Council of the Spanish-Speaking, the Bishops' Committee for Migrant Workers, and the Inter-American Catholic Social Action Conference.

"The record will show," he said, "that most of these organizations were started ahead of their time and moreover might not be in existence even at this late date had it not been for the almost clairvoyant vision of a single-minded priest of God who, oddly enough, was good-naturedly but mistakenly caricatured even by some of his friends and admirers as an inefficient administrator. He was admittedly rather indifferent to the details of administration in the accepted sense of the word, but unless efficiency is to be defined exclusively in terms of neatness and punctuality he was, I submit, a most gifted and efficient administrator in the field of Catholic social action. He was efficient in the sense of being able to see the forest for the trees—of being able to anticipate, sometimes by a decade or more, the needs of the Church in the field of social reform."

Higgins took on a growing number of assignments in the department as McGowan showed signs of slowing down. In May 1954 (along with Father McManus) he was given the title of papal chamberlain. Six months later, when ill health finally forced McGowan to resign, Archbishop Francis P. Keough of Baltimore, episcopal chairman of the Social Action Department, announced the name of his successor.

The new chairman would be 38-year-old Msgr. George G. Higgins. With all that he had accomplished, and with all the recognition he had received, one technicality had never been resolved. It made no practical difference, but just for the record, George Higgins had never been assigned to the conference.

CHAPTER THREE

DEAN OF
CATHOLIC SOCIAL ACTION

"As dean of Catholic social action, he moves with dignity and competence as easily through the halls of Congress as he does in the barrios of the farm workers. His weekly column, The Yardstick, gives voice to the social teachings of the Church. Possessing astute judgment and deep wisdom honed through experience and study, he is cautious of utopian solutions, skeptical of piety substituting for social policy, and critical of empty rhetoric posing as civil discourse. . . ."

The citation for the honorary doctorate George Higgins received from the University of Notre Dame in 1979 (written by Msgr. Egan) hardly exaggerates the facts. Higgins indeed has been the dean of American Catholic social action, a role he has followed in direct line with Msgr. Ryan and Father McGowan, not only by reason of the official titles they held in the bishops' conference, but in fact as well.

The names of Higgins and Ryan have carried a special association. "Pity the man who thinks that we have nothing to learn from those who went before us," Higgins wrote in 1968. "From a John A. Ryan, for example. The Church in the United States should be so lucky as to come up with another social reformer of his extraordinary stature in the present generation."

Many would argue, of course, that Higgins is just the man, some with special credentials to do so. Father J. Bryan Hehir, the U.S. Catholic Conference's brilliant specialist in international issues, wrote in 1978 that "John A. Ryan, John Courtney Murray, and George Higgins are the only names presently guaranteed to be in the history of Catholic social thought in the United States." Presumably the particular connections would be less important to Higgins than the fact that he is linked so directly with a long and noble tradition: the historic association of the American Catholicism with causes of social justice.

Two of the most prominent names in that tradition are those of Cardinal James Gibbons of Baltimore and Archbishop John Ireland of St. Paul, who, as Higgins has pointed out, played vital roles in the critical years at the turn of the century when the American Church was finally able to change its primary social focus. Instead of channeling all its energy into meeting the needs of its ever-growing immigrant population, it was able to devote more and more attention to the broader social issues of the national scene. Another important figure was Archbishop John J. Keane of Dubuque ("our personal favorite in the hierarchy of that generation," Higgins once noted).

While the three were not "social reformers" as such, Higgins said, since Catholic social action was only one of their interests and responsibilities, their openness, vision, and willingness to take papal social teachings to heart helped to pave the way for the success of activists such as Father Peter Dietz. Dietz was a native New Yorker (born in 1874) who was regarded as America's first "labor priest." Working largely in the Midwest following his ordination in 1904, he dedicated his priestly career to the task of making American Catholics aware of the social implications of the teachings of Pope Leo XIII. He is credited with a number of significant "firsts": founding the first Catholic labor college and the first Catholic school of social service, establishing the first association of Catholic workingmen, inaugurating the custom of the Labor Day Mass. "As time goes on," Higgins said, "he will be honored as one of the greatest of all the American pioneers in one of the most important areas of the apostolate."

The National Conference of Catholic Charities, founded in 1910, played an important part in advancing the cause of social activism in the American Church (although in its early years it lagged behind secular agencies in the social field). One of its organizers, and its first executive director, Msgr. John O'Grady, had a vital behind-the-scenes role in the development of one of the most significant documents in the history of the American Church: the program of social reconstruction issued by the National Catholic War Council in 1919.

Known popularly as the Bishops' Program, it was a position paper of remarkable, not to say incredible, far-sightedness for that time. Msgr. Ryan originally had turned down the bishops' request to prepare the text for a document, but it was O'Grady, secretary of the NCWC's committee on reconstruction, whose persistence finally won the day. His repeated urgings convinced Ryan not only that a document was needed, but that Ryan was the only man equipped to do the job. The statement that emerged has stood over the years as a Magna Carta of social action for the American Church.

"The four bishops who signed the statement, long since called to their eternal reward, probably did not realize at the time how far-reaching their recommendations were," George Higgins wrote in an anniversary column 30 years later, in 1949. "They concentrated on moderate measures of reform which seemed at the time to be feasible and practical. They consciously refrained from advocating a 'fundamental scheme' for the reconstruction of industrial society because 'such an undertaking would be a waste of time as regards immediate needs and purposes for no important group or section of the American people is ready to consider a program of this magnitude'. . . . Events were to prove that the bishops, in many of their proposals, were far in advance of their times. Most of their legislative recommendations were eventually translated into fact, but not until a period of almost 15 years had elapsed, and then, in many cases, only partially and inadequately."

The program the bishops recommended was of the kind that had been recommended by Father Dietz and Father William J. Kerby, a positive declaration by the hierarchy on matters of trade unionism and related issues. As finally propounded by Ryan and signed by Bishops Peter J. Muldoon, the chairman; Joseph Schrembs, Patrick T. Hays, and William T. Russell, the statement called for government regulation of public service monopolies; growth of industrial cooperatives; equal pay for women (although it recommended that heavy industrial jobs be reserved to men); a living wage as the minimum demanded by justice; public housing projects and insurance programs; the right of labor to organize and bargain collectively; and a ban on coercion of non-union members by unions. In all, 11 of its proposals would become federal law under the New Deal.

"It was," Higgins wrote in 1955, "perhaps the most important single document and the most significant landmark in the history of the Catholic social movement in the United States."

The bishops' statement stunned the American business community. The document was "partisan, pro-labor union socialistic propaganda," complained the president of the National Association of Manufacturers to Cardinal Gibbons, and an official of the National Civic Federation said that the "near-Bolsheviki" element in whose name the statement was issued did not speak for the vast majority of American bishops.

If its recommendations went unheard during the Twenties, though, they began to be reflected in legislative programs, first, those of the New Deal and, later, the Great Society. They were given strong support all along the way by the Church's social action leadership under Ryan, McGowan, and Higgins himself.

"Happily," Higgins wrote in 1955, "the climate of economic and political thinking has changed for the better during the intervening decades (since the bishops' program was written). Most of the 'socialistic propaganda' of the bishops' program has long since been enacted into law by the federal government. . . . The program is now accepted by the majority of the American people as a moderate program of social reform."

Higgins continued to refer to the historic statement many times over the years, including a comment on its sixtieth anniversary in 1979:

"Surely U.S. Catholics will want to read the Bishops' Program again and refresh their understanding of its contents. Perhaps they will also want to say a little prayer of requiem for the four bishops who signed the document as the Administrative Committee of the National Catholic War Council, and a prayer of thanksgiving that these pioneers should have recommended back in 1919 a social reconstruction program so farsighted and advanced that it is timely in certain major respects three generations later.''

Over the years, Higgins has related the social activist tradition of the American Church to two principal factors: first, the demands of the Natural Law, and second, the teachings of the Church, especially as reflected in the gospel and the great social encyclicals.

A Catholic should work toward social reform, is *obliged* to work toward social reform, simply because such activity is part of the Christian ideal calling for harmony in the social order. Higgins has applied that basic argument many times, as he did in a 1952 Yardstick column: "The Christian has a temporal mission to perform in and through society," he wrote, "a mission which is part and parcel of his supernatural development and not something added as an elective."

Some wrongly attribute Catholic social activity to expediency, he noted, or to ulterior motives designed to further the general purposes of the Church. He rejected that argument, as well another that Catholics who engage in social work do so in something of a penitential sense, depriving themselves of luxury in order to lead a life of virtue. That answer, he said, "is closer to the truth but still doesn't tell the whole story." He continued: "It is a negative reason at best and really doesn't get to the heart of the matter, which is the responsibility of the Christian, for the most positive motives in the world, to see to it that the will of God be done even on this earth as it is in heaven."

For his own version of the full answer, Higgins turned to the French Jesuit, Yves de Montcheuil. In speaking of "the communion of each man with God," implying the Christian ideal of the communion of all men in God, de Montcheuil had encapsulated the reason behind all human activity in the social sphere, Higgins said. He quoted de Montcheuil: "Every factor of hate or discord which divides, which opposes mutual understanding and love, will unceasingly be opposed by the Christian. . . . Therein lies the basis for an untiring activity in the political, economic, and social domain (and) also a fight against all the injustices, all the distorted institutions which are opposed on the human plane to the communion of men and which gives rise to isolation, envy, hatred."

The concept, the argument was as real to Higgins as his morning newspaper, as self-evident as the light of day. A Catholic was obliged to do what he could in the cause of social justice simply because it was part of God's natural plan for him to do so. Higgins might argue in a civil tone with someone who questioned a church position on a matter of collective bargaining, or community organizing, or engaging in a boycott, but he had little patience for those who wondered whether it was any of the Church's business to be there in the first place. It was not only a right, but a duty, he pointed out time and again, down through the years.

If that argument were not enough, he had the rich tradition of the Church's social teaching—its gospel values and its great encyclicals of the last 90 years—to fall back on. Higgins's teachings and commentaries on the encyclicals constitute a study course in themselves, a brilliant reflection of the application of the teachings of the 20th-century popes to contemporary social problems.

The classic social encyclicals of an earlier era, Leo XIII's *Rerum Novarum* (1891) and Pius XI's *Quadragesimo Anno,* published on the fortieth anniversary of its predecessor in 1931, figured prominently in the early columns written by George Higgins. He used them to bolster his own arguments on behalf of collective bargaining and related issues, to explain his unrelenting stand in favor of the Industry Council Plan (of which more will be written in a subsequent chapter), and to refute (in those combative days) the railings of Paul Blanshard, the era's most constant critic of things Catholic. In 1951 he responded angrily to a charge by Blanshard that *Rerum Novarum* was nothing more than "a vague and sentimental appeal for justice for the working man. . . ." by citing the laudatory comments of both William Green, then president of the American Federation of Labor, and his counterpart at the CIO, Philip Murray.

"Take your choice," snapped Higgins. "It's Paul Blanshard versus two of the most important and most influential labor leaders in the history of the United States. If Blanshard is correct, Mr. Green and Mr. Murray are a couple of morons and/or sycophants unworthy of the high honor and privilege of speaking for approximately 15 million American workers. But if Mr. Green and Mr. Murray are correct. . . . what? Then, the time has come for all fair-minded

Americans, non-Catholics as well as Catholics, to stand up and publicly repudiate the prejudices of a former clergyman whose gospel of secularism is just as much opposed to Orthodox Protestantism as it is to Roman Catholicism.''

He was in a mellower mood a decade later, writing on the encyclicals' anniversaries, the seventieth for *Rerum Novarum* and the thirtieth for *Quadragesimo Anno.*

The two documents, he said, had had significant influence in the United States, at least to the extent of making people aware of the ethical aspects of economic life, and of their responsibilities in the political and economic sphere, both individually and as members of groups. Before the encyclicals were written, he said, few Americans thought in terms of economic morality, and even fewer thought it a field for Church involvement. The rugged individualism condemned by the popes was the dominant philosophy of America's economic life. But progress had been made, Higgins noted. Even though "economic liberalism" was still an influential force, "more and more Americans. . .find themselves agreeing with Pope Pius XI when he says that 'even though economics and moral sciences employs each its own principles in its own sphere, it is, nevertheless, an error to say that the economic and moral orders are so distinct from and alien to each other that the former depends in no way on the latter.' ''

He distinguished between the "social reforms" some saw as the encyclicals' ultimate goals, as desirable as those might be, and the broader purpose they had in mind, especially *Quadragesimo Anno.* To that end he quoted his old mentor, Msgr. Ryan: "The term 'reconstruction,' in other words, rebuilding, is the only adequate expression. What the pope demands is a new kind of society, a new social order, an industrial organization which will differ radically from the economic arrangements which have existed for the last 150 years.''

Higgins applauded the progress made in the direction of "reforms," citing the pattern of change which resulted in government intervention in areas of wage benefits, labor safety, family relationships, areas in which earlier administrations had maintained a hands-off policy. But there was more to be done, he insisted, a wider vision to follow. The pope who would chart it was John XXIII, the "transitional pope" whose five-year reign would crumble walls that had been years abuilding.

Higgins acknowledged the forward strides made during the pontificate of Pius XII, even though no major social encyclical emerged during that time. He points out, in fact, that despite the lack of a single complete and definitive summary of the pope's social teaching in encyclical form, "he spoke about the problem in season and out of season." Higgins predicted, therefore, that as future church historians compiled and synthesized Pius's social teaching, "His Holiness, who, in the field of socioeconomic reform, might have appeared during his lifetime to be content to live in the shadows of Pope Leo XIII and Pope Pius XI, will be acclaimed as one of the original and most influential of all the social-minded popes in the history of the Church." Higgins devoted several columns in the Forties and Fifties to refuting "misinterpretations" of papal discourses that indicated, to some, opposition to trade unionism, to any form of nationalization, and to the closed shop. (The latter was the most difficult to deal with, since in his 1952 Christmas message Pius specifically criticized the practice in which "access to employment or to places of labor is made to depend upon registration in certain parties or in certain organizations which trace their origin to the labor market." American right-to-work proponents who pounced on the papal words to support their cause were off-target, Higgins explained, since the pope was referring to European labor abuses in which workers were forced to join the Communist Party or Marxist-dominated unions. "It would be a moral problem were a man forced to join a Marxist union in order to secure work," Higgins said. "Because of this, European Catholic social writers have generally opposed the closed shop. Likewise, Europeans have formed separate Christian unions when the Socialists controlled a national movement. Conditions in America are different. A good Christian can belong to most American unions without such membership involving any moral compromise. For this reason the bishops of the United States have never advocated the formation of Christian unions here.")

It was John XXIII, however, who would be remembered more than Pius XII for dramatic breakthroughs in papal social teaching, particularly in his encyclicals *Mater et Magistra* (1961) and *Pacem in Terris* (1963). Higgins was naturally attracted to the popular pope, whose open style and desire to update the Church won him affection throughout the world. Higgins had John's teaching on ecumenical relations and world peace in mind as much as the social encyclicals when he wrote in June 1963, a week after the pope's death: "In the field of socioeconomic reform and the related field of international affairs, Pope John's impact has been unprecedented from the point of view of immediate and measurable results."

Pope John XXIII had been in office nearly a year before he was the subject of a Higgins column. In the Labor Day column for 1959, he wrote approvingly of the labor-management section of Pope John's encyclical *Ad Petri Cathedram,* citing its emphasis on the moral purpose of economic progress and prosperity, and stressing the particular application of that teaching to the United States.

Higgins was in Rome—conveniently enough, in the Vatican press office—when the first copies of the historic *Mater et Magistra* were distributed, and he recalls sitting that day with Redemptorist Father Francis Murphy in the office of Raimondo Manzini, then editor of *L'Osservatore Romano,* the Vatican daily newspaper, to discuss the encyclical. Manzini was particularly enthused about its new directions. "I had the feeling that Manzini might have been exaggerating in describing it as an important step forward in the development of Catholic social teaching," Higgins said. "My first reaction was that while the new encyclical was obviously very important from the pastoral point of view, it didn't really break much new ground." He changed his mind after a few readings, as he told his column readers on August 7, 1961: "The encyclical, as many commentators have pointed out, is more pastoral in tone than previous social encyclicals. At the same time, however, it comes to grips with and resolves a number of substantive problems, some of them very controversial, in the realm of social theory."

Some of Higgins's most reflective comments on *Mater et Magistra* are contained in an address delivered August 26, 1961 at the University of Detroit, during the fifth annual convention of the National Catholic Social Action Conference. The encyclical's essential theme, he says, is that of Christian social humanism, and its most distinctive feature is "its repeated emphasis on the universal scope of the virtue of social justice and the consequent necessity of effecting a more equitable balance in social relationships at every level and in every sector of the economy." He reviews at some length the document's teaching on trade unionism and labor-management relations, international social justice, wages, property, the role of the government, and other topics before summing up: "These random comments don't begin to do justice to an encyclical which may well prove to be one of the most important ecclesiastical documents in our generation. In any event, the important thing is not to discuss the encyclical theoretically but to try to discern its practical meaning and to look for opportunities to apply its principles to contemporary problems."

Higgins devoted all or most of seven consecutive weekly columns to *Mater et Magistra* in August and September 1961, an unusual pattern of single-issue concentration which indicates his early recognition that the papal letter would become a historic social document. In several cases he referred to the "fundamental principle" of Christian social ethics which John had spelled out: "that individual human beings are and should be the foundation, the end and the subjects of all the institutions in which social life is carried on."

Mater et Magistra, Higgins said, "clarifies and refines our understanding of labor's right to share in management and our understanding of the role of government in economic life." On August 28 he related an encyclical passage calling for labor-management cooperation to the original theme behind the American celebration of Labor Day. He devoted a full column (September 11) to Pope John's use of the word "socialization," which the pope had meant to describe the interplay of relations in society, and which some commentators had mistakenly identified with socialism. Socialization, the pope had written, finds its expression for the most part not in government programs but in a wide range of groups and movements and institutions. Higgins cautioned against reading into that a rejection of governmental action in the social sphere. That mistake, he said, "is more likely to be made by ultraconservatives who interpret the principle of subsidiarity so rigidly as almost to exclude the possibility of effective governmental action. To make this mistake would be to ignore the numerous references in the encyclical to legitimate governmental programs in the field of social welfare and social reform." When governmental action does take place, Higgins said, in any phase of the economic order, the pope insists that it "must be exercised so as to protect the essential personal rights of individuals and the rights of the family."

"Surely one of the most distinctive features of the encyclical," Higgins wrote on September 25, "is its consistently positive and constructive tone—its tone of quiet and reassuring optimism and unaffected benevolence so characteristic of its author." Earlier he had conceded that on most of the social and economic issues it addressed, *Mater et Magistra* "takes what most Americans would probably regard as a liberal line." Predictably, Higgins noted, it drew criticism from some conservative circles, but only one "really nasty comment," a "supercilious and wiseacre sort of editorial" in William F. Buckley's *The National Review,* which referred to the encyclical as a "large sprawling document" which "may become the source of embarrased explanations" in years to come and "must strike many as a venture in triviality." The comment drew a rare burst of editorial anger from Higgins: "This snide comment on the encyclical is a rather disgraceful performance, but it will not have been written in vain if it served to open the eyes of those Catholics who have hitherto looked to *The National Review* for guidance in the field of social ethics."

Pacem in Terris appeared only a few weeks before Pope John, by that time one of history's most universally-loved world leaders, entered the final stage of his fight with cancer. People throughout the world greeted the encyclical's message with the same affectionate enthusiasm they felt for its author, some expresssing surprise at what they regarded as its revolutionary call for peace. Higgins, though, saw *Pacem in Terris* as one more logical step forward in the orderly development of Catholic political and social thought.

In an article written for *Extension* magazine in April 1963, Higgins described the then new encyclical, Pope John's "great 'appeal to love,' " as "one of the most important religious documents of modern times and possibly one of the most important in the entire history of Christianity." Reviewing the encyclical according to its chapter headings, Higgins applied the teachings it contained to contemporary problems: those on "Order Among Men" to America's racial turmoil; those on "Relationship of Man and Political Communities with the World Community" to support for the United Nations, and so on. Welcoming the favorable reception given to *Pacem in Terris* but warning that its ultimate test would be the practical application to which it might be put, Higgins nevertheless told his readers not to underestimate "the unprecedented fact that the entire free world and to some extent, the Communist world as well (with whatever mixture of good, bad and indifferent motives) have publicly applauded the new encyclical.''

He carried that thought forward in the closing paragraphs of his column for April 29, 1963, expressing the wish that all who loved the pope—an incalculable number, surely—would follow his teaching more closely:

"There is a vast difference between Catholic social theory and the everyday practice of individual Catholics. While it is true. . .that four centuries of modern history stand behind the pronouncements of the encyclical *Pacem in Terris,* the practice of Catholics during those same four centuries has too often been at odds with the traditional teaching of the Church.

"Towards the end of the encyclical, Pope John himself laments this inconsistency between Catholic theory and Catholic practice and calls upon the faithful to reestablish an internal unity between their religious convictions and their manner of acting in the temporal order. Let us hope that American Catholics will be among the first to rise to this challenge.''

A little more than a month later John XXIII was dead, and in his column Higgins offered a brief, deeply felt tribute: "Pope John XXIII had the shortest reign of any pontiff in recent history. Yet his influence for good in the temporal as well as the spiritual order was phenomenal and may well have been greater than that of all but a small minority of his predecessors in the annals of the papacy.''

Higgins revealed much more of his profound feeling of loss at John's death in a eulogy he prepared privately for delivery by a bishop-friend (one of many such "ghostwriting" requests he has cheerfully filled over the years): "Long after the Vatican Council and the other public acts of His Holiness have faded in the fine print of the history books and have ceased to be of immediate and overriding interest to the average man and woman—let us say 1,000 years from now—the memory of Pope John's lovable personality, which so faithfully reflected the compassionate charity of our Blessed Savior, will still be as fresh as ever and will be as much of an inspiration to the people of that distant day as it has been to the overwhelming majority of our own contemporaries,'' he wrote. In less than five years, he continued, Pope John had accomplished "veritable wonders that most of us never even dreamed of witnessing in our own lifetime.'' He was not referring, he pointed out, to the great encyclicals or the Council, but that in stamping his personality on these things he had "prepared the way for what promises to be an extraordinarily important epoch in the history of human society—an epoch which, hopefully, will be characterized by truth, unity and peace.''

Higgins wrote about Pope Paul VI less frequently than he had about John XXIII, despite Paul's much longer reign and despite Higgins's generous praise of *Populorum Progressio,* the landmark social encyclical Paul issued in 1967. In the early years of the pontificate, Higgins discussed briefly Paul's first encyclical, *Ecclesiam Suam,* noting with approval the judgment of one commentator that with its publication the pope ''is in fact very much in the progressive mainstream;'' and quoted Paul's full-fledged endorsement of the United Nations to rebuke that organization's American critics (although curiously no Higgins column commented on the Pope's U.N. visit in 1965).

Higgins devoted only one Yardstick column to *Populorum Progressio* (April 17, 1967), taking the occasion to castigate the *Wall Street Journal* and *Barron's,* the national business and financial weekly, for their criticism of the encyclical's rejection of laissez faire capitalism. ''It is obvious,'' Higgins says, ''that the pope is not condemning capitalism as such or in all its forms. What he is condemning, and what many earlier encyclicals have condemned with equal vigor, is the false philosophy of excessive individualism to which some exponents of capitalism subscribe. While it would be unfair to exaggerate the number of capitalists who are committed to this philosophy, by the same token it would be naive to pretend that there are no such capitalists left in the world today.''

Eulogizing Pope Paul in August 1978, he acknowledged the pope's concern for social justice and praised his consistently pastoral and collegial style. ''Pope Paul did not pretend that his treatment of contemporary social and economic problems was exhaustive. His only purpose was to bring them to the attention of his readers and, hopefully, to start them thinking about alternative ways and means of solving them in the light of the Gospel message and of human values.'' He said the pope's final social document, the letter *Octogesima Adveniens* (1971), written to mark the eightieth anniversary of *Rerum Novarum,* was ''a pastoral letter in the literal sense of the word pastoral'' and an effective call to social action. ''The same can be said about the many other statements made by Pope Paul on social problems during his 15-year pontificate,'' Higgins concluded. "His aim in this area, indeed the overall aim of his entire pontificate, was to engage in a fraternal dialogue with the modern world, a dialogue characterized, in his own words, by 'courteous esteem, understanding, and goodness on the part of the one who inaugurates the dialogue.' I have no doubt that history will say that Pope Paul's commitment to this eminently Christian way of teaching was one of the most distinctive features of his pontificate.''

Higgins has been as fascinated as any other observer by the total-involvement papal style of John Paul II. He devoted a friendly column (October 22, 1979) to the American press for its coverage of the papal visit (far from being cynical, as frequently charged, the journalists "went absolutely gaga over the pope" and were "unashamedly sentimental not only about the man himself but, by and large, also about his pastoral mission").

He wrote more reflectively (August 4, 1980) about John Paul's Brazilian trip, seconding one reporter's observation that because of his constant talks on social justice, the journey had become a "traveling encyclical." Wrote Higgins: "The pope knew that merely exhorting Brazilian Catholics to take seriously the teaching of the Church on social justice would not bring automatic results. He also knew the odds against a sudden and dramatic improvement in the lot of the poor and oppressed of Brazil. Nevertheless, as a man of faith, the pope looked to the future with confidence and felt compelled to do what he could to keep alive in the hearts of the poorest of the poor in Brazil the indispensable virtue of hope. . . . He also knew that the people still hoped to find in the Church the strength, courage and hope they so desperately need to struggle, to suffer and to win in their continuing struggle for liberation. So he did everything in his power to lift their spirits and raise their hopes.''

The great papal social encyclicals of the twentieth century were anything but new teachings to George Higgins. They were merely confirmations of what he had known as a student and as a young priest, lending support to what he had been saying all along because of what he knew of the gospel and the natural law: that the Church had an obligation to be involved in the worldly matters of social and economic justice, and that individual and family interests stood at the front line of concern.

He was one of many American Catholics who were preaching the social gospel. Some did it as organizers and crusaders, activists in the most literal sense of the word, especially in an earlier era. The role of Higgins (and some of his contemporaries) has been quieter. He has been a teacher, a defender, an exemplar, and, not to put it too strongly, a conscience. That association carries profound meaning for him, as he has made clear in numerous columns, articles and addresses through the years.

No accident is responsible for the column being listed first. Week after week—in season and out, as he is fond of saying—The Yardstick has appeared in diocesan weeklies across the country, charting a social action course for any who were concerned enough to follow it. The collection of Yardstick columns stretching out over the years, mimeographed, duplicated, set on photo typesetters and sent out over the NC News Service wire stands as the most complete tangible legacy of the incredible body of his social commentary over the years, the compendium he never formalized, the book—regretfully for him; regrettably, for students—he never wrote.

CHAPTER FOUR

THE YARDSTICK

"Writing a weekly column is, if the truth must be told, a beastly chore under the best of circumstances," George Higgins wrote on August 5, 1968.

Less than a year later he made a further confession: "I have been writing this column for almost 25 years. If it seems longer than that to some of our readers, as it does to the writer himself on deadline day, *c'est la vie.*"

He spoke of the column again in June 1970: "It became a chore in much less than six months and has remained a chore ever since—only more so." But he added: "On the other hand, it's the kind of chore that has its own (non-pecuniary) compensations or rewards, and, for this reason, among others, I have opted to stick with it until the bitter end." (He appended another line that would have an ironic ring a few years later: "I plan to hold on to my NC franchise until the powers-that-be move in on me by stealth and take it away by sheer force.")

Chore or not, George Higgins has churned out The Yardstick, with few exceptions, each week for some 35 years. "Within a few weeks," he wrote home on November 30, 1945, "I will take over Father McGowan's Yardstick as a regular assignment." And so it has remained, even after his formal retirement in 1980. Higgins has made The Yardstick synonymous with his social philosophy, his daily work, and his creed.

The Yardstick had been a fixture of the Social Action Department for some years, a vehicle through which first Ryan and then McGowan reached the Catholic public through diocesan newspapers which subscribed to it through the NC News Service. Higgins had frequently substituted as a columnist for McGowan during 1945, and at that point already had some column experience on his own, writing regularly on social issues for *The Tidings,* the Los Angeles archdiocesan weekly then edited by Father Thomas McCarthy. (In a letter to his parents written March 17, 1944, Higgins reported he was "back on schedule" with *The Tidings* column, adding an approving account of how McCarthy had physically ejected two prominent Catholic laymen from his office for protesting the amount of "pro-Negro" material the Los Angeles paper was carrying. Of the laymen and their organization, Higgins commented brusquely: "What a bunch of fakers.")

Some fairly obvious attributes gave Higgins first-rate credentials to do a regular column so early in his career: a marvelous grasp of the general subject area of social action, a clear writing style, an analytical mind, and important contacts, particularly in organized labor. In addition, he always demonstrated a professional news sense. (This was a talent which would prove especially valuable during the Second Vatican Council. Father Andrew Greeley wrote in 1970 that during the council, at a press panel briefing, "a very distinguished journalist" turned to him and said, "You know, of all the men up there Higgins is the only one who understands what a newspaperman has to look for.")

And there were other elements in his makeup—elements less obvious to the general public, perhaps, but recognized by his intimates—that have contributed mightily to the columns over the years. Again, it was Greeley—writing sardonically in 1970 in reply to a young priest who had made the patronizing comment that he and other young clergy respected Higgins but had nothing to learn from him—who pointed some of them out: "Good heavens, yes! George Higgins does not have a beard, or even sideburns, and cuts his hair short; he does not smoke pot, but only long black cigars; he is not self-righteous or moralistic; he has a passion for facts and for clarity; he is incapable of taking himself seriously (and probably has stopped reading this column long before this paragraph); he does not engage in broad, sweeping generalizations. . .and, oh, yes, George Higgins's ultimate crime is wit—the somber, middle-class Catholic rebels can abide just about anything but a priest with a sense of humor. (It's a good thing for the rest of us who write columns for the Catholic press that Monsignor Higgins's wit does not creep too frequently into his columns. The rest of us, I should think, would be very quickly put out of business.)"

Msgr. John Egan credited Higgins's family background for the sense of curiosity which has made him a lifelong student of the world and the Church, and for another attribute critical to a columnist's ability to hold readers' interest: "What I always admired about George was that he was always in the midst of controversy. He never knew how to run away from an argument, and he was a member of a class of great arguers. There was nothing they loved more than to get into a good fight. Now, as a person George is not controversial, but the positions he takes often are. He would have made an extraordinary criminal lawyer. He has a razor-sharp mind, which came from his reading and studying, but mostly from the controversy. But with all the fights he's been in, up and down the gamut of the Church, I never met a person who didn't like George Higgins. They respect him."

("Well, I can say that controversy doesn't bother me personally," Higgins confirmed, "and I've never lost a minute's sleep over a good fight. I've never seen any good reason why you couldn't have a real good argument and still be good friends.")

Egan continued with further thoughts about Higgins, all of which are reflected in Yardstick columns down through the years: "His spiritualness, his deep prayerfulness, religion which was never worn on his sleeve; his marvelous intellect, his love for the Church, his priestliness, his obedience, his respect for authority, his being truly on the right side of every issue, his just detesting hypocrisy, his fear of McCarthyism in the Church at any time, his love of democracy, his respect of the labor movement in America, and for the best self of our republic. . . . It seems to me it forced George not only to be a student of America, with its traditions and how it relates to the poor, but his love of the Church, the Church across the world."

Egan added a final thought that relates to Higgins as a columnist. "You'll never get George shooting off his mouth on something he doesn't know anything about," he said. "But there aren't many things he doesn't know something about."

If that is true, and few who have dealt with Higgins would question Egan's assertion, his amazing reading habits unquestionably have a great deal to do with it, and with providing background material for column after column. Higgins's passion for reading is of legendary proportion to his friends, who seem to vie with each other in recording and measuring it.

Father J. Bryan Hehir remembers with awe his introduction to the Higgins reading phenomenon, when he moved into the U.S. Catholic Conference staff house in his first Washington assignment and found himself across the hall from Higgins, a hero since his seminary days. ("It was like being across the hall from the Trinity," he said with a laugh.) Early on the morning of the Fourth of July, with almost everyone either away for the holiday or about to leave, Hehir remembers passing by the open door of Higgins's room and seeing him sitting in a chair, reading, with a tall stack of books by his side. Late that afternoon Hehir returned to find Higgins in the same position, still reading, with the stack of books reduced almost to floor level.

"On Saturdays George would read morning, afternoon, and evening," said Auxiliary Bishop John McCarthy of Galveston-Houston, recalling with disbelief a typical Higgins schedule. "And you know what he'd do on Sundays? The same thing; he'd read morning, afternoon, and evening. He'd break only for meals, Mass, and a walk. And I never saw him vary that. He never went to afternoon barbeques. If the car needed work, somebody else had to do it or the darn thing would stop. I don't know when he got a haircut.

"I figured one time that George was reading close to 40 hours a week: 15 hours minimum on the week nights, and at least 12 hours combining Saturday and Sunday. So not counting newspapers and anything he read at the office, he read at the staff house close to 40 hours a week. And remembered just about all of it." He paused. "No, change that. He read 40 hours a week, and he remembered everything."

Higgins chuckled when an interviewer read him the quote from Bishop McCarthy. "Reading's a habit," he said, "and I keep needling McCarthy because he thinks he has the habit but he doesn't. He never got in the habit of closing the door and saying, 'It's nine o'clock and I think I'll read until midnight.' I wouldn't think of going through a night without reading for a couple of hours. If I could control my schedule I'd be very happy to spend three or four hours each day reading."

Higgins's family background obviously had planted him firmly in the direction of the kind of reading habits he acquired, especially the example set by his father. (The elder Higgins remained a prime focus of family folklore, and good-natured kidding as well. In 1953 George wrote home to congratulate his parents on the birth of a grandson named Charles Vincent in honor of the patriarch. "If the baptismal name takes," cracked Higgins, "they'll have to get the poor kid a subscription to *Commonweal* for his first birthday.")

But it wasn't just the volume of reading toward which C.V. Higgins had steered George that was all-important, Msgr. Egan pointed out; it was the quality as well. "Mr. Higgins would give George a book after he'd read it, and that signified something," Egan said. "It would be a good book because it had been selected by a person who knew the value of literature and could discuss it with George. I think that accounts for the precision of George's writing and, of course, his thinking. It helped him to develop a reflective and critical evaluation of whatever he was going to read. Very early in his life he developed a sense of discernment as to what was good writing, and what was bad. He never wasted his time in reading trivia."

Another habit Higgins acquired early—and never lost—was that of sharing something he had read with those he thought might use or appreciate it.

"George has a mind that understands every conceivable network," said Bishop McCarthy. "Now, I'll read a good article in a magazine and say to myself, 'I wonder if old Harry or somebody would like this.' George can read the same article and think of 22 people who ought to read it, and he makes sure that's what they do. He's really one of the great communications institutions of the Church. One of the reasons I'm still moderately well informed on the whole social scene is because George has not allowed me to become uninformed. He sends stuff constantly."

The late Bishop James S. Rausch of Phoenix, former general secretary of the bishops' conference, made substantially the same point in an interview. "I'd say that no three days passed during my time as general secretary that George Higgins didn't send something to my desk saying this was something I should read," he said. "Sometimes it would be a book and he'd write, 'Read pages 82-85 and you've got it.' This was an invaluable service to a person as busy as the general secretary. You'd get the meat of the thing and digest it, and you could speak intelligently about the subject or the author. He'd mark the margins of articles, and boil down a lengthy piece to one or two pages. It was a tremendous service."

All the diverse elements that had gone into George Higgins's background—family, studies, Church, friends, reading, contacts—helped to form the tools with which he worked on his major task: teaching, urging, challenging his readers through The Yardstick to meet the obligations of social action which were theirs as American Catholics.

He started out with some fairly rigid strictures regarding subject matter. In 1951, for example, he apologized for discussing an international conference of the Moral Rearmament Movement (MRA): "We ourselves are not competent to express a worthwhile theological opinion about MRA in all of its ramifications; and even if we were, the subject would fall outside the ordinary scope of this particular column, which is supposed to limit itself more or less to the field of socioeconomics." Nevertheless, he managed to make it clear that Pope Pius XII had not endorsed MRA, as some of its backers had implied, and he left no doubt about the extent of his personal misgivings about the movement.

As the years went on, Higgins widened The Yardstick's sights, ultimately addressing topics as diverse as professional football, commercial television, and Little Orphan Annie. For the most part, though, the topics were familiar ones to Higgins readers. The majority of them have dealt in one way or another with organized labor. He has written regularly about interracial justice, Catholic-Jewish relations, questions of international peace, the Second Vatican Council and all the Church-related issues it spawned, the social encyclicals.

Those are fairly obvious divisions of his concern. He has also returned to favorite themes connected in a more general way with social action in the Church. He has pointed out, for instance, that those engaged in Christian social action should not regard it solely as a secular concern, but must be mindful of the importance of liturgy to the social apostolate. Similarly, he has stressed the obligation of the laity to take the more direct role in social activism, for the most part leaving the clergy to leadership, motivational, and guidance positions. (This line of thought surfaced more frequently in the years before the Second Vatican Council.) Many columns have advised those new to the field of social action to remember their debts to their pioneering predecessors—the Gibbonses, Dietzes, Ryans, and McGowans.

And, from time to time, Higgins has used the column to talk about column-writing itself.

In 1955 he lamented the bitterness that had arisen in some disputes among Catholics (mild, it seems, in contrast to the nearly incessant internal battles of the post-Council years) and endorsed a new approach to dealing with inter-Church controversy:

"This new approach. . .would be based on three simple rules: 1) an open-minded study of Catholic social teaching in its entirety; 2) a fair and objective study of both sides of debatable issues, and, 3) a greater measure of fraternal charity which would impel all of us to respect the integrity and good faith of those who disagree with us, unless we have conclusive proof to the contrary. The last of these three rules would seem to be the most important at the present time. Surely we need more knowledge of principles and problems, more scientific research, both doctrinal and factual, but more than anything else we need a spirit of fraternal charity and/or a better sense of humor."

In his first column of 1959 Higgins set down some New Year's resolutions about column writing that stand today—as much as they did then, and as much as his thoughts, cited above, on dealing with controversy—as a personal credo to which Higgins the journalist has always adhered.

He resolved first to be more positive than negative, and quoted an unidentified Irish writer who claimed that too many preachers rail on about neglect of duty, and not enough speak of

God's love. "Amen!" wrote Higgins. "Change the word 'preachers' to 'columnists' and you have the perfect diagnosis of what ails so many of the latter and the perfect remedy for the ailment."

In making a second resolution, to be more tolerant of controversy, he simultaneously served warning that he would never sidestep tough issues. "I shall not hesitate to express my own opinion frankly and forcefully during 1959," he wrote, "but shall try to avoid writing anything which would in any way reflect upon the sincerity, integrity, or theological orthodoxy of those who hold different opinions on the application of Christian social principles to the problems of the day. In return—and this brings us to the first of my New Year's hopes—I would appreciate it very much if some friends on the other side of the fence would reciprocate."

Critics were on Higgins's mind in April 1969, as he discussed correspondence received from readers over the years. Most of it, he said, was on the critical side, and much of it was scurrilous in tone. "Letters of protest have outnumbered congratulatory notes by a ratio of approximately ten to one," he estimated, "and roughly 75 percent of these protest letters have challenged either my integrity, my sanity, my patriotism, or my theological orthodoxy."

Higgins's most revealing written reflections on column-writing appeared in June 1970, as he marked his twenty-fifth anniversary in that role. This was a column in which he admitted, as noted earlier, that column-writing became a chore six months after he started, but that he intended to stick with it. He explained why:

"Not the least of the incidental compensations. . .is that anyone who writes a regular column over an extended period of time is almost compelled, in spite of himself, to do a little more serious reading than he might otherwise be prompted to do. Not that reading doth a columnist make, but other things being equal, it helps to prime the pump and, once it has been primed, helps to keep the well from going dry.

"Secondly, writing a column is an inexpensive form of psychic therapy, a safety valve that keeps the lid from blowing off the boiler when the pressure builds up."

There were perils attached to weekly column-writing, too, he conceded: "Generalizing from the depths of one's ignorance and inexperience about the problems of the universe; turning the pen into a slingshot; making fun of popular idols; . . . trying to be perky or sassy or, worst of all, trying to be funny."

"Having decided not to call it quits," Higgins said, "I can only resolve and hereby publicly pledge on my silver anniversary as a columnist to watch my manners more carefully."

Higgins finally discussed his long-time practice of writing in the first-person singular, pointedly offering no apologies. "For better or for worse, until death or impeachment or forced retirement [another foretaste of the years ahead?] do us painfully part, I shall probably go on speaking to the readers of this column (if there are any left after all these years) in the first person singular instead of pretending, by the use of more impersonal forms of speech, that I am authorized to represent the official point of view of some anonymous corporate entity."

It has not been, ever, an "anonymous corporate entity" that Higgins has represented, but simply the teaching and tradition of the Catholic Church, applied to contemporary situations. In that process, he developed a vision of Church, state, and society in which government, management, and labor worked for the common good in an ordered cooperation blessed by the Church. It was closely allied to the blueprint drawn in the Bishops' Program of 1919, and reflected most faithfully in the Industry Council Plan, the topic of an unusually high number of columns in the Fifties, a subject that will be treated in more detail in the following chapter.

Thus, he was able to write in 1955: "We still have a long way to go, but we have made enough progress in the field of legislation and in the organization of labor unions to warrant our concentrating most of our attention now on what might be called the unfinished business of the Bishops' Program. In other words, having effected a great number of specific 'reforms,' we are now in a position to give our attention to that fundamental 'reconstruction' of the social order which is called for so insistently in Pius XI's encyclical *Quadragesimo Anno,* and in so many of the pronouncements of our present Holy Father Pope Pius XII.

"The 'reconstruction' of the social order, as recommended in the social encyclicals, calls for a democratically organized system of cooperation between labor, management, agriculture, and the professions in a joint effort to establish order and stability and justice in an economic system which, for too many years, has drifted along without adequate moral direction and control and, to some extent, is still distributing its phenomenal benefits unevenly and inequitably.''

In applying the principles he espoused to specific situations, Higgins has frequently run into flak but rarely, even in the early days, encountered censorship problems. Occasionally, though, a diocesan editor would pull a column dealing with issues considered sensitive at the time, many of which seem tame today. It happened even in his own archdiocese. Father Thomas Meehan, then editor of *The New World,* wrote apologetically to Higgins in 1954, informing him that "on instructions" he had withheld from publication a column on the World Council of Churches. It developed that Cardinal Stritch, the ordinary at the time, had decided to ignore a WCC international convention which was to take place in Evanston, and wanted no mention of it in his archdiocesan paper.

The lone written reference Higgins made to an outright attempt at censorship appears in a letter to his parents in February 1951, when he told them there was "trouble" over a column which was critical of Clarence Manion, the archconservative dean of the Notre Dame Law School. According to Higgins, Bishop John F. O'Hara of Buffalo (later cardinal archbishop of Philadelphia), a former Notre Dame president and close friend of Manion, phoned NC News Service in an attempt to get the column quashed, but the problem was worked out amicably by Archbishop Patrick A. O'Boyle of Washington. For his role in settling the matter, Higgins gave O'Boyle, a close friend over the years, one of his highest accolades: "He's a gentleman and a fighter.''

The Higgins reading audience has never been immense by syndicated column standards, but as a specialized group, concerned with social issues and the intellectual vitality of the Church, it was an important audience, influential far beyond its numbers. The postwar American Church was youthful, imaginative, and incredibly energetic, and it was George Higgins's Yardstick that motivated many of its members, those for whom the social mission was a primary concern. General readers, too, found that he could deal with complex economic and social questions in a way they could understand.

He appreciated positive comments about his writing from professionals in the field, and made certain his earliest and most demand-

fessionals in the field, and made certain his earliest and most demanding mentor, C.V. Higgins, knew about them. In 1947 he sent home a copy of a letter from C.G. Paulding, the editor of *Commonweal,* which praised an article he had done: "You have an ease and a freedom, a pace, that you did not have in the old days, a personal style. . . . You'll never lose it." Similarly, he forwarded a brief but welcome note from Bob Considine, the Hearst papers' columnist, responding to a Higgins piece on Gen. Douglas MacArthur: "You wrote yourself a darned good column."

Higgins's friends have joined historians, theologians, political figures and labor leaders, among others, in lamenting the fact that he has never written a book. Higgins shares that regret.

"I suppose if I could live my life over I probably would have disciplined myself to do a little more writing," he said. "I could give excuses and say that I was too busy, but nobody is too busy. I've never been able to block out the time and just sit down and write. In the nature of the job you get caught up in the activity and travel. But one thing: I've never let the job keep me from reading."

So while there has been no Higgins book—not to date, at any rate—there is a permanent record in The Yardstick of an incredible outpouring of words, of insightful and significant commentary on the major questions of our time faced by the Church in the past 35 years.

He has touched on many individual topics in that time, but as noted, a handful of special subjects clearly stand as his own favorites. And of those, he has written more columns—twice as many, in fact—on the one broad topic area with which he has been most closely identified: organized labor.

CHAPTER FIVE

THE LABOR MOVEMENT

LANE KIRKLAND, PRESIDENT OF THE AFL-CIO, CALLED IT A "gold-watch send off," hardly overstating the case. Some 750 guests packed the banquet room of Washington's dazzlingly-refurbished Sheraton-Washington Hotel, long a favorite of the labor crowd as the Wardman Park, to pay tribute to Msgr. George Higgins, whose retirement became official two days earlier—Labor Day, 1980.

Cesar Chavez was at one of the front tables, acknowledging, as he had often done before, all that Higgins has meant to the farm labor movement. Ray Marshall, then the Secretary of Labor, was there as well, bringing an appreciative message from Jimmy Carter. The presence of Senator Daniel Patrick Moynihan, sitting next to Chavez, called to mind his off-the-cuff remark at a "preretirement" dinner for Higgins earlier in the year: "I've been an acolyte at the altar of George Higgins for more years than either of us cares to remember.''

Kirkland's remarks were warm, generous, and to the point.

The crowd was there, he said—a crowd that included international presidents, office workers, shop stewards, local leaders, names known to the world press and names known only to a small circle of friends—to let Higgins know that all he had done for labor over the years was neither unnoticed or unappreciated.

"In looking back through the events in the history of the labor movement for the last 40 years," he said, "it is difficult to find a time when Father Higgins was not there to stand up for the rights of working people. . . .   Father Higgins understands that the American trade union movement speaks and fights for human rights and human dignity. It not only celebrates the strength of collective action to achieve democratic goals, but also never loses sight of the worth of the individual. Father Higgins has found the strength to be a defender of the labor movement and these same principles are in total consonance with the teachings of his Church and the promptings of his heart.''

Veterans of the Catholic social action movement who were on hand responded appreciatively to Thomas R. Donahue, the AFL-CIO's articulate secretary-treasurer. Donahue, a Manhattan College-educated lawyer, referred to Higgins's place in the "singularly important line" of Haas, McGowan, and Ryan—"each, in their turn, the clear, identifiable voice of the Catholic hierarchy on matters of Catholic social action and its application within the labor movement.''

Beyond that, Donahue said, Higgins has sustained "dozens and dozens...of other priests who have been the defenders, supporters, advancers of this workers' movement.'' The audience knew the names that Donahue called off from that "long honor roll of stalwarts'': Msgrs. Charles Owen Rice, John Monaghan, Daniel Cantwell, Higgins's contemporary from Chicago, and Clement Kern, a veteran of the Detroit labor scene; Msgrs. Frank Lally and Lawrence Corcoran from the conference and, of course, Jack Egan; a handful of bishops, including Higgins's long-time friend, Bishop Donnelly, and two who were present, Archbishop James Hickey of Washington, and Bishop John McCarthy; the "labor priests" whose support for Catholic labor schools had inspired a generation: "Father Mortimer Gavin in Boston, Father Vincent Fox in New York, Fathers Carey and Cronin and Toner, and so many more.''

All of them, Donahue said, owed Higgins a debt which flowed from his inspiration and guidance, and for the courage he had shown in the face of criticism. Similarly, he added, Higgins had taught and guided America's Catholic trade union officials—"dozens in this room, and hundreds across the nation"—and provided them with the institutional framework within which the Church's social teaching and policy was to be understood and implemented.

"And so," he concluded, "we honor you as the premier translator of the American labor movement to the Church, and of that Church to this movement. All of us who have taken inspiration from you in the past fully expect to continue to be able to do so for lots of years to come."

Higgins, predictably, wowed the crowd. He introduced his old associate, Father John Cronin, who attended in a wheelchair, and Nevila McCaig, his secretary, "who has run my office, not only in my absence but even when I was there, for 27 years." He told a couple of funny stories about George Meany, and then drew a roar of applause when he said his "retirement," ostensibly the reason for the dinner, was a hoax: "I am not, have never been, and do not expect to be in the future a retiree in anything but the technical sense of the word. . . . I hope to continue what I've been doing in the past, and specifically I hope to continue my very close relationship with the labor movement."

The humor, the quips, the banter were put aside then, and so was the easy exchange with old friends from old campaigns. For the next 20 minutes or so, George Higgins talked in straight and serious and personal terms about the Church and the working man. His words summed up as much as any single talk or column his own feelings toward the labor movement—his love for it, his hopes and fears for it, his total immersion in it as priest and pastor.

His own family tradition, Higgins said, prepared him to accept almost without question an observation by Yves Simon, the French philosopher, about the accomplishments of organized labor: its faults and failures notwithstanding, they stand among mankind's greatest works for what they have done to meet human needs and promote justice. "I believe that," Higgins said. "I believe it sincerely, I always have, and for whatever time I have left in the years ahead I intend to do what I can to support that movement in every possible way."

The family background was critical, of course—the long discussions, the books, the lectures, reading aloud from *America* and *Commonweal,* the underlying insistence that God's gift of life was too profound to have it wasted, even in leisure, on trifles. Charles V. Higgins's incredible degree of influence on his son's life began early and never ceased. "I would never see him," Higgins said, "even until the time he died, that he wouldn't be asking about the latest editorial in *Commonweal,* or *America.* Did I agree with it? Did I disagree? He never stopped wanting to discuss what was going on. . .the important things that were going on."

His education in Chicago's seminary system and, later, at Catholic University—the people who taught and guided him, and the friends he made—followed up naturally on the formation he'd been given at home. So did the very times themselves, filled as they were with news, day by day, of social upheaval: labor unrest, vicious battles between strikers and strike-breakers, mass emigration from the Dust Bowl, bread lines and soup kitchens. There was the accident of timing, too. It was just at the time of his ordination that the Chicago Archdiocese resumed sending its new priests to Washington for further study; a year earlier and Higgins might never have gone to Catholic University. Four years later, as he prepared to return to Chicago and probable seminary faculty assignment, an unexpected vacancy in the conference's Social Action Department created a natural opening for him.

And finally, there was the matter of a great tradition to continue.

The Catholic Church had an established, comfortable relationship with American workers and the associations they formed that dated, at the official level, back to 1887, when Cardinal James Gibbons of Baltimore defended the Knights of Labor while in Rome. Speaking on behalf of the American hierarchy, Gibbons pleaded— successfully, as it turned out—to have a Canadian-inspired prohibition on the Knights lifted by the Congregation of the Holy Office.

Workingmen, the cardinal said in his petition, love the Church and were concerned about their personal salvation. But, he continued: "They must also earn a living, and labor is now so organized that without belonging to the organization, it is almost impossible to earn one's living. . . . To lose the heart of the people would be a misfortune for which the friendship of the few and powerful would be no compensation."

Edward Marciniak, a Chicagoan who has written extensively on the social and moral dimensions of labor, points to the absence of a protracted class struggle in America as a primary reason for the good relations that have traditionally existed between the workforce and the American Church. The Church has never had to face—as it has in Europe—a hostile and dechristianized working class, he notes. Too, the background of the American bishops was totally different from that of European bishops, who frequently came from titled families. "Every one of our bishops," Archbishop Richard J. Cushing of Boston told the CIO convention in 1947, "is the son of a workingman and a workingman's wife." The labor movement's academicians enthused over Church teaching on work and workers' rights, particularly the right to organize, as it was expressed formally in encyclicals and such documents as the 1919 Bishops' Program. Rank and file workers who were Catholic, along with their fellow parishioners, had probably barely heard of the social encyclicals, let alone read them, but still felt the Church was on their side. The priests they saw at church every Sunday came from the same kind of families, and spoke the same language.

Higgins fit easily into the framework of that Church-labor alliance. It was a topic to which he turned in his columns often.

The relationship between religion and labor might have been vague in the minds of labor union pioneers who began the custom of "Labor Sunday" (which became Labor Day), he wrote in 1954, but "all things considered, they were on the side of the angels." The tradition they started has developed to a point, he said, that "it is no exaggeration to say that within recent years Labor Day has almost come to be regarded as an unofficial holy day in the United States."

From time to time he would note that defending the right of workers to organize was good, but not good enough—as he did in 1950: "The time has come to focus on the 'duty' of people to organize—whether workers, employers, farmers, or professional people—and on the corresponding duty of labor unions and business, professional, and agricultural organizations to cooperate with one another and with the government in joint councils designed to promote the general welfare."

The new social order he envisioned would not be possible, he repeatedly warned, without the "renewal of the Christian spirit"

Pius XI called for in *Quadragesimo Anno,* and he often cited the need for better relations between the social action movement and the liturgical movement to help that renewal develop. "The Labor Day Mass," he wrote in 1954, "attended in ever-increasing numbers by workers and employers alike, is a good beginning, but it is not enough. There must be a continuing program of religious education adapted to the needs of workers and employers and designed to convince them of the importance of corporate worship in their daily lives and to show them the connection between the liturgy and social action."

In enriching the lives of workers, the Church needed the active cooperation of labor organizations and employers, Higgins said in a 1958 column, written as he reflected on a Mass for AFL-CIO convention delegates. "I refer," he said, "to the responsibility which labor jointly shares with management to create conditions of employment which will help the average worker, particularly in the mass production industries, to take pride and to find satisfaction in his job, and to look upon it as something more than a means of earning a livelihood for himself and his family."

From time to time, Higgins has reacted with thinly-veiled irritation to the charge that in its long tradition of pronouncements related to the rights of the workers to organize, the Church "takes sides" on behalf of labor.

"Man is by nature a social being with social responsibilities," he wrote in 1961, and those responsibilities cannot be carried out effectively by unorganized individuals. In the same column he quoted from the 1947 pastoral letter of the American bishops, which stressed the social nature of man and of work, concluding that the organization of men according to their function in economic life is both desirable and necessary. "If this be unwarranted interference in politics," said Higgins, "politics will have to make the most of it, for it is the duty of the Church to teach the moral law." He went on to suggest that those who object to the Church's call for more extensive organization in economic life weigh the "more dangerous" alternative—excessive governmental intervention in economic life.

A column on October 3, 1977 summed up Higgins's response to those who contend that the Church is blindly supportive of organized labor and hypercritical of management. What the Church can generally be counted on to do, he said, is to:

1. Defend the right of labor to organize and encourage the labor movement to organize the unorganized.

2. Support the labor movement in its demand for adequate labor legislation and for the repeal or the amendment of discriminatory laws.

3. Approve of labor's request for adequate representation at every level of the economy.

4. Criticize those employers who refuse to bargain collectively in good faith, and criticize the philosophy of unregulated economic freedom in the name of which this refusal to bargain is so often rationalized.

"Unions cannot count on the support of the Church," Higgins added, "when they discriminate against blacks, Hispanics, or other minority groups, when they engage in unjustified strikes, when they resort to violence, racketeering, or other lawless practices." However, he continued: "In my opinion, the majority of American unions are not guilty of such offenses. Most are honestly trying to do the right thing. They have their faults and their weaknesses, of course, but in general they are on the side of the angels in their principal objectives and methods and are deserving of the support they are receiving from organized religion in general and from the Catholic Church in particular."

The people of the organized labor movement are important to George Higgins. Those who walk with him through the corridors of a union-convention hotel will find themselves waiting a dozen times while well-wishers, most of whom he knows on a first-name basis, stop to tell him about a son or a daughter, or to report the illness of an old-time union companion. At home as much on the convention floor as he is on the dais, he genuinely looks forward to mixing with the people—at a regional farm workers' meeting in a dusty Texas border town, or a top-level executive meeting in a Washington hotel. For men and women in the labor movement beyond counting—Catholics as well as those of other faiths, and some of no faith at all—George Higgins is their parish priest.

"George has helped me through some bad days on the domestic scene," a Jewish official said privately during a union convention in 1980. "And I know personally of five or six people he's helped directly, either as a counselor or a friend during a trying period. Who knows how many others there are in this union alone? Or how many people in other unions? Or the number of people he's helped in a more general way? I'm not embarrassed to call George my pastor. He's really a pastor to the whole union movement.''

Higgins himself looked at his role as that of a pastor on occasion—as in the address he delivered at the United Auto Workers convention in Atlantic City in 1957. "It's going to be a sermon rather than an address," he told the delegates. "I am going to talk to you this morning not as a labor economist or a labor journalist, but man-to-man as a Catholic priest who is primarily interested in spiritual and moral values." His 20-minute "sermon" centered on the labor movement's problems with dishonesty and corruption—not in themselves, but as symbols "of a decline in moral and spiritual values on the part of the rank and file, which shows itself principally in a lack of interest in union affairs and an unwillingness to relate the principles of religion and morality to the everyday problems of the labor movement."

He has gone even beyond a pastor's role on occasion, becoming, in effect, a family member. In one especially notable case, he assumed the guardianship of two children whose father, a union official, died with no close surviving relatives, and whose mother was physically unable to care for them. The arrangement was a costly one for Higgins in terms of time and personal concern, and it continued well after his retirement from the Conference.

"There's something to be said for long-term assignments," he said in a 1979 interview. "Whatever field it is that you're in, you establish a certain credibility just by being there a while, and you find you're able to do things you wouldn't be able to do if you were there for only a few years. My work with the labor movement is something like that. I know all the weaknesses of the labor movement—I could write books about it—but I consider it important that somebody is here who has that ongoing contact with a very important movement, and I don't think there's any other way of doing it except to be around for a long time. We, the Church, ought to have a regular presence in the labor movement. Labor should know that the Church is more than an ecclesiastical institution, just concerned with its own affairs. It's taken more of my time than it probably should have, with weddings and funerals and memorial services and what have you. But I've never regretted that time. You know, a lot of priests with jobs like mine say they'd rather be in parish work, that this wasn't what they were ordained for, and so on. But that's never bothered me. There's a form of parish work even in my job which is just as important."

Anyone so inclined could explain away Higgins's involvement with union people by noting that most of them seemed to be Catholic anyway, a fact true enough, and a phenomenon that Higgins had examined in a 1959 column. It was too easy to attribute the working-class makeup of the Catholic Church simply to the fact that most American Catholics are descendants of immigrants, he said; another reason is the social teaching of the Church and its insistence on the right of labor to organize. "Catholic workers, to a greater degree than many of their fellow workers, have been encouraged by their Church to exercise this right," Higgins said, adding a pastoral warning: "The fact that Catholics are proportionately more numerous in American unions than are the members of other religious groups means that they have a proportionately greater responsibility for what goes on, and what doesn't go on, in the labor movement."

From the beginning—from the marathon early-morning conversation with Philip Murray about which he wrote his parents in 1947—to the present, Higgins has been on a first-name basis with every major figure in American labor, as Tom Donahue would put it at his retirement dinner, serving as "the premier translator of the Catholic Church to the American trade union movement and of that movement to the Church." For the most part, he liked them. To a man, they respected him.

Murray's was the first name Higgins mentioned when an interviewer asked him in 1980 to identify the labor leaders who stood out in his mind. "He wasn't only a great labor leader, but a very warm friend, a friend of many people," said Higgins of the late CIO president. "And he was one of the finest speakers I ever heard in my life. Walter Reuther was a different type altogether, much more articulate and intellectual, a man with a lot of vision and imagination. George Meany was another completely different type, with none of Reuther's flair but much more staying power. I never knew John L. Lewis except from a distance, but he was a great leader in his day despite his faults—and he had some bad ones."

He has known each labor secretary over the last 30 years, and formed especially close friendships with two of them: James Mitchell, who served under Eisenhower, and Arthur Goldberg, appointed by Kennedy and subsequently named associate justice of the

Supreme Court and then U.S. ambassador to the United Nations.

The bond with Mitchell was particularly affectionate, but Higgins disputes a friend's recollection that news of Mitchell's death left him in tears. "I don't know that I was that visibly upset," he said, "but Jim Mitchell was a very good friend of mine. It was a personal thing; we were drinking buddies. Mitchell was in the wrong party, of course; he should have been a Democrat. His family was made up of New Jersey Democrats, but he got into this Eisenhower group. He was a wonderful human being. He didn't like the social life of Washington, but he loved to sit around for a long quiet talk. He'd skip all the parties, so I used to spend many evenings with him. He was a real good friend."

Higgins's friendship with Goldberg dates back to more than 30 years. "A wonderful man and a very close friend," Higgins said. "He's put me on the spot a few times, and all I can do is just laugh it off. He once got Cardinal Cody aside at a dinner in Chicago— this was my bishop, of course—and wondered why I hadn't been made a bishop. Then it happened again, and that time I wrote to Cody, a good-humored letter, I thought, hoping that he would realize I hadn't known anything about it, and so forth. He never answered."

Goldberg puts a closer tag on the beginning of the friendship—a Washington dinner with young Father Higgins and his predecessor, Father Ray McGowan, along with Philip Murray, shortly after Goldberg came to Washington as general counsel for the CIO in 1948. As a frequent lecturer at the labor schools flourishing in the Chicago Archdiocese under the aegis of Msgr. Hillenbrand, the future ambassador was familiar with "Catholic issues" involving labor. He and Higgins hit if off immediately, and the friendship has endured over the years. They have collaborated in matters involving Catholic-Jewish relations on occasion, but their professional relationship, as Goldberg pointed out in an interview, involved labor matters. "The years that we spent together were labor years," he said. Goldberg appointed Higgins, or had him appointed, to a variety of mediation boards, fact-finding panels, arbitration boards. "He was involved in the issues I always deemed important," Goldberg said. "Equality in America, freedom from prejudice, for Blacks, Jews, farm workers, anybody, across the board. The one common reaction I had from people toward George was that they all accepted him, a great testimonial to him."

Still another labor secretary for whom Higgins had a special fondness was Martin P. Durkin, who came from a poor family struggling to survive on Chicago's South Side and rose to national prominence. "He didn't go around feeling sorry for himself," Higgins wrote when Durkin died in 1955. "He tried to improve the situation by collective bargaining and progressive social legislation. For 40 years he dedicated himself, in the labor movement and in government service, to the cause of social justice; and when he died, a few weeks ago, he was one of the most highly respected men in American public life."

Higgins's standard technique over the years has been—with rare exceptions, generally involving highly specific situations—to praise labor leaders in public and reserve his criticism for private sessions, as often as not over a number of scotches in the early morning. Occasions such as these provide Higgins with the opportunities to "needle" his friends in the movement (his expression) and get them to look favorably on minority training, support for the farm workers, and other issues close to his heart.

"George would be constantly meeting with people at our conventions," I.W. Abel, the former Steelworker president, said in a 1980 interview, "and we wouldn't think of having a convention without him. He'd get us talking not just about the proceedings of the convention, but about the things he was interested in, like the farm problem or the civil rights movement. And nobody resented it. I've never heard a word about him that wasn't completely complimentary."

Higgins found his technique successful, and thinks that it worked well for several reasons. For one thing, he said, the message he was delivering on questions such as civil rights was a message the union people knew they should be hearing, with Higgins, again, filling the pastoral role. Secondly, he had entree to the top officials because—in his own evaluation—he had been around "long enough" to gain credibility. That was one of the reasons he was annoyed that the U.S. Catholic Conference had no one ready to replace him when he retired.

"I stayed here long enough to establish a contact with the labor movement that couldn't have been developed any other way," he said in an interview at the time of his retirement. "It takes years. I'm afraid that won't continue after I leave. I'd say in all modesty that if they found a priest tomorrow for the staff and told him, 'The only thing we want you to do is keep in touch with the labor movement,' he couldn't do it in less than five years. Or 10 years. It would take him that long to get his credibility established. Look at the UAW. They only meet every three years. A fellow would have to be here 10 years before they'd even let him in the hall. Well, they might let him in the hall, but they wouldn't know who he was.''

One reason Higgins reserved his criticism of labor leaders for private conversations was his awareness of their resentment of a public rebuke. "Labor leaders," he wrote in 1972, "are hypersensitive to public criticism, even when they happen to agree with and might even be willing to admit that the criticism is well founded."

When he did go public with his praise in the Yardstick, though, it was from the heart and, certainly in these instances, written from an insider's perspective:

Philip Murray (November 17 and November 24, 1952): "As a graduate student of labor economics at the Catholic University of America, I managed, through the good offices of a mutual friend, to be invited to Mr. Murray's apartment for an evening's conversation—or so I had expected—on labor-management relations. Fortunately, from my point of view, we never got around to such a prosaic subject. The only formal education I received that evening was an undergraduate course in poker. Mrs. Murray, a lovely woman to whom our heart goes out in deepest sympathy in her bereavement, ended up with almost all the chips. . . .

"Philip Murray has been repeatedly eulogized these past 10 days as one of the greatest labor leaders in the history of the United States. He was more than that. He was a great human being and will be honored as such in the folklore of American trade unionism long after the details of his phenomenal career as a labor statesman have ceased to be of interest to the average American.

"(He) was a symbol, perhaps the most perfect symbol in the history of the United States, of the wholesome relationship which prevails and, please God, will continue to prevail between the Catholic Church and the American labor movement. Murray was the perfect combination of the practical Catholic and the practical labor leader. His intense loyalty to the faith of his fathers and his equally intense loyalty to the cause of organized labor, far from being in conflict with one another, were opposite sides of the same coin, the former loyalty providing the motivation for the latter."

Walter Reuther (May 18, 1970): "Devotion to the labor movement and to the cause of the poor and the underprivileged came to him quite as naturally and quite as instinctively as devotion to his family and his nation. . . Those of us who were privileged to know him as a friend can testify to the fact that few men in the history of the American labor movement have ever served that tradition more faithfully, more unselfishly, and with greater effectiveness. . . .

"The labor movement is a means, a noble and indeed an indispensable means, through which workingmen and women express and put into practice the spirit of justice and charity which has its roots in the very depths of their conscience. This is what the labor movement was for Walter Reuther. He had profound respect for his fellowmen and all his life tried to show this respect by serving them unselfishly. . . .

"The UAW is his lasting, everlasting, monument. What he did for the million-odd members of this great international and, through this international, for the nation as a whole will be regarded for all time as one of the greatest contributions made by any man of this or any other generation in American history to the cause of social justice and the advancement of human progress."

George Meany (December 3, 1979; January 28, 1980): "The great outpouring of respect and affection which was showered on Meany as he handed over the AFL-CIO president's gavel to his long-time associate, [Lane] Kirkland, was richly deserved, not only because of his many accomplishments as one of the truly great figures in the history of organized labor, but also, and even more importantly, because of his sterling personal qualities. As I noted in my invocation at the opening session of the convention, he is a man of 'granite-like integrity, great sincerity and strength of character'—a man who, without fear or favor, always means what he says and says what he means, sometimes bluntly, to presidents and kings as well as to his associates and peers in the movement to which he has dedicated all his energy for 60 years or more. . . .

"I owe him a great personal debt of gratitude for many favors over the past 40 years, but I would find it difficult to express my gratitude in words. In lieu of that, upon my retirement from the U.S. Catholic Conference staff, I will present my entire labor library, in his honor, to the George Meany Center for Labor Studies. . . ."

(Excerpted from Higgins's homily at Meany's funeral Mass): "Coming back to the prayer with which he so appropriately concluded his farewell address at the AFL-CIO convention two months ago, let me simply underline the fact that his priorities as a public figure were always kept in the proper order. After giving thanks to God for granting him more than one man's share of happiness and rewards, he prayed, in this order, for the nation which he loved so dearly and the labor movement which he served so effectively for more than half a century. . . . In standing up consistently not only against communism but against any and all the forms of totalitarianism, George Meany was not defending the so-called American way of life as such. He was defending the cause of human rights which, for him, were indivisible and were meant to be universal in their application.''

George Higgins is fond of saying that as head of the conference's Social Action Department, he rarely knew what his day's agenda would be until he'd looked at the front pages of the morning's *Washington Post* and *New York Times*. Roughly translated, it meant that if a breaking story somewhere demanded comment, background information, or deeper study from the Church, Higgins wanted to be ready to get onto it right away. It probably made for sometimes haphazard administration (as Higgins himself concedes), but it was a policy that enabled him, and through him, the American Church, to be in the thick of contemporary issues where moral and ethical values were at stake. As often as not, where Higgins was concerned, a labor connection was involved at least indirectly.

That approach helped to make Higgins much more than a theorist in matters involving labor and the Church—although the extent of his philosophical background lent added weight to the stands he was to take. He liked, rather, to wade into specific issues. He made his position clear in private talks with labor officials, in speeches across the country, in the convention invocations for which (because of their content and, at times, their length) he achieved a certain notoriety, and most of all through The Yardstick. Its currency and its wide distribution made it a natural vehicle for Higgins to address contemporary social issues, and it was read avidly (as it continues to be today) by labor leaders, by the rank and file, by other commentators and by the general public to determine where Higgins, and, inferentially, the institutional Church, stood on a current topic.

In the labor field, few issues were as long-running or as historically significant as the merger of the AFL and the CIO, and Higgins gave it the attention it deserved.

On December 8, 1952, he provided an historic backdrop to a hoped-for merger—which had been given added impetus by "the almost simultaneous decease" of Murray and the AFL's William Green. "To our way of thinking," Higgins said, "there has been no fundamental, and certainly no irreconcilable, difference between the two. By the time the CIO was organized the AFL had already begun to modify, if not to abandon, its traditional philosophy of voluntarism or 'pure and simple' unionism. . . .'" The difference between the two unions over social and labor legislation, dating back even to the Thirties, was one "chiefly of degree," Higgins said.

Less than a year later, on October 12, 1953, he noted progress toward a unified labor organization: a no-raid pledge made by the AFL, and a similar resolution due from the CIO. The AFL was "our largest and most powerful labor organization," he said, but because of the CIO's influential role in collective bargaining the AFL should treat it as an equal partner. While the presidents of both organizations favored the merger that was to come, Higgins sounded a warning: "It is an open secret that some of the associates of Meany and Reuther are not prepared to ratify the no-raiding agreement. Meany and Reuther will have to use all of the influence and prestige at their command to keep the peace within and between their respective federations."

As the merger drew nearer, opposition from the right grew louder and more extreme. In his column of May 16, 1955 Higgins attacked a mysteriously written Washington news letter that suggested that a merger would ultimately lead to the formation of a labor party in the United States, and that it was a part of a "master plan" to take over the federal government. Higgins ticked off the names of notable Republicans who looked favorably on the merger, including President Eisenhower and Secretary of Labor Mitchell. "A man of less integrity than Mr. Mitchell," he said, "could have found a number of fairly plausible excuses for keeping this opinion to himself."

Higgins played no direct role in bringing the merger about, but behind the scenes (more from the AFL side than the CIO's, according to the Steelworkers' Abel) served as a listener, adviser, and friend to the principals. It was fitting—and predictable—that he was there to deliver the invocation at the first joint convention of the AFL and CIO in December 1955. His invocation at the final separate convention of the CIO, held just prior to the joint session, looked ahead to the success of the new organization with an eye on history:

"We approach this historic turning point in American history fully conscious of the possible dangers as well as the potential benefits involved in the establishment of labor unity. Labor unity is not an end in itself. It is only a means to an end. If it helps to advance the cause of social justice, as we expect it to do, it will be a great boon to our beloved country. If, on the other hand, it fails to serve people whom it will be privileged to represent, if it fails to respect the rights of management and the public—if, in short, it fails to serve the general welfare—it will not and should not be permitted to survive."

As closely identified as he was with the labor movement, George Higgins never excused hints of corruption or racketeering associated with unions. Indeed, he faced the issue head on many times over the years, invariably warning that even suggestions of impropriety were inexcusable.

The vicious 1956 attack on Victor Riesel, the New York labor reporter, drew a quick and angry comment from Higgins. Riesel was permanently blinded when intruders, assumed to be thugs hired by certain labor interests, splashed sulphuric acid in his eyes during an early-morning attack in his home. The assault apparently was in retribution for columns Riesel had written on union corruption.

"The solution to the problem of labor racketeering is anything but simple," Higgins wrote on April 16. "The impression . . .that the problem can be solved by the labor movement alone. . .is a great over-simplification." That is a joint responsibility, Higgins continued, of labor, management, politicians, and law enforcement officials.

Higgins approvingly noted in a column on April 8, 1957, "the statesmanlike and intelligent manner" in which the labor movement had reacted to the forthcoming investigation by a Senate committee headed by Senator John McClellan of Alabama. He singled out Meany and members of the AFL-CIO's executive council: "These men readily admit that there are serious abuses in the labor movement, and when they say they are determined to eliminate these abuses, they mean it. Naturally they would prefer to clean house on their own initiative. . . through the Ethical Practices Committee. They realize, however, that the job is too big for them, and consequently. . . welcome the assistance of the McClellan committee."

The union officials would stand by their pledge to support new legislation designed to eliminate abuses, Higgins said. "This I know from discussing the matter with many of them privately and off the record." Their example, he continued, should be followed by other economic organizations such as the National Association of Manufacturers, or the U.S. Chamber of Commerce, management-oriented organizations with which Higgins has often been at odds over the years. He concluded that labor's willingness to clean house was perhaps overdue, but welcome nevertheless. He urged reasonable legislation to correct abuses. "Punitive legislation," he said, "is no solution to the problem of racketeering or corruption. On the contrary, it would only make the problem worse."

In November 1957, taking pains to emphasize that he was not overdramatizing the scope of the problem of union corruption, Higgins hailed the Senate investigation as a "godsend." Corruption in the ranks of organized labor is limited to a relatively small group, he wrote. "Nevertheless," he said, "it is sufficiently extensive that had it continued for another decade without public notice and without a determined effort on the part of the labor movement itself to correct the situation, the cause of trade unionism in the United States might have suffered irreparable harm."

In a column dated May 12, 1958, he urged union cooperation with the subcommittee headed by Senator John Kennedy, charged with preparing legislation to correct union abuses. It was The Yardstick's first mention of Kennedy, a man Higgins found distant and ambitious. (He was equally unenthusiastic about Robert Kennedy, he told the author in 1980, contending that the "ruthless" label some found appropriate for the New York senator was, indeed, just that. On the other hand, Higgins had high praise for Senator Edward Kennedy of Massachusetts, a good friend whom Higgins finds warm, outgoing, sincerely interested in poor people and working men and women, and, generally speaking, "right" on the labor question.) His reservations about the author aside, Higgins enjoyed reading Robert Kennedy's *The Enemy Within,* an account of the workings of the McClellan committee, which Kennedy had served as chief counsel. Reviewing the book in a 1960 column, Higgins noted approvingly that Kennedy described union officials "with few exceptions" as honest and dedicated. Kennedy also pointed out that while the AFL-CIO had moved against unions such as the Teamsters and Bakers because of certain corrupt practices, no management group had acted similarly in dealing with members who were found to be in collusive deals.

Throughout his career, George Higgins has demonstrated little room for compromise, if any at all, on questions involving racial equality. If that was true of his position on racial questions in general, a subject which will be treated in a subsequent chapter, it was even more so where unions were concerned. Higgins used his columns, his influence, his personal friendships, and the prestige of his office to get union leaders—often recalcitrant, at that— to see not only the moral necessity but the practical need as well of promoting genuine racial equality in the labor movement. The entire field serves as a prime example of what Higgins was able to accomplish simply by being, as he likes to point out, on the job long enough.

He attacked the problem in some of his earliest columns. In connection with a survey of a large, unidentified union issued at the time, he wrote on March 17, 1952: "The failure of all too many Catholic members of this union to apply the principles of their religion to the problem of race relations is discouraging to say the least." In 1958 he singled out for praise three unions for positive accomplishments in the field of race relations: Rubber Workers, Electrical, Radio and Machine Workers (IUE), and the United Steelworkers.

"George was always pushing us," one union official said in a 1980 interview. "We'd be sitting around after a meeting, having a drink or two, and George would manage to get the conversation around to civil rights. 'What are you people doing?' 'Wouldn't it be better to do these things yourself than have to be forced to do it?' 'Can't you see how unfair your policies are now?' If it wasn't that, it was the farm workers. George never let up."

As the subject of racial equality heated up in the Sixties, Higgins turned to it more frequently in his columns. He issued one of his most direct challenges to the labor movement with a column (August 26, 1963) that took labor leaders to task for sitting out the landmark civil rights demonstration that would take place in Washington on August 28. Higgins pointedly noted that each year, in what was usually his Labor Day column, labor could expect a pat on the back. However, he said:

"We are now at a turning point in the history of the United States and also in the history of the American labor movement. This is the year of decision for all of us in the field of race relations and civil rights.

"On Labor Day, 1963, therefore, the labor movement, like every other organization in American society, is on the spot. For the moment it must expect to be judged almost exclusively on its performance in the field of civil rights and must expect to be told, even by its friends, that its record on the issue of civil rights has been somewhat disappointing."

Higgins then referred to the civil rights demonstration. "Perhaps there is something to be said for labor's decision to sit this one out but, if so, labor hasn't said it very convincingly," he said. He continued.

"Negro leaders are also asking, quite legitimately, when the labor movement is going to lower the boom on those unions which are still practicing racial discrimination. When an employer tries to discourage the organization of his workers or refuses to engage in collective bargaining, the labor movement will go to almost any length to bring him to time, and, if necessary, will drive him to the wall. Negro leaders are disappointed that it tends to react much less vigorously when one of its own affiliates is guilty of practicing racial discrimination."

A year later, in a sermon he delivered at the annual Labor Day Mass of the Washington Archdiocese, he made basically the same points, adding that the record of American industry and American management is no better than that of organized labor. Expanding on the theme in a subsequent Yardstick column (September 14, 1964), Higgins said that the record of labor's top leadership—beginning with Meany, he noted—was better on the race question than that "of many second and third echelon union officers and infinitely better than that of many rank-and-file union members at the local level."

Higgins missed few opportunities to get that message through to the rank and file, too. It popped up in his sermons during convention Masses, in his chats with delegates, in his "invocations," where he rarely omitted a pointed petition to the Almighty.

Later on, Higgins saw signs of progress. He applauded efforts to "tackle the issue of race relations head on" in the 1968 election, and in 1971 (Yardstick, October 4) challenged labor's critics who claimed or implied that unions, all unions, were guilty of racial discrimination.

Higgins's emphasis on the rank and file—in this case, developing the commitment of individual members for the formal positions taken by union leaders—reflected his genuine interest in their welfare, their appreciation for the sacrifices of their predecessors, their support for the principles of sound unionism. As noted earlier, his long record of attendance at certain meetings, the AFL-CIO, UAW, and Steelworkers among them, has brought him into regular contact with delegates. Whether he knows them by name or not, he makes it a practice to draw them into conversations as he does cabdrivers and others with whom he comes in contact during his frequent travels— simply to find out what they're talking about.

He made that point in a 1952 Yardstick column (January 14) which took issue with a conservative magazine's claim that rank-and-file members, relatively conservative individuals, were disinclined to support union leaders' collective bargaining demands. He cited a recent Steelworkers' convention to make his point. He had been attending "five or six" labor conventions a year for 10 years, Higgins said, and the rank-and-file delegates he encountered at the Steelworkers' session were "more radical and more militant" than any he had come across.

"We arrived at this conclusion," he said, "not merely by listening to the spirited discussion from the floor, but also by engaging many of the delegates in private conversation between the acts. All those who spoke from the floor and all those with whom we talked privately made it abundantly clear that they are doing their own thinking. . . . They may be right or wrong, but right or wrong they certainly are not being victimized by Philip Murray and the other officers. . . ."

In a number of comments extended over the years, Higgins was pessimistic about union workers meeting their responsibilities to participate in local deliberations. That was particularly so, he noted, in mass production industries in large industrial centers. But he continually matched the personal concern he felt for rank-and-file members with a theoretical appreciation of their worth that he outlined in an early column (July 13, 1953):

"The importance of the attitude [of the rank and file toward their local union and its elected officers] can hardly be exaggerated. For if it be true that the health of the whole labor movement is forged in the councils of its thousands of affiliated locals, intelligent rank-and-file participation in local union affairs is almost a matter of life or death for the movement as a whole."

One tangible means that Higgins has used to demonstrate his concern for the welfare of individual union members has been his enthusiastic participation in the United Auto Workers' Public Review Board, an outside "watchdog" committee which Higgins has served as a member since its formation in 1957. He became its chairman in 1962, a post he continues to hold. Each year the board of seven members, most of whom are from the academic world, issues a formal report on a case-by-case basis, explaining decisions it has made on individual appeals, many of which involve local elections and various personal grievances.

He bristled at a conservative columnist's suggestion when the PRB was founded that it would be little more than window dressing, especially since its work had not yet begun. In The Yardstick for April 29, 1957, he said: "Nothing could be more futile than to engage in an a priori controversy. . .as to the value of the board and/or the integrity of its members. As one of the members of the board, the present writer is perfectly content to let the record speak for itself."

In his report as board chairman to UAW delegates at their 1979 constitutional convention in Anaheim, California, Msgr. Higgins said that while the volume of appeals handled during the year was high, "the cases with which we had to deal were of the type which one would normally expect to rise in the day-to-day conduct of the affairs of the union." He continued; "No case, however, involved issues or subjects which would give rise to concern over the continued commitment of the union to its traditions of trade union democracy or the integrity of its leadership." Commenting on the fact that the UAW had expanded the scope of PRB activities, Higgins added an informal note of congratulations. The UAW pioneered in turning over grievance matters to outsiders, he said, and now was showing "courage" in giving the board an even wider range of jurisdiction. "I wish others would copy your example," he said.

George Higgins's position in the conference, his knowledge of internal union operations, his acquaintance with labor and government officials and his perception of social justice concerns gave him a unique vantage point from which to study major labor-related disputes over the last 40 years. First among them, of course, was the continuing struggle of the farm workers, which will be discussed in the following chapter. A few of the specific cases on which Higgins has spoken out, with comments culled from Yardstick columns:

The Kohler strike (July 2, 1962): "One of the longest, bitterest, and most tragic strikes in the history of this nation: the eight-year strike of UAW Local 833 against the Kohler Company of Sheboygan, Wisconsin. . .The press can help to hasten a constructive settlement. . .by reporting negotiations calmly and factually and with a minimum of sensationalism. . .Community leaders in Sheboygan can also help to release the bitterness of the past by patiently building bridges. . . . The clergy have a particularly important role in this regard."

The Farah boycott (October 10, 1977): "Doctrinaire anti-unionism was the real cause of the company's current crisis. If Willie Farah had concentrated on running the business efficiently instead of leading a fanatical crusade against trade unionism and collective bargaining, he would have saved himself and his company a lot of grief. Actually, that's what the boycott was all about. Its sole purpose was to persuade Mr. Farah that, whether he wanted to or not, he would have to respect the right of his workers to organize for the purpose of collective bargaining."

The Campbell boycott (May 19, 1980): "Church teachings hold that through work, men and women must be able to achieve at least a minimum standard of living, allowing them to live in the divine image. The most basic problem Christians have with the Ohio migrant issue [basically, the issue on which the boycott turned] is that the wages and living conditions of these children of God represent a denial of his law in this respect. . . . It is incorrect to conclude that the Church is against the growers in this controversy. The Church is not against anyone; she is for God's law and its application to human affairs."

The Nestle boycott (June 9, 1980): "The tragedy of this whole affair lies in the fact that the boycotters ask a minimum of Nestle. The company is not asked to remove itself from the infant-formula market. It is simply asked to stop all direct consumer promotion; stop the use of company milk nurses in Third World countries; cease distribution of free formula samples to new mothers and health-care institutions; end all gifts to the medical profession and fully inform health-care personnel of the dangers inherent in the use of the product under poverty conditions. Why Nestle cannot turn around the increasingly adverse public image it is receiving and go along with such demands remains a mystery.''

The J.P. Stevens boycott (April 28 and November 3, 1980): ''The southern bishops' March 12 endorsement of the J.P. Stevens boycott has been severely criticized by some southern Catholic business executives. This criticism has been shallow and simplistic. . . . During 36 years at the U.S. Catholic Conference I have known no other case in which a group of bishops made such an intensive study of a particular problem before taking a position.'' One would have to be naive to think Stevens ever would have settled with the union had it not been for the boycott and other forms of economic pressure exerted by the Amalgamated Clothing and Textile Workers Union and its supporters. Stevens' 17-year battle with the ACTWU has been costly not only for the company, but the union as well. . . . (The) historic agreement has been described accurately as a 'truce,' because Stevens has said it will continue to oppose the union in its other plants. . . . The company certainly has a right to take this position, provided it observes the letter and spirit of the law, as I gather it has now agreed to do. Legality aside, however, I think it is making a bad mistake. Sooner or later the textile industry in the South is going to be organized. For the good of all, including the company, why not sooner rather than later?''

George Higgins's support for the right of workers to organize extended not only theoretically, but on the practical level as well— to an area which steered him into sometime difficult waters: workers in Church-related institutions, especially hospitals and schools.

On March 25, 1968 Higgins, emphasizing that he was speaking for himself and not as director of the conference's social action department, said ''the time has come'' for Catholic institutions to catch up with what others had done 30 years earlier; namely, ''to begin to take seriously the right, or, if you will, the obligation of people to organize into their own economic organizations. . . .'' Administrators of Catholic institutions, not having been ''out in front of the field'' in labor-management relations, should start making up for lost time, he added. ''The notion,'' he said, ''that because we are connected in some way or another with Catholic institutions, or even worse, the notion that because we graduated from a Catholic nursing school and are now working in a non-Catholic hospital or health situation, and therefore should not get involved in this rather 'dirty' business of trade unionism, is as dead as a dodo.''

On several occasions in 1976 Higgins had encouraging comments to make about Catholic educators trying to deal with the relatively unfamiliar problem of teachers' unions. "I have the impression that many of the delegates [to a National Catholic Educational Association symposium on collective bargaining], despite their confusion and concern about the impact of collective bargaining, are prepared to live with it if and when they are required to make a decision," he wrote (November 1). "I am afraid, however, that some administrators will go down fighting and will be tempted to adopt a negative and legalistic approach to unionism and collective bargaining." He especially hoped, he added, that administrators would not stall the issue while the question of National Labor Relations Board (NLRB) jurisdiction was being decided on constitutional grounds.

On January 22, 1979 Higgins expressed support for teachers in Catholic schools who wanted to dissociate themselves from the American Federation of Teachers (AFT) because of that organization's opposition to federal aid for parochial schools. "I have always been a staunch supporter of the AFT," he said. "I reserve the right, however, to disagree with my friends in that organization when I think they are wrong, and I think they are dead wrong in taking such a doctrinaire stand on the federal aid issue. They are out of touch with reality if they expect the rest of us to agree with them or refrain from taking issue with them in the public forum. That's not the way the game is played in our society."

After the Supreme Court ruled (March 21, 1979) that teachers in church-related schools were not covered under the National Labor Relations Act, Higgins warned Catholic school administrators not to use the decision as an argument against dealing with teachers' unions in their institutions. Were that to happen, he said (April 9, 1979), parochial school teachers who wanted to organize for collective bargaining purposes would have no recourse but to strike for recognition. Instead, he said, administrators should negotiate bona fide contracts and move to establish voluntary substitutes for the NLRB, in conjunction with Catholic teachers' unions and the professional assistance of outside experts.

Higgins's most recent comments on unions and Church-related institutions have had decidedly pessimistic overtones. In a column on October 29, 1979, he chided a Catholic college for sponsoring a "union-busting program," and in an interview by Dan Morris, editor of the (Oakland, California) *Catholic Voice,* predicted that friction between Catholic institutions and employees who seek unionization "will probably get worse before it gets better."

The 1979 column criticized Loyola College of Baltimore, which sponsored a program called "Management in a Union-Free Environment: A Unique One-Day Labor Relations Program." The purpose of these programs is "the denial of democracy in the workplace," Higgins declared, and their "bottom line is unchallenged management rights." He quoted from the brochure which described the program: "Without unions, there are no restrictive work rules . . . no strong union officials. . .no time wasted in processing union grievances and arbitrations. . .no time lost in contract negotiations, strikes or other non-productive activities." Said Higgins: "I can't imagine how a Catholic college can justify or rationalize lending its good name to this kind of anti-union propaganda which runs directly counter to traditional Catholic teaching (and directly counter to long established federal policy) on the subject of trade unionism and collective bargaining." Some of the management consulting firms, Higgins said, employ rough tactics in helping their clients keep free from union activity; others are concerned only with preventing workers from organizing for the purpose of collective bargaining. "I find it impossible," Higgins concluded, "to reconcile this with the basic principles of Catholic social teaching."

Higgins cited such consulting firms in his interview with Morris, noting that some Catholic hospitals have used them to avoid unionization. "I think that's a mistake," he said, "and it's going to leave a lot of scars." He said hospital administrators fear third-party interference with their operations, and use that fear as an argument against the formation of unions. "Much of that fear, I suspect, is ungrounded," Higgins said. "But they perceive it as a problem. My guess is that 20 years from now many of those fears will be seen as academic. People will wonder what all the shouting was about."

Higgins saved some of his sharpest criticism, especially in the last 10 or 15 years, for liberal critics of individual labor leaders or of the labor movement as a whole. He seemed increasingly disturbed by liberals, or, as he often preferred to label them, phony liberals, who felt they had outgrown the old-fashioned liberalism associated with labor. Higgins could be as tough as any critic when he felt labor deserved a rebuke, but he was even tougher on those who were once friendly but now characterized, or more properly, caricatured, the labor movement as lazy, tired, and out of touch with the times.

On October 14, 1974 he gave something of that treatment to Wilfrid Sheed, the novelist and critic, who had written a book linking the Catholic Church, the Mafia, and the labor movement as three "vanishing species." The publisher's blurb had said that each was based on "a value system formed during a pretechnocratic immigrant-oriented age," and that each is "guided by chiefs whose own personal values reflect the obsolete realities of this earlier period." Higgins commented wryly: "I don't know what the Church and the Mafia will think about that inflated rhetoric, but as a long-time observer of the labor movement I wish, for his sake, that Mr. Sheed had forbidden his publisher to put it into cold print. Frankly, it makes him look a little silly." He questioned Sheed's credentials as well as his research, wondering aloud if he had really interviewed George Meany. "Yet," said Higgins, "to read his 'provocative analysis of the condition of labor today', you would think that he knew Mr. Meany inside out. All I can say is that better men than he have lived to rue the day that they made his same mistake."

Higgins used the same column to castigate the editors of *The Nation* for their "Labor in '74" issue, principally on the same personal issue. "I stopped counting [the number of pejorative references to Meany] when I got to 10," he said, "for by that time I was convinced that Meany's critics were slightly paranoid." He continued:

"The labor movement has its faults, and I assume that Mr. Meany would be perfectly willing to admit that he, as president of the AFL-CIO, is not immune to criticism. On the other hand, I can't help but yawn when I find serious writers repeatedly trying to caricature President Meany as a reactionary bumbler, a kind of neanderthal man who is standing in the way of progress in the labor movement. I haven't heard the word in a long time, but when I was a boy they used to call that tommyrot.

"Just a few days after *The Nation's* Labor Day edition appeared, Mr. Meany made the strongest, toughest, speech I have ever heard in support of Cesar Chavez and The United Farm Workers of America. His critics might be surprised to learn that Chavez was exuberantly happy about the speech. . . . Needless to add, Chavez knows very well, even if Meany's critics are unwilling to admit it, that Meany's support of UFW is worth considerably more than that of any UFW's supporters in the ranks of the intelligentsia, and may well be the decisive factor in bringing about a victory for Chavez' union in its struggle for survival."

The Yardstick for September 19, 1977 was one of several others in which Higgins took a similar tack. He was particularly hard on a *New York Times* column by Tom Wicker in which Wicker confessed to being "heartened" because Meany had spoken on problems of unemployment as they affected Blacks. "What Meany said was a substantial development," said Wicker, "and if that means [here Higgins interjected "notice the 'if' "] that George Meany and the AFL-CIO is coming out in a broad sense for social objectives, then I think he is coming back into the fold, and I am in favor of that."

Higgins fumed: "While I have great respect for Tom Wicker as a journalist and commentator, I must say that's an insufferably pompous statement. It suggests that Wicker is beginning to lose his sense of humor or that he hasn't been reading his own paper in recent months." He listed some of Meany's accomplishments in that area, and added: "It is also a matter of record that Meany has been supporting 'social objectives' with much greater vigor than most of labor's sideline critics, who are now using these social programs as a litmus test of Meany's liberal orthodoxy. In short, it is laughable for a journalist who only dabbles in economic matters to be patronizing a man of Meany's stature, and downright insulting for him to say that he is now magnanimously prepared to welcome Meany back into the fold."

Washington Star columnist John Fialka came in for his share of criticism in the same Yardstick piece, having used his Labor Day column to announce "very solemnly" that he had completely given up on the labor movement. He said American unions were living in the past, that the passion of the early labor organizers had died "and in their place was a fat, narrow-minded complacency."

Higgins responded with a rare public display of the impatience and irritation he occasionally shows in private when confronted with similar comment.

"Whenever I read the kind of stuff that Wicker and Fialka handed out so pompously over the Labor Day weekend," he said, "I keep asking myself why I haven't run into them more frequently during the 30 years that I have been following labor matters almost full time and at very close range. Could it be that they have really been out there leading the troops in the struggle for economic justice and that I just happened to miss them? I think not. The more likely explanation is that while Meany and company, with all their limitations, have been working full time in the field of social reform, many of their liberal critics have been busy about other things. That's fair enough, but common sense would seem to dictate that they refrain from talking down to the people on the firing line.''

Liberal critics of modern unionism, especially those who didn't have their facts straight, brought out a streak of peevishness in Higgins, but for the most part he has remained cheerful and upbeat about matters involving the labor movement and its leaders. He has been consistent as well, returning to established themes in light of changing conditions over the years: the right to organize, certainly; collective bargaining; labor schools and ''labor priests'' (''We object to being characterized as a 'labor priest,' as does every other priest to whom the label has been applied'': July 25, 1955); and over and over again—in season and out, as he would put it—the Church's teaching and its application to contemporary problems.

The annual Labor Day statements he produced for the conference reflect his singular dedication to advancing labor's cause in light of that teaching—warning, encouraging, exhorting; summing up the state of things and trying to predict the future. An occasional pessimistic note slips in, as it did in 1981 (September 7): ''The labor movement is beset by a crisis of identity and credibility which only the painful process of self-criticism and internal renewal can resolve.''

For the most part, though, the prophecies were positive, the reflections warmly nostalgic. As he wrote on August 28, 1978:

''I haven't heard anyone complaining about the fact that Labor Day, with all its rich traditions, has become, for practical purposes, a relic of another age. To the contrary, I have the impression that most people, including most workers, really couldn't care less. And maybe that's just as well. There is no point in living forever in the past.

''And yet wouldn't it be unfortunate if the American people, and especially the younger generation, were to become so future oriented as to break their links with the past and lose sight of where they came from? Correct me if I am wrong, but I have the feeling this has already begun to happen in the case of the labor movement.

''By and large, young adults, including young priests and

union members under 40, seem to know very little, and care even less, about the history of organized labor. At best, they are only vaguely aware that the labor movement, as we have come to know it, had to struggle for its very existence against almost insurmountable odds, and that over a period of many decades.''

Higgins, then a year-and-a-half away from formal retirement, recalled the labor tradition of the Catholic Conference on February 5, 1979, in a column which contained excerpts of a talk he delivered while accepting the Hubert H. Humphrey Civil Rights Award from the Leadership Conference on Civil Rights:

"The National Conference of Catholic Bishops-U.S. Catholic Conference remains fully committed, as always, to a progressive program of social reform. . . . I am grateful to the conference of bishops for having given me unlimited freedom over the past 35 years to carry on, however inadequately, in the great tradition of the late Msgr. John A. Ryan, first director of our Social Action Department— a tradition that was developed and refined over the years by my colleagues, the late Father Raymond A. McGowan and Father John Cronin, who is now retired. [Msgr. Ryan's] views and the work our conference has tried to do (in industrial ethics) during the past 60 years can be summarized, at the obvious risk of oversimplification, by quoting two sentences from one of Msgr. Ryan's books which he wrote at the height of the Great Depression: 'Effective labor unions are still by far the most powerful force in society for the protection of the laborer's rights and the improvement of his condition. No amount of employer benevolence, no diffusion of a sympathetic attitude on the part of the public, no increase of beneficial legislation, can adequately supply for the lack of organization among the workers themselves. . . .''

Higgins noted with regret that the majority of wage earners remained unorganized, as they had been in Ryan's time. Because of that, he continued: "We remain committed, as Msgr. Ryan was 50 years ago, to do whatever we can to help organize the unorganized, especially those whose right to organize is being openly violated by anti-union forces in our society. Despite the progress of recent decades, the right of workers to organize is still a live issue. The right itself is seldom, if ever, explicitly or directly challenged as a matter of theory, but in practice hundreds of thousands of workers still struggle against difficult odds to achieve the protection and benefits of collective bargaining long since enjoyed by their fellow workers in most of the basic industries in the United States.

"We have no choice, in the light of our own tradition, but to continue to stand up and be counted in defense of labor's right to organize. There is one school of thought which says that, in doing so, we are beating a dead horse or, alternatively, that the labor movement is passe. We disagree with both arguments.

"The labor problem is not a matter of ancient history. It is an ongoing problem which calls for active involvement on the part of those who believe in social justice. While the labor movement is undoubtedly far from perfect, there is no other movement in sight which would enable American workers to protect their legitimate economic interest and at the same time play an effective and responsible role in helping to promote the general economic welfare."

Higgins continued to spend time countering the arguments of labor's critical commentators such as Msgr. Robert G. Peters, long-time editor of *The Catholic Post,* Peoria diocesan newspaper. Peters had complained that some people were addicted to the "myth" that unionism is "as sacrosanct as the Holy Grail" and as a result were overly hesitant to criticize its faults. His specific complaints were that labor was guilty of holding back modern technology to protect jobs, that labor's top echelon people were bureaucrats, far removed from the working person, and that "some unions" were corrupt, tainting all unions.

Conceding "an element of truth" in each charge, Higgins said it did not justify the vigorous anti-unionism of various management interests. The crux of the matter, he continued, is that "many of labor's antagonists are not simply criticizing labor for its abuses, but are deliberately and, in some cases, avowedly agitating against the very principle of trade unionism. . . . It would be a great mistake to confuse this kind of destructive anti-unionism with objective criticism of labor's admitted faults and imperfections."

On September 5, 1980, as he looked out at the hundreds who were present for his AFL-CIO-sponsored retirement dinner in Washington, Higgins made many of those same points. Yes, he said, labor had its faults, but they were far outweighed by its positive accomplishments over the years. Those accomplishments were threatened by new pressures, he maintained, not the least of which are economic, and that as a result a "growing spirit of resentment" was increasingly a problem. Then he touched on the historic link between the labor movement and the nation's poor.

"Under the pretense of managing our economy," he told the audience at the Sheraton-Washington, "social programs are being severely cut back, labor's right to organize is being effectively thwarted in many industries, unemployment is at intolerable levels and the poor and the aged, in too many cases, are being left to their own devices of survival.

"This tendency to try to turn back the clock while ignoring the plight of the poor and the disadvantaged raises serious questions about the future of our society. Are we in danger of becoming a society in which private gain is placed above social and religious values? Will our national and global communities be torn apart by the struggle for limited resources? Will our economic problems be solved at the expense of the poor and the weak, both at home and abroad? The answer depends on our willingness to place the values of human dignity and equality at the heart of the debate over our nation's future.

"The labor movement, in my judgment, has an absolutely indispensable role to play in seeing to it that these values prevail in the months and years that lie ahead."

One way in which George Higgins expressed his commitment to both causes—to organized labor and to the disadvantaged—would give him more satisfaction than any other single endeavor. It was centered around one man, whose name first appeared in a Higgins column on April 18, 1966, when he wrote: "Thanks be to God, he is still a relatively young man—young enough to complete the job which he has so successfully begun. . . . More power to him. We haven't seen anyone like him in the American labor movement in many a long day."

The organization the young man headed called itself the National Farm Workers Association. The man's name was Cesar Chavez.

CHAPTER SIX

THE FARM LABOR MOVEMENT

"MY INVOLVEMENT IN THE FARM LABOR PROBLEM HAS given me greater satisfaction than almost anything else I have done during my 36 years at the conference," Msgr. Higgins said as his retirement neared.

"I doubt that anybody has done as much for us as Msgr. Higgins has," Cesar Chavez said in 1980.

The two sentences sum up as concisely as possible the relationship between Higgins and the farm workers who had found their champion in Chavez. For Higgins farm labor was a cause to which he gave his personal, even passionate dedication; for Chavez and the farm workers, Higgins was an advocate whose enormous influence might have been—and in the eyes of some observers, probably was—the difference between success and failure.

"I never analyzed the reason I got so deeply involved," Higgins said in an interview early in 1980. "It's a combination of things. Here was a country that was fairly affluent, and we suddenly discovered through the media—and through Cesar's ability to sell his story—this group of people in a very rich country who are at the bottom of the heap. I guess that's what started it all."

The farm labor problem, more properly, the plight of farm laborers, had occupied Higgins for many years. Some who rallied to the marches and boycotts of the Sixties and Seventies did so because the emotional protests they heard appealed to their sense of justice. Higgins, predictably, came to the battle with much more, based on his years in Washington: an understanding of the economics involved, a knowledge of the laws that had worked and those that hadn't (and those that were never given a chance), and a broad vision of the overhaul that was needed if farm laborers were ever to hope for a place in America's affluent society.

Cesar Chavez was still a young field worker, his first strike a year or two behind him, when Higgins first devoted a column to the farm labor problem. It was April 16, 1951, a time when the nation was mesmerized by the televised hearings on organized crime by a Senate subcommittee headed by Estes Kefauver. Acknowledging the scope of "public immorality" the hearings had exposed, Higgins regretted the fact that a report issued at about the same time hadn't stirred up similar indignation.

The report was prepared by the President's Commission on Migratory Labor (which included Archbishop Robert Lucey of San Antonio) and, according to Higgins, it "uncovered at least as much immorality as the Kefauver Committee did." He cited abuses of migrants by American farm owners discussed in the report, adding: "These are crimes that cry to heaven for vengeance; but by American standards, as of 1951, they are still rather respectable crimes. The men who perpetrate them are the very pillars of respectable society in their local communities." The scorn displayed for the criminals spotlighted in the Kefauver hearings was proper, Higgins conceded. But, he continued: "We ought to save a little of it for respectable growers who made a deliberate policy of hiring women and children, often in violation of state and federal legislation, to pick their cotton or their beets." Interspersing phrases from the commission's report, Higgins concluded: "The migratory workers of America, who 'move restlessly over the face of the earth, but. . .neither belong to the land nor does the land belong to them,' are our 'brothers under the skin,' our brothers in Christ.''

A tragic bus accident that took the lives of 16 migrant workers in Arizona led to a Yardstick column on July 6, 1959. In this column Higgins noted that transportation was only one of many areas in which migratory workers were not properly covered by legislation. ''The shocking truth of the matter,'' he said, ''is that there is practically no social legislation of any kind, either federal or state, for the protection of agricultural workers in general and migratory workers in particular.'' He cited the Fair Labor Standards Act, Unemployment Compensation, Workmen's Compensation, the Labor-Management Relations Act and Child Labor Laws as particular laws which failed to protect farm laborers, resulting in ''substandard wages, excessively long hours, poor housing, inadequate health facilities, and a number of other depressing conditions.'' Departing from his general policy of not recommending public support of specific Congressional bills, a significant departure, perhaps, in view of what would be his advocacy role in relation to the United Farm Workers, Higgins endorsed bills that would provide a minimum wage for farm workers (75 cents an hour), regulate child labor in agriculture, and require the federal licensing of crew leaders (many of whom had gained reputations for unscrupulous conduct in dealing with the laborers under them). ''Farm workers in general and migratory workers in particular, being completely unorganized and having no lobby of their own, must of necessity look to sympathetic friends in other walks of life to fight their legislative battles for them,'' Higgins wrote.

He returned to this theme in his column two weeks later, singling out the Labor-Management Relations Act as the most important of all the pieces of legislation which was being denied to farm workers. (In later years, Higgins joined other friends of the United Farm Workers in defending the union's decision, based on strategic considerations in its battles with growers and with the Teamsters, not to seek inclusion under the National Labor Relations Act since it forbade the secondary boycotts which Chavez had utilized so effectively.)

The reason farm workers needed this legislation, Higgins said, was to help them to organize and bargain collectively. ''In the absence of an organization of their own,'' he said, ''they are unable to counterbalance the political influence of the growers, who are extremely well organized and have a very effective political lobby at the federal as well as the state level.''

Although such formal organization was not likely to take place for some time, Higgins continued, the trade union movement, hitherto quite indifferent to the farm labor problem, "is now beginning to make up for lost time." He especially welcomed the formation by the AFL-CIO of an Agricultural Workers Organizing Committee, with a pilot project in northern California, aided by the "vigorous support" of a number of priests there.

One reason the situation of American farm workers failed to improve was the existence of the so-called *bracero* program, which allowed (under Public Law 78) Mexican contract workers to enter the U.S. for specific farm jobs. Noting that some 500,000 had come to the U.S. the previous year, Higgins commented on November 2, 1959, that while no one would object to the fact that the *braceros* were guaranteed decent housing, free transportation, and a 50-cent minimum hourly wage, "it is morally indefensible to deny to our own American migrants even the admittedly substandard guarantees which are provided for the *braceros*."

In subsequent columns Higgins took a stronger stand against the *bracero* program, pointing out its adverse effects not only on farm laborers, but on small family farms, even then in danger of extinction. He explained its workings, and its advantages to corporate farm operations, in a Yardstick column on May 20, 1963: "A *bracero*-seeking grower offers work at perhaps 60 cents an hour in Arkansas. If the wage is inadequate to attract farm workers, he does not have to raise the pay. He simply tells the federal government that he cannot get farm labor, and asks for *braceros* from Mexico. The poverty of northern Mexico is so great that *braceros* are available at these wages. The result is that poverty competes against poverty to produce more poverty. . . . Most *braceros* are used by large growers, sugar refining corporations and vegetable and fruit processing companies to harvest their crops. Public Law 78's mass importation of Mexican farm workers helps the corporation farms drive out family farms which use little or no hired help."

Higgins joined representatives of other religious groups in calling for the repeal of Public Law 78, or its formal expiration at the end of the year.

"The mass importation of foreign workers is one of the major reasons why American farm workers, the poorest work group in the United States, were able to earn an average of only $881 in agriculture during all of 1961 and were able to obtain only 134 days of farm work in the entire year."

The efforts of Higgins and other critics of Public Law 78 were ultimately successful. The program, begun in 1951, was phased out at the end of 1964, an event that went unnoticed, and certainly unmourned, in The Yardstick.

No column summed up as effectively the Higgins overview of the farm labor problem in the pre-Chavez era as The Yardstick for January 2, 1961, in which he again criticized Congress for having failed to enact legislation which would aid farm workers. Congressional inaction, he contended, was helping to perpetuate a farm labor system that was based on poverty and destitution at home and abroad. Poverty at home, he said, provided a pool of workers willing to migrate from harvest to harvest at substandard wages under poor living and working conditions. Foreign poverty made it possible for agricultural employers to obtain hired hands willing to work for even less.

"If this pool of underprivileged workers were not available," Higgins said, "American growers would have to compete on the open market for their labor. They, like industrial employers, would have to plan their production schedules in accordance with the labor market situation. They would have to offer wages and working conditions that would appeal to domestic workers, who are covered by such protective legislation as minimum wage, unemployment insurance and workmen's compensation. In short, they would be forced to raise employment standards in agriculture.

"However, because there is poverty at home and abroad, the American grower does not have to worry about such things. Because his workers are exempt from most social and labor legislation, he can ignore taxes for unemployment insurance, insurance rates for workmen's compensation, industrial child labor laws, and laws which guarantee workers the right to organize into unions. Most important, because there is no floor on wages for agricultural workers, he can recruit workers at wages far below the level necessary to maintain human dignity.

"As a result, American farm workers, especially migratory workers, are among the least privileged of any major occupational group in the nation. Anyone who has seen the conditions under which most of these workers live knows that it is not necessary to go abroad to observe human beings living in abject poverty. . . .

"There is no way that this problem can be rationalized out of existence. The basic causes of the farm labor situation—low wages and unemployment due to labor surpluses in some of our rural areas—must be eliminated once and for all. It should be public policy to adopt those measures which will achieve this goal.

"To put it in a more positive manner, it should be public policy to accomplish in agriculture what we have already accomplished in other sectors of our economy—the restoration of respect and dignity, based on good wages, good working conditions and steady employment, to the men and women who labor for hire on American farms."

Chavez had already begun his rise to national prominence; by 1961 he was serving as director of a California self-help organization, and within a year would begin his organizing efforts in the grape fields, founding the National Farm Workers Association. He and Higgins had not yet met, but their paths were already merging. Their eventual encounter would have a profound impact on the social action role of the American Church.

Cesar Estrada Chavez had lived the terrible migratory life about which Higgins wrote so effectively. Born in 1927 near Yuma, Arizona, to Librado and Juana Chavez, who had a small farm in the north Gila River Valley, Chavez and other members of the family began the migrant life when the mortgage on the farm was foreclosed during the Depression. They packed what they could into the family car and headed for California. They tied carrots in Brawley, harvested vegetables near Oxnard, joined the grape harvest in the Fresno area, spent a few months in a cotton camp near Mendota, where home was a 15'-x-15' tarpaper and wood cabin. A single electrical bulb hanging from the ridgepole provided the only light.

"We couldn't play in those camps like we did on the ranch," Chavez once told writer Ronald B. Taylor. "We had been poor then, but we had a big adobe ranch house, with lots and lots of space. We had a special place where we would play, by this tree that was our own. And we built things—playhouses, bridges, barns—we could come back the next day and they would be there. . . . I bitterly missed the ranch. Maybe that is where the rebellion started. Some had been born into the migrant stream. But we had been on the land,

and I knew a different way of life. We were poor, but we had liberty. The migrant is poor, and he has no freedom.''

The Mexican-American migrant had other handicaps. Tolerated but not accepted, he lived in a world of segregated movie houses, "White Trade Only" diners, and schools where his national background was a source of ridicule.

"They wouldn't let you talk Spanish," Chavez told Taylor. "They would make you run laps around the track if they caught you speaking Spanish, or a teacher in a classroom would make you write 'I won't speak Spanish' on the board 300 times. I remember once a teacher hung a sign on you that said 'I am a clown, I speak Spanish.' " Despite the best efforts of Mrs. Chavez to give her children a good educational background, Chavez dropped out after the eighth grade. By that time he had lost count of the number of schools he attended. He has estimated it at 30 or 40.

He began a hitch in the Navy in 1944, when he had just turned 17, and when he was discharged two years later, after serving in the South Pacific and on Guam, went back to the cotton fields. He took part in his first strike in September 1949, when the fledgling National Farm Labor Union conducted a walkout by several thousand cotton pickers to protest a cut in the pay rates. The strikers went back to work two weeks later with the pay cut restored, but Chavez was disturbed by the lack of organization and effective leadership in the union. He was interested enough to want to learn more, and when a congressional subcommittee held hearings on farm labor strikes in Bakersfield two months later, Chavez took time off to be there. (The subcommittee's members included a freshman California congressman named Richard Nixon, already a favorite of the influential agribusiness community. As Nixon observed during the hearings: "Agricultural labor has been exempted from all labor relations (laws) ever written. The evidence before the subcommittee shows that it would be harmful to the public interest and to all responsible labor unions to legislate otherwise.")

Priests had played significant roles in the life of Cesar Chavez long before he had heard of George Higgins. One of them was Father Donald McDonnell, one of four priests (the others were Fathers Thomas McCullough, John Garcia, and Ralph Dugan) who formed the original San Francisco archdiocesan mission band, organized to work with the rural poor. A later member of the same mission band and a long-time social activist, Father Eugene Boyle, calls McDonnell "the man who discovered Cesar Chavez." Knocking on doors in a San Jose *barrio* called *Sal Si Puedes* ("leave if you can"), McDonnell met Chavez quite by accident—and found him a ready listener, anxious to know as much about labor organizing as he could.

Ronald B. Taylor, a veteran California labor reporter whose 1975 book *Chavez and the Farm Workers* (Beacon Press) chronicles the early Chavez years in great and highly readable detail, quotes Chavez on the impact of the chance meeting:

"He told me about social justice and the Church's stand on farm labor and reading from the encyclicals of Pope Leo XIII, in which he upheld labor unions. I would do anything to get the Father to tell me more about labor history. I began going to the *bracero* camps with him to help with the Mass, to the city jail with him to talk to prisoners, anything to be with him. . . ."

McDonnell soon introduced Chavez to Fred Ross, a community organizer who had studied under Saul Alinsky and was a faithful disciple of the Alinsky techniques: a strong, grass-roots organization built around shared concerns and a strategy that confounded the power structure by bold and confrontational tactical moves. He joined Ross in the Community Service Organization, a group which registered many Mexican-American voters, aided countless other migrants with naturalization procedures and citizenship classes, and generally gave the rural poor, the bulk of them Mexican-Americans, a voice and a sense of power. (Others who joined the CSO and later became Chavez' closest associates in the United Farm Workers were Dolores Huerta and Gilbert Padilla.)

By the end of the Fifties, Chavez was ready to translate the CSO operational techniques into the formation of a union, under CSO auspices, but the organization's board turned him down. Several other farm labor organizations were struggling to make a go of it: the NFLU (which had called the original 1949 strike in which Chavez was involved); the Agriculture Workers Association, formed by Father Thomas McCullough and composed principally of Mexican-Americans; and the Agricultural Workers Organizing Committee (AWOC), established in 1959 at the direction of the AFL-CIO executive council. (AWOC's effort, surprisingly, turned out to be somewhat amateurish, mainly because its early leaders were totally unfamiliar with farming and farm labor. It eventually succeeded in organizing some workers, many of them Filipinos in vineyards and vegetable fields.) As interested as some CSO officials were in farm labor, others were not, including most of the board members. When they turned down his request, Chavez decided to go it alone. He resigned his CSO position in 1962, moved his family to Delano, and launched his union, the National Farm Workers Association.

He spent time crisscrossing the state's farm areas, talking to people in the fields during the day and in the barrios at night. Some 250 or 300 laborers attended the new union's first convention in Fresno in September 1962. Chavez was elected president; Dolores Huerta and Gil Padilla vice presidents, and Antonio Orendain, who would split with Chavez in later years, secretary-treasurer. The union banner which would soon become familiar across the country was unveiled for the first time. Designed by Manuel Chavez, it featured a black Aztec eagle against a white circle, all on a deep red background.

Chavez continued spending much of his time as he had done before: organizing, talking, listening to people. The new union was pushed into two small strike operations before it was ready to conduct them, and although both failed, they provided valuable lessons. It wasn't until 1965 that the National Farm Workers Association became embroiled in its first major strike, and it came about only because another union had initiated the action. The other union was AWOC, the joint target of its combined effort with the NFWA was the table grape industry, and the events of the next few months, largely directed by Chavez, would make his name a household word across the country.

From the beginning Chavez made his union, under whatever title it went by, an organization dedicated as much to the cause of the Mexican and Mexican-American people as to traditional union concerns: better working conditions, better wages, and the like. That aspect of his activity—the cause, or, as it came to be known, *La Causa*—helped to attract a growing number of clergy to his side.

Many had been there long before: Fathers McDonnell and McCullough, Father Boyle, Father James Vizzard of the National Catholic Rural Life Conference and Father Keith Kenny of Sacramento, a pilot who flew Chavez low over the fields so he could greet laborers through a bullhorn. The Protestant clergy counted many staunch Chavez supporters in its ranks, none more dedicated or involved for a longer time than Rev. Wayne (Chris) Hartmire, who had been with the California Migrant Ministry. He helped to enlist others such as Jim Drake, who aided significantly in the early organizing years.

"Cesar always recognized the need for clergy involvement," Father Boyle observed. "For one thing, it was useful in fending off the charges of communism that were always raised when his name would come up, but more than that it was tied in with the people he represented. There was a deeply imbedded cultural factor there that made the church involvement a natural part of things."

Others with deeply-felt concerns about social rights took up the NFWA cause as they heard more and more about Chavez. In a decade remembered for its social activism, the rights of farm laborers, especially migrant laborers, would become a major concern. Much of that was due to Chavez himself and the mystique he projected—partly by design, to be sure, but highly effective nevertheless. Word about Chavez was already filtering back east. Among those who began hearing about Chavez was George Higgins, and all that he heard was good.

"By 1965 it was clear that Cesar was different," Higgins said in an interview. "Most of what I knew came from reading and hearing about him, since I spent so much time in the early Sixties with the activities of the Council in Rome. I first met him at a Catholic social action meeting in Boston, but it wasn't until the bishops' farm labor committee became active in 1970 that I really got to know him."

As noted earlier, Higgins first mentioned Chavez in his column on April 18, 1966, when he said of him, "We haven't seen anyone like him in the American labor movement in many a long day." He repeated the theme three months later, on July 18, when he referred to "the inspired, not to say charismatic leadership" of Chavez and noted: "From all accounts, he is a man of extraordinary genius and unimpeachable integrity."

The great grape strike would bring the Chavez name to many more people. When Chavez convinced some 1,000 NFWA members, partly by quoting the words of Leo XIII, that they should join AWOC's strike against the grape growers, he launched the union into a role of prominence from which it has not since retreated. One factor was the strike itself, and some of the events which accompanied it: a boycott of table grapes, which soon became nationwide; Senate hearings that spotlighted abuses suffered by migrant workers;

visits by prominent supporters such as Walter Reuther; the short-sighted anti-strike techniques of police, which included jailing workers for using the Spanish word *huelga* instead of the English *strike;* a 300 mile march from Delano to Sacramento, which began with less than 100 and wound up on Easter Sunday 1966 with some 4,000 participants, including a number of celebrities; Chavez' own well-publicized fast, which he ended by breaking bread after Mass with Senator Robert F. Kennedy.

Every bit as critical to the union's eventual success was the presence on the scene of William Kircher, whose name, although perhaps not familiar to the general public, holds a permanent place of honor in the union's history. "I would think that if Cesar were completely honest," Higgins said, "he would admit that Bill Kircher did more for that union than anyone except himself."

Kircher had been named director of organization for the AFL-CIO by its executive council in 1965, and one of his first assignments from George Meany was to resolve what had become an unhappy situation with the Agricultural Workers Organizing Committee. Under the AFL-CIO constitution, an organizing committee is an affiliate of the national organization, without the autonomy of a full-fledged union. The organizing committee period is one of trial, and as far as AFL-CIO headquarters in Washington was concerned, the AWOC had not proven itself.

"Meany's suggestion to me," Kircher said in an 1980 interview, "was that we find a union to take AWOC off our hands. So I went out to California convinced that the only way it could succeed was with a unified base of operations. And I set my course to try to accomplish that."

Kircher met Chavez in January 1966, impressed with the man but also with those who had been attracted to him, so many of them typical of the aggressive, committed young people drawn to important causes during the turbulent Sixties.

"They were very anti-establishment, and they knew just so much," Kircher said with a smile. "As far as they were concerned, there was really no difference between AT&T and the AFL-CIO. We were both establishment, massive and structured and impersonal. So I was about as welcome as the president of a giant utility corporation. But I knew I'd overcome them. I talked with them, spent time with them, even marched with them, all the way to Sacramento. Then things got a little bit warmer, and they thought that maybe I was for real.''

A year later, over the objections of some Chavez followers and the misgivings of others who had dreamed of an independent union, AWOC and the NFWA were merged into the United Farm Workers Organizing Committee (UFWOC) of the AFL-CIO, with Chavez as president. The merger proved to be a turning point for the farm workers.

"Bill Kircher was the number one support the farm workers had in the labor movement," Higgins said. "He and Meany were always at it; Meany accused him of spending too much time on the farm labor thing. But he'd go right back at him. Fortunately for the farm workers, Bill was in the position as director of organization to make his support count for more than that of just any other one person. He could easily have said he didn't really have time to devote to this one issue, but he didn't. He was committed. He helped them with the techniques of organizing, how to handle publicity, how to work out contracts. He practically lived out there. He'd get into his old clothes and just be one of the boys.''

Meanwhile, the grape boycott wore on. Some wine producers, susceptible to the fear of a national boycott, began negotiating labor contracts, but the table-grape industry was standing firm against Chavez. His personal fast effectively dramatized the nonviolent nature of the struggle, and boycott centers across the country—50 of them, throughout 1968 and 1969—helped to publicize the cause. Still, more help was needed.

Kircher and Higgins had discussed the issue many times, out of the background that comes with long-time friendship, mutual respect, and common concerns.

"George Higgins was easily the most knowledgeable and accepted cleric in this nation with respect to trade unions," Kircher told the author. "It's hard to talk to a trade union leader and mention George Higgins's name without them knowing him personally, or at least knowing of him. With union people George didn't have a religious agenda as such; he had a strong, Christian concept about trade unions and their role in the social order. Most of the time that made him supportive of what trade union leadership was doing. But the good thing about him was that when those same leaders were doing things that that concept couldn't support, he very articulately let them know about it.''

That was precisely what happened with Meany and Higgins on the farm labor issue, Kircher recalls. Periodically protests would arise from supermarket workers: retail clerks and meatcutters who were upset because their stores were being picketed by Chavez supporters backing the grape boycott. When they reached the top through union channels, Kircher said, Meany would denounce the picketers and pull in certain farm labor assistance, or insist on concessions from Chavez.

"When Higgins found out about these things," Kircher said, "he went straight to Meany to complain about it. I'm sure the complaints were gentlemanly, but the point was made nevertheless. He was a great counterbalance as far as the whole farm labor scene was concerned."

There was widespread church support for the grape boycott, and a formal endorsement by the recently-reconstituted bishops' organization, the NCCB-USCC, would surely give it a major boost. Higgins had used his column to outline the issues on several occasions. As early as January 1966, he endorsed the migrants' right to strike, citing Vatican II's *Constitution on the Church in the Modern World* for its reaffirmation of that right. He noted that when the document was being drafted, some Council Fathers argued against inclusion of that section on the grounds that the rights to organize and to strike had been defined often enough in church pronouncements. But the majority, he continued, "successfully countered this argument by pointing out that, while the specific rights in question are undoubtedly more widely recognized today than they were a generation or two ago, they are still being violated. . .at times, in certain industries and trades in nations which are highly industrialized."

He tackled the boycott question head on in The Yardstick for January 6, 1969, responding to charges that by not specifically endorsing the grape boycott at their meeting in November 1968, the bishops were opposed to it. "This isn't true at all," Higgins said. "If the bishops didn't support the boycott, neither did they oppose it. They said nothing about it, one way or the other. I wish they had, but, in fact, they didn't—so that's that."

There was no mistaking Higgins's own position:

"This column is strongly in favor of the boycott, not as the best of all possible ways of persuading the growers to recognize the right of their workers to organize, but as a legitimate last resort.'' To support his position he turned to an old mentor, Msgr. Ryan, citing his predecessor's theory that a boycott is legitimate ''when the injustice inflicted by the employer is grave, and when no milder method will be effective.'' To deny this, Ryan had continued, could be to argue that the employer can pursue his advantage to any lengths, no matter how unreasonable. The laborer, therefore, is entitled to seek reasonable benefits by reasonable means, including, ultimately, a boycott.

"In my judgment," Higgins concluded, "the California grape boycott is a perfect case in point. I therefore wholeheartedly support it and hope that it will soon achieve its one and only purpose, namely, to persuade the growers, at long last, to recognize their workers' right to organize."

Higgins had the boycott endorsement proposal back on the agenda for the bishops the following year, in November 1969, but some California bishops—especially then Archbishop Timothy Manning, recently-named coadjutor of Los Angeles, and Bishop Hugh Donohue, who had been bishop of Stockton and succeeded Manning in Fresno—preferred a more conciliatory approach. They reasoned that if the bishops, rather than simply endorsing the boycott, could get the growers and the farm workers to sit down together and talk over the issues, they would stand a better chance of resolving the matter. Higgins agreed, with some reservations.

"All right," he told Donohue privately. "I'll kill the resolution. But let's see where we go from here." He arranged to have Donohue talk the matter over with Kircher, a committed Catholic concerned about the Church's role in the dispute, and from that private talk emerged the idea of an ad hoc committee that would offer its services as mediator.

The proposal sat well with all hands. Before the bishops' meeting was over, Cardinal John Dearden of Detroit, then the conference president, appointed the Bishops' Ad Hoc Committee on Farm Labor. Its members were Manning, Donohue, Bishop Donnelly, then Bishop Humberto Medeiros of Brownsville, later cardinal archbishop of Boston, and Bishop Walter Curtis of Bridgeport. Higgins was named a consultant. The group got together before they left Washington and, significantly, elected Donnelly as chairman.

On the surface the reasons Donnelly was chosen instead of one of the Californians were plausible enough: Donnelly had at least

20 years of experience in labor-management affairs, and for many years had been chairman of the Connecticut state mediation board. But others wondered if the California bishops wanted to stay in the background—if, in effect, they didn't want the committee to pursue its task overzealously, especially if it appeared to favor the workers. When Donnelly discovered a few weeks later that the formative steps which were supposed to have taken place in California were still being delayed, he took action, calling a meeting for the following week. "If I take this job, I'm going to take it seriously," Donnelly told Higgins.

Higgins's respect for Donnelly, particularly for his role in the farm dispute, is almost boundless.

"If it had not been for Donnelly," he said in an interview, "the farm labor movement would have gone on without us and everybody would be saying, 'Where was the Catholic Church? Where were you people when we needed you?' I don't think they're saying that now. We couldn't have accomplished what we did if it weren't for seniority. Because of Donnelly's experience, the bishops had a high respect for him, and I was around for so long that there wasn't much they could do about me."

He put the tribute in more formal words in a Yardstick column shortly after Donnelly died unexpectedly on June 30, 1977. "No single individual outside their own ranks did more than Bishop Donnelly to assist the farm workers in their courageous struggle for self-determination."

If the praise is similar to that Higgins accorded to Bill Kircher, the similarity is appropriate. The three men—Higgins, Donnelly, and Kircher—were unquestionably the key figures in whatever the institutional Church did to contribute to the UFW's early rise to success in the fields. "We turned the thing around," Kircher says matter-of-factly, and it comes through as a simple truth rather than a reflective boast. But before it turned, there was work to be done.

When the bishops' committee gathered at Fresno in January 1970, Bishop Donohue brought along his young chancellor to help with the paperwork. Msgr. Roger Mahony, later Donohue's auxiliary in Fresno, and still later bishop of Stockton, would become the committee's permanent secretary and one of its most valuable contributors.

He was no stranger to the farm labor scene, having ministered to workers in *bracero* camps since his seminary days. He had also helped the California bishops formulate statements on farm labor before the ad hoc committee was formed.

Once it was formed, the members, prodded by Higgins and Donnelly, wasted no time getting to work. Within days of their first session, they arranged an historic meeting between Chavez and the principal growers in the San Joaquin Valley, a meeting that no one else had been able to effect.

"It was the first real breakthrough in five years," Mahony recalled, "the first time the parties had ever gotten together across the table. We invited 20 growers, and 16 or 18 of them were there. In the morning we met separately with the growers and the union representatives, and then after lunch we invited both groups to a joint session in which there was no agenda, and no expectations set. We were amazed when all the growers except one showed up for the afternoon session."

That was the first of literally hundreds of sessions in which the committee played a role over the next four years, a period in which Higgins and Donnelly spent more time in California than they did in Washington or Hartford. Mahony was their near-constant companion, driving up and down the valley, arranging meetings, keeping valuable records. The initial involvement centered around the business of getting people together, looking for common ground, and generally lending an air of credibility to the proceedings. After 1971 the accent was on contract negotiations, where the grower agreed that the union did indeed represent his workers, and specific contract points had to be hammered out.

Through it all, Higgins played a unique role. One observer who saw most of it close up was Gerard E. Sherry, a veteran Catholic journalist who was then editor of the *Central California Register,* the Fresno diocesan newspaper. In addition to reporting on the farm labor question, he frequently assisted the committee in preparing statements for the press.

"George's background in labor made him the perfect consultant for the bishops' committee," Sherry said in an interview. "He never overstepped his role; it was, after all, the bishops' committee. But he led them. Manning was unsure of the right of the Church to pressure the growers, and the same could be said of Medeiros and Curtis. They were for complete impartiality. But George kept bringing them back to the fundamental issue, not a contract; that could be sorted out later. The fundamental issue here was the right to collective bargaining by the workers. George kept reminding the bishops' committee that this was their job, to convince them of this right. The committee couldn't have mediated contracts if it hadn't first mediated the principle.

"George educated the bishops' committee, but more important he facilitated the acceptance by the growers of a union and got them to accept the fact that the union wouldn't strain them. And he also got the farm workers to recognize the fact that to be successful in representing workers they also had to be businesslike and that there had to be some give and take; that nothing was done by simply making demands."

Higgins's personal style had a great deal to do with the committee's effectiveness, Bishop Mahony noted.

"He was, and he is, virtually unflappable. He was beyond that point, ostensibly, of becoming frustrated by the parties. He was always able to confront the reality of the situation; able to say at the end of a meeting, for example, 'Well, there's no reason for us to continue meeting until somebody changes their mind. We're at an absolute deadlock, so let's just take a week off.'

"And he was so effective in the caucuses, where we'd be floating back and forth. He might say to the growers, 'Well, the union hiring hall is so essential to the union that if you think they're ever going to give that up you'd really better start thinking differently. It's not going to happen.' Then he'd talk to the union on their side of the caucus about the growers' position on seniority, or returning field hands from previous years. 'They're not going to change that,' he'd say. 'They're not going to take a bunch of amateurs who've never been in their field before. So you guys might as well be realistic.'

"That was a special asset. He was tremendously effective in pointing out the issues that were genuinely non-negotiable."

Both Sherry and Mahony were pointing to a Higgins gift which those on the outside found hard to understand: his ability to win the confidence of growers when he was perceived publicly as such an outspoken advocate of the union.

Chavez himself attributed it to Higgins's "savvy" in an interview with the author. "He knows how to move with people in this whole field of labor relations. The growers knew that he liked us, but he never lost his credibility with them for a minute.''

Bishop Mahony cited the difference between Higgins's sentiments in the farm labor dispute, both privately and publicly stated, and his role as consultant to the bishops' committee. There were some growers who wanted nothing to do with the committee, but more and more they came to see that the Catholic Church had become an important element in the situation, and that its presence, reflected in the committee of bishops, could help them effect settlements.

''During the meetings themselves the bishops didn't try to get the growers to accept the union's position,'' Mahony said, ''and that word got around with other growers very fast. Bishop Donnelly or George Higgins would often tell the union people, very pointedly, that their position on a given item didn't make any sense, that it wasn't going to fly. That certainly helped. When the growers experienced what the committee was trying to do, they felt a lot more at ease about the presence of the bishops. And, of course, they were trying to get the best contract they could from their own perspective, and they knew the bishops had a lot of clout with the union. In a way it was really to their own advantage to have the committee there.''

Higgins's own socializing abilities were an important part of the equation as well. He relishes the company of people whose interests parallel his own, especially if the conversation is intellectually challenging and the debate is sharp-edged. The right setting helps: a comfortable room late at night, a generous supply of ice and scotch, a cigar or two to flavor the atmosphere. Higgins's sentiments might have lain entirely with the farm workers, but he could talk the growers' language with no trouble at all. They found—probably to their surprise, in more than one instance—that this bookish priest from Washington with the liberal reputation was one of the boys, after all.

On one occasion, not long after the committee had been formed, Higgins, Donnelly, and Mahony stopped outside of Bakersfield to talk to a grower named Jim Camp, whose father had come to California from North Carolina during the Depression and developed extensive farm operations in the San Joaquin Valley. He politely received the committee members in his office, and after a period of exploratory conversation, in which the parties were sizing each other up, Donnelly interrupted the talk.

''Mr. Camp,'' he said, ''I wonder if I could get a glass of water? I have to take some pills periodically.''

Camp had barely said "Of course" before Higgins waved him off. "You can have water if you want, Donnelly, but I'll give you odds that there's a bar here," Higgins said. "It's got all the ear-marks of a place with a bar hidden away someplace, and I think it's about time we broke up and had a drink."

"God Almighty," Camp replied, "let's get going."

A bond of mutual respect developed steadily in the weeks to come. Camp encouraged the committee to work with other growers, and obviously helped in spreading the word among them that the bishops were genuinely interested in working out a fair settlement in the dispute.

Several weeks after their initial meeting, Camp called Higgins in Washington on a Sunday morning and told him he was going to negotiate that evening with Chavez at the Los Angeles Airport.

"I want you to be there," Camp said. "I don't want to go into this without observers."

"But it's ten o'clock in the morning here," Higgins protested.

"There's a three hour difference," Camp answered. "You can make it."

Higgins did indeed make it, and a settlement followed not long after.

Camp was one of several growers with whom Higgins hit it off. He also helped in the negotiations with a grower named Hollis Roberts, a tall, heavy-set former Texan who—despite a background which provided for relatively little formal education—had trans-formed a sprawling tract of land near McFarland into acre after acre of lush farmland, making him a wealthy man in the process. He had been among the most bitter and vehement critics of Chavez, hint-ing at communistic ties and un-American tactics. At a press con-ference announcing his settlement with the union, Roberts astounded Higgins, Mahony, and the reporters who were there by throwing his arms around Chavez, all but lost in the folds of the grower's em-brace. The reporters couldn't believe it. After all the things you said about Cesar, they asked, what brought about this dramatic transition?

"Well, boys," Roberts said, "as you know, I thought at one time that Cesar was a communist, but now I recognize that he's a God-fearing man who's doing the best he can for his people." He paused. "Besides that, I can't get my goddam peaches picked!"

Few of the meetings on Higgins's frequent trips provoked the kind of laughter that Roberts's remark drew. Most were arduous, at times marathon negotiating sessions in which Higgins, Donnelly and Mahony would meet with one side or the other, and at times with both, before absenting themselves to wait in the wings while private talks went on. The waiting was the worst part. During one 18-hour meeting in the Monterey County Courthouse in Salinas, Donnelly wisecracked to Sherry that he and Higgins had gotten to know the first name of every pigeon on the courthouse steps. It was two in the morning at that point, and the only difference separating the growers and the union was a half-cent an hour.

Aside from his deep personal interest in the farm labor problem, Higgins was able to get to California as frequently as he did—almost literally, at times, on a moment's notice—because of shifting responsibilities within the bishops' conference. Following the 1966 reorganization which changed the old National Catholic Welfare Conference to the National Conference of Catholic Bishops and its action-related arm, the U.S. Catholic Conference, Higgins saw a rapid succession of title changes. At first he retained the title of director of the social action department. In 1969 he became director of the USCC's division of urban life, a designation that hardly began to hint at the sweep of his activities; in 1972 secretary for research, and in 1976 secretary for special concerns. But whatever the title, Higgins was largely unburdened with administrative responsibilities and free to make his agenda whatever the day might call for.

Expenses for the trips and, indeed, for all the ad hoc committee's business were picked up by the conference. Then Bishop Joseph L. Bernardin, the general secretary, and Bishop James S. Rausch, who succeeded him in that post, were supportive of the committee's efforts, and at that time the budget problems which were to plague the conference in later years had not yet begun. Most of the bills were submitted by Bishop Mahony, who recalls that Bishop Donnelly paid most of his own accounts. The total bill rarely ran over $5,000 a year, most of it for lodging, meals, travel, and rental of rooms for meetings. (The late Bishop Rausch often needled Higgins about the amount budgeted for "refreshments," the scotch and mixers that kept the marathon sessions from falling apart.)

All the traveling and all the meetings began to pay off before long. The bishops committee achieved its first breakthrough in April 1970, only three months after its first California meeting, when

Lionel Steinberg, who ran the largest table-grape farming operation in the Coachella Valley, signed a contract with Chavez following a round of negotiations mediated by the committee.

The agreement was considered so significant—it was, after all, the first contract that UFWOC had achieved with a major grower—that the signing became a public event. It took place in the Los Angeles archdiocesan chancery office, with the press and all the members of the bishops' committee on hand. Soon afterward a neighbor of Steinberg's, K.K. Larson, signed a contract with Chavez covering his vineyards, and the long logjam seemed clearly to be broken.

Near-total victory appeared to be Chavez' three months later when, on July 29—again, following negotiating assistance by Higgins, Donnelly, Mahony and Kircher, among others—the 26 major grape growers in Delano who were the original targets of the strike and boycott finally signed with UFWOC. The farm workers agreed to $1.80 an hour, 40 cents more than they had requested when the strike began five years earlier. The growers agreed to pay 10 cents an hour to the Robert F. Kennedy Health and Welfare Fund and two cents an hour into a social service fund. Work schedules were to be arranged through a hiring hall rather than through a labor contractor, a key point in union negotiations. The new contracts, added to those Chavez already had in his pocket, gave his still-struggling union more than three-fourths of California's table-grape land, and if the past had been grim, the future looked bright. But the farm-workers' jubilant mood lasted only a few hours. That night they heard incredulously that the Western Conference of Teamsters had signed agreements with 30 lettuce growers in the Salinas Valley, covering 5,000 workers. Chavez had to begin a new battle for survival as the Teamsters' move added a new dimension to California's complex farm labor problems. It meant a new dimension, too, for the Church, the bishops' committee, and for George Higgins.

The Teamsters' raid, for that is how Chavez and his supporters viewed it, changed the rules of the game. The committee maintained a posture of neutrality in the long, bitter, and even bloody skirmishes that would take place between the UFWOC and the Teamsters over the next few years, but Higgins personally wasted no time pretending. From the beginning, he took on the Teamsters and their leaders in direct, forceful, uncompromising terms. Their move, he said, was "obscene," the word he used in a personal conversation ("it turned into a shouting match") with the late Frank Fitzsimmons, then the Teamster president.

The Teamsters had long been active with packing house and shed workers in California's agricultural industry, but had shied away from field operations. Their agreement with the Salinas lettuce growers to move into the field stunned Chavez and his followers. They saw it as nothing more than a sweetheart pact aimed ultimately at shutting out the United Farm Workers.

"I think the reason they got involved was that they saw Chavez winning his long fight with the Delano grape growers and figured that this man might be a real winner, on his way to taking over the whole industry," Higgins told the author. 'We're not going to be able to control him,' they must have thought. 'He's an irresponsible sort of maverick who's leading a social movement which we don't understand, with an undisciplined work force. He's going to call strikes, and then our cannery workers are going to be out of work because there won't be any food delivered there, and then our people in the markets are going to be out of work as well. We've got to get this thing under control before it's too late.'

"Now," Higgins continued, "I've never seen them say that in print. But it's the only logical explanation. It didn't make any sense for the Teamsters to be so worried about the low-paid field workers whom they had never organized before; they must have felt that they had to organize the whole industry or else their people were going to get hurt."

Whatever the reason—and the one advanced by Higgins seems to be the only plausible explanation—the Teamsters' move into the field threatened to kill off the still-struggling UFWOC. Chavez had to deploy his chief lieutenants in the Delano area to start the complicated business of implementing the grape contracts before he could seriously concern himself with the second front opened by the Teamsters in Salinas.

Higgins and the bishops attempted an early rescue operation, convening a meeting between the two unions that resulted in a jurisdictional agreement hammered out under committee auspices. The meeting, held in Salinas, was chaired by Higgins in Donnelly's absence, with Mahony providing assistance. It began at 10:30 AM Tuesday, August 11 and continued almost uninterrupted until 6 o'clock the following morning, when the agreement was announced.

"We told the parties. . .that we were hoping for. . .a document which would be more than an armistice, more than a legalistic nonagression pact," Higgins wrote in The Yardstick dated August 24, 1970. "We urged them to try to come up with an agreement which would be thoroughly positive in tone and would be calculated not so much to defend or protect their separate interests as to promote their mutual interests and the general interest of the entire agricultural industry. We think they have done just that and have done it very well."

The basic points of the agreement were simple enough. The Teamsters would prevail on the lettuce growers to rescind their newly-signed contracts and negotiate with UFWOC instead; UFWOC agreed to limit its organizing endeavors to field workers, and leave the packing sheds and canneries to the Teamsters.

But Higgins's enthusiastic comments (he went so far as to refer to the agreement as "a truly historic document in the annals of the farm labor movement in this country" proved more a hopeful wish than an accurate prophecy. The difficulty centered on the rescinded contracts, and on personalities and politics within the Teamsters. Einar O. Mohn, then the director of the Western Conference (one of four regional Teamster divisions), was a sincere and respected union official whom Higgins had known for years. He seemed genuinely interested in avoiding a war with UFWOC and the AFL-CIO. But his chief negotiating lieutenant was William Grami, director of organizing for the Western Conference and a combative opponent at the bargaining table. He hinted to Higgins that he might have a problem in working actively on contract rescissions because he expected the issue to be a highly controversial topic at a forthcoming Teamster convention. As he told Higgins, "We'll let Einar Mohn explain this to the convention."

Said Higgins, "I should have sensed then, as I did shortly after, that what he was really saying was 'You're not going to see my signature on any of these rescission agreements, because it's going to be a political hot potato among our members. We'll let somebody else explain it.' That should have been my tipoff."

The agreement called for a 10-day implementation period. Higgins stayed on in Salinas, attending to a number of details that included sitting in on Grami's meetings with the lettuce growers.

"They'd come in to a conference room, three or four or five

at a time, and Grami would explain to them, while I was there, what the Teamsters' agreement with Chavez called for. My recollection is that he really didn't convey to them any sense of urgency about tearing up their new contracts with the Teamsters. I think that if they'd gotten that message they would have had enough respect for the muscle of the Teamsters that they would have said, 'Well, we have no place else to go except to Cesar.' But Grami just gave them the terms of the agreement, told them they could ask out if they wanted to, and left it at that.''

The agreement collapsed within days, the Teamsters charging Chavez with violating the pact by continuing to picket some growers, and Chavez contending that the Teamsters were not genuinely interested in canceling out their lettuce contracts. On August 20 a grower announced that he and all the others in the valley would honor the Teamster field contracts; Chavez responded with a call for a general strike and a boycott of all lettuce.

That touched off a war in the fields that went on for several years, with the bishops' committee periodically trying to arrange truce pacts. Twice prospective agreements went out the window when a combination of growers and Teamster locals failed to provide the necessary co-operation. Chavez and the United Farm Workers Union, no longer an organizing committee at this point, but a fully-charted union within the AFL-CIO framework, received a boost when the California Supreme Court called the Teamster-grower contracts "the ultimate form of favoritism," but at the same time the court found itself unable to invalidate them.

Increasingly, Higgins took a strong line on the Teamsters; a dozen columns in 1973 alone dealt with the dispute in hard-hitting terms.

On May 28 of that year, he criticized the Teamsters for failing to agree to a request that they agree to secret-ballot jurisdictional elections under neutral observers. "This means," he said, "that all of their pious talk about the sacred right of farm workers to belong to a union of their own choosing is somewhat less than sincere. I suspect it also means that the Teamsters are deathly afraid that they would lose the election and thus have to leave the Coachella Valley in disgrace. They are not about to take that risk.

"So be it," Higgins continued. "If the Teamsters are determined to have a fight to the finish, that's precisely what they are going to get. The Farm Workers Union is prepared to carry on the fight forever if it takes that long to bring the Teamsters to their knees.

"The Teamsters may win a skirmish here and there, but I am confident that they will eventually lose the war. Time and public opinion are on the side of the Farm Workers Union."

On July 16 he criticized the Teamsters for failing to discipline a 6'4", 300-pound "security guard"—the quotation marks were his—who had "without the slightest provocation beat the living daylights out of Father John Bank," a Youngstown diocesan priest working as a volunteer with the farm workers.

On July 23 he struck back at Fitzsimmons ("an old friend"), who had lashed out at "the nearly total vacuum of knowledge in the collective bargaining process by those (clergymen) who fanatically support that twentieth-century mystic, Cesar Chavez." Said Higgins: "I am not surprised that the Teamsters are so upset about the role the clergy are playing in the current farm labor dispute. . . . What they really mean is that they are angry at the clergy for supporting the United Farm Workers and opposing the Teamsters. . . . If the reverse were true, you could bet your bottom dollar that they would welcome the intervention of the clergy and would not be arguing that the clergy are technically incompetent to express an opinion in this area. In other words, it all depends on whose ox is being gored."

At about the same time Higgins issued an open letter to the American labor movement, urging its support for Chavez in the bitter struggle. A condensed version of a homily he delivered at the annual Memorial Mass of the Chicago Building Trades Council in May 1973, it stands as the definitive Higgins statement on the moral questions raised by the Teamsters' battle with Chavez.

He opened by disavowing any personal grievances with the Teamsters, and regretting the need to enter an argument between two unions. He hailed the decision of the AFL-CIO executive council, made a few days before, to support Chavez with a $1.6 million strike fund, then lamented the probability that it would end up being used against another union. He continued:

"It makes no sense in 1973 for the biggest and probably the wealthiest union in the world to engage in a life and death struggle with a union that can speak for, at most, no more than 50,000 farm workers, the most exploited workers in the American labor market.

"I urge you, in the good name of the American labor movement, now that the AFL-CIO Executive Council has acted unanimously on this matter, to take the leadership in your own community to help these poor people get organized into a union of their own choice.''

He was speaking out, Higgins said, because he felt his own credentials were in good order: "I don't think any priest in the United States has done any more than I have to defend the organized labor movement, but I will not defend the movement in this case unless it does what organized labor had traditionally done in other struggles of this kind, and that is to come out four square in favor of the farm workers' right to decide which union they want to represent them.''

He rejected the Teamsters' argument that a wealthier, more powerful, and more influential union could do more for farm workers than Chavez.

"That's a phony argument," Higgins said. "Clearly aside from the fact that Chavez' contracts are better than the Teamsters' contracts, no self-respecting trade unionist has ever judged the value of a union purely in economic terms.

"He doesn't want to be handed an increase in wages by a paternalistic employer or a paternalistic union. He wants the right to have a voice in determining his own wages and working conditions. That's what this fight is all about.''

The farm workers were depending on all of organized labor to help them, Higgins said. No one in the Church is interested in tangling with the Teamsters, he noted, but at the same time Church people are willing to do that if necessary to see that "these poor exploited farm workers" achieve the right to self-determination. He concluded:

"I urge you to make the nation proud of the labor movement by taking the lead in seeing to it that these people achieve the basic goal for which the labor movement was established. The basic goal of your movement, in addition to better wages and better working conditions, is the freedom of workers to determine which union will represent them. That's all the farm workers are asking. You owe it to them—and to the good name of the labor movement—to assist them in achieving this modest goal.''

That kind of partisan language was bound to attract critics—which, of course, fazed Higgins not in the least. ("I don't mind a good fight," he has told the author on more than one occasion.) A well-known California priest, Msgr. Thomas Earley, then a pastor in Salinas and vicar general of the Monterey Diocese, addressed a letter to all priests in the country in October 1972, criticizing the bishops' committee and enclosing an anti-Chavez pamphlet entitled "The Lettuce Story." Earley's swipe at "poorly informed churchmen" for allegedly complicating the local issue brought a "Dear Tom" response from Higgins, who said, "I sincerely regret that you felt it necessary to take a swipe at those of us who happen to read the situation somewhat differently."

At the height of the struggle in April 1973, Richard Thornton, executive director of the Grower-Shipper Vegetable Association, told the author during an interview in Salinas: "We wouldn't trust the bishops' committee to be objective or fair. The Church is well-intentioned but misguided. The people involved were old-time labor men who would've backed any union. The Church has definitely overstepped its role. It started taking sides without knowing all the facts, and lost its credibility and effectiveness as a result. It should bow out gracefully and leave the job to the professionals."

In a 1980 interview at his retirement home in Menlo Park, California, Einar Mohn, the former Teamster leader, was only slightly less critical of the committee. Its members had the best of intentions, he said, but remained highly partisan. He said he had once told the committee, "If you give us the same support for six months that you've given the United Farm Workers, we'll organize all the workers in the state of California."

Mohn said that while his encounters with the committee were always cordial, he resented its one-sided approach. "You can't be a peacemaker if you're going to be that partial," he said. He thinks the Teamsters suffered from the publicity the protracted struggle created, partly because of the David-Goliath image involved in their contest with Chavez. "We were big, strong, and wealthy," he said. "All Cesar had was a slingshot."

Mohn is a friendly man in a quiet way, and his reflective comments on the farm labor situation are of more than passing interest. If he had any regrets, they centered on the violence that became part of the struggle. "You could blame both sides for the physical encounters," he said. "There was a lot of taunting, a lot of name-calling. You never ordered violence, but sometimes you could see that it was just going to happen."

Mohn left the field of battle with an interesting evaluation of Chavez. "He's a visionary, a man with a great compassionate feeling for his people," Mohn said. "He believes that if you feel your cause is just, you're going to win. I don't think he ever sat down to assay how he could take on the strength of a powerful group like organized agriculture, but he just felt that since he was right and carried a banner and marched that it would all work out. But things don't happen that way. I have a feeling of frustration in having tried to deal with him, but none of antagonism. Actually, I have a lot of respect for him.''

The long and costly struggle between the Teamsters and the UFW finally came to an end in 1976 (after two more false signals that jurisdictional agreements had been reached). By that time the California Agricultural Labor Relations Act had gone into effect, requiring officially sanctioned elections instead of the kind of grower-union arrangements which had served the Teamsters so well. The bishops' committee—which still exists on paper, but has not met in years—was not in on the final agreement, but Mahony, by then a bishop and the first chairman of California's state farm board, played a major role in bringing it about. As he recalled in 1979, it was not that much of an effort:

"It became obvious in 1976 that except in those ranches where the Teamsters had a real strong footing that the UFW was beating them right and left in elections. Also, life was becoming very difficult for the Teamsters. The UFW had so many volunteer attorneys to represent them in all kinds of procedures before the board; if the Teamsters wanted any kind of decent representation they had to hire attorneys. So in 1975 they started talking about moving out of the farm labor field. The agreement was reached in 1976, whereby the Teamsters would have jurisdiction over occupations covered by the National Labor Relations Act and the UFW over things covered by the (California) Agricultural Relations Act. From what I can tell, it's still working out fine.''

Chavez' union has continued to struggle. Some who had been connected with it tired of Chavez' own determination to involve himself in minor details, of the continued insistence on an all-volunteer staff, of the remote and unbusinesslike setting of the UFW's national headquarters at La Paz, a Tehachapi Mountain aerie. Some long-time associates like Jerry Cohen, for years the union's chief counsel, and Gil Padilla, veteran Chavez lieutenant, have left after disagreements with Chavez. The union announced a major internal restructuring in 1982, including a team-management system designed to promote more shared leadership and bring younger people into the decision-making area.

Whatever the changes, those who remember the early days have found recollections of Higgins and of the bishops' committee, and of their decisive role in the union's survival.

Cohen credits Higgins and Donnelly with making the UFW realize the necessity of compromise and negotiation. "They were able to open up communication where no one else could," he said. "If it hadn't been Msgr. Higgins and Bishop Donnelly telling us certain things, I don't know that we would have believed anyone else."

Chavez has acknowledged his debt to Higgins on occasions beyond counting, and makes it a point to be present when Higgins is being honored or receiving an award. (The round of Higgins retirement dinners in 1980 kept him particularly busy.) One moment in his years of association with Higgins stands out in his mind, he told the author in a 1979 interview at La Paz.

"This was early in our struggle with the Teamsters," Chavez said, "and Msgr. Higgins had just come from a meeting with some of the top Teamster people. We were at a hotel near the San Francisco Airport. He told me the Teamsters said we had to stop fighting them or they would crush us, and he said he believed them. But I said no; we had nothing to lose. We had to go on with the fight, and it had to be all out. People who knew the situation gave us a million-to-one chance of winning. But I sensed that Msgr. Higgins—although he didn't say anything—once he was sure that we understood what he had told us, and we still didn't change our minds, was kind of happy that we had made that decision. I think he was proud that we had decided to fight."

Higgins retains a lively interest in the farm labor situation as well as a friendly relationship with Chavez. He is an honored guest at UFW functions from coast to coast, and is still ready to postpone other activities if an emergency call comes out from Chavez. At the same time, Higgins will be critical if he feels the situation demands it, as he did when several UFW people spoke out against a news story Gerard Sherry wrote on a farm labor issue because it did not fully support the union's position. "I told them that Gerry has done more good reporting for them than any other reporter in the country," Higgins said, "but that he's still a reporter and has to do his job as he sees it. I told Gil Padilla that I wanted Cesar to know I was serious about this, that I was going to defend Gerry to the hilt, and that I'd go public on it, letting people know they were trying to manipulate the press. They got the message."

The occasional heat of Higgins's declarations on the farm labor issue, whether directed toward a grower, a Fitzsimmons, a Grami, or to Chavez himself, stems from his passionate concern for the farm worker himself. It is as fervent today as it was when he first wrote on the subject more than 30 years ago, and he is as ready now as then to take on all comers who see the case differently. Once, not long after the bishops' committee was established, its members were at an informal get-together when he heard one of the California bishops complain about the amount his diocese was being assessed to finance the activities of the U.S. Catholic Conference. Higgins shot back that it was "peanuts" compared to the efforts being expended on the farm labor issue alone, where, he noted archly, "what we're really doing is bailing you guys out."

"Now, George," the late Cardinal Medeiros interrupted, "we didn't come out here to argue."

Higgins replied simply and to the point, "You're talking to the wrong man."

CHAPTER SEVEN

THE SECOND VATICAN COUNCIL

IN THE FALL OF 1963, IN ROME, AT THE SECOND SESSION OF the Second Vatican Council, the place to be was the Casa Villanova.

It was the place to be at the third and fourth sessions as well, but there was something special about the fall of 1963. It was a splendid time to be part of what was happening in the Church. A feeling of purpose was in the Roman air; the first session of the Council, largely exploratory, had come and gone; now, in September 1963, the Council Fathers were about to get down to business. And exciting business it was: new roles for the laity; new relationships with other faiths; new patterns of worship; a new understanding of the Church itself.

These were the ideas being thrashed out at the Villanova, an international residence in Rome's Parioli district—a clubhouse of

Council regulars and irregulars, really—which became Vatican II's intellectual crossroads. Cardinal and bishop, priest and layman, European and American, liberal and conservative were all part of the cast which lived, worked, prayed and talked there. A key Council document was hammered out there, and it served as home for some of the major names for which the Council would be remembered.

And at the center of it all, encouraging and goading, convening and presiding, arguing and reconciling, was George Higgins. He gloried in the Council, for what it meant to the Church. He attended virtually every working session through the four years, and sparked some of the liveliest Rome evenings off the Council floor. He instructed bishops, ran interference for journalists, turned out speeches, lobbied for some documents and helped give birth to others. The Council was a highlight of George Higgins's life and career.

"When George first heard about the Council, he resolved that he'd be there," said Bishop Mark Hurley of Santa Rosa, an old friend. "He couldn't possibly be anywhere else."

As it turned out, Higgins was one of the handful of Americans who went to Rome to work on the Council before it began, serving as a member of its preparatory commission on the lay apostolate. But he downplays that role. "I don't know how many times I went to Rome in that preparatory stage, maybe 10 times, but I didn't make much of a contribution. I took part in the discussions, of course, but it was slow and gradual. Everyone there was trying to find his way."

Higgins had gone over the objections of then Msgr. Paul F. Tanner, NCWC secretary, who felt that because the council was an international undertaking the conference should not have been responsible for the expenses of those who were participating. Higgins raised his own traveling fund, thanks mainly to the generosity of old friends in Chicago, but deeply regretted the attitude that had made it necessary. "It was the same attitude," he said, "that would explain why the American bishops didn't organize properly during the first session of the Council. Somebody told them that this didn't have anything to do with national conferences, and to stay out of it."

Whatever the extent of his contribution to the preparatory

commission, an appointment he attributes to the influence of Msgr. Luigi Ligutti, another commission member, Higgins shared in its heavy workload. There were five formal meetings of the commission during 1961—in January, April, June, July and October—and in between there was a voluminous amount of background reading, most of it in the form of suggestions which had been sent in by bishops around the world.

Tanner greeted him after the final preparatory session with the hope that he would remain in Washington, but Higgins replied that he intended to go to the Council itself. Again Tanner objected, serving notice that no funds from the conference would be available to finance Higgins's travels or other expenses. And again Higgins said he'd make those arrangements himself. A few days later Higgins received a formal invitation from Bishop Coleman Carroll of Miami to serve as his Council *peritus* (the Latin word for expert; that is, a readily-available consultant on theological or related matters). His presence in Rome was thus assured, but not long after that he became one of 175 priests from around the world appointed by Pope John XXIII to collaborate with various Council commissions in compiling, preparing, and correcting documents (others among the 10 Americans so honored was Father Theodore Hesburgh, president of the University of Notre Dame). The appointment would give Higgins entree to all major Council events, including all the general sessions, even though the consultants were not permitted to take part in the debates. It was just the ticket that Higgins hoped to have.

The right company would be an important part of the Council proceedings, Higgins knew, and together with two of his oldest friends, Bishop Ernest Primeau and Msgr. John Quinn, got together a group which put up at the Hotel Mondial on the Via Torino, across from the Rome opera house. Quinn, for many years the presiding judge of Chicago's archdiocesan marriage tribunal, had been invited to the Council by Cardinal Alfredo Ottaviani, a friend from the days when he had studied in Rome. Their companions at the Mondial, mostly Chicagoans or former Chicagoans, included Bishops Martin McNamara of Joliet and William O'Connor of Springfield, Archbishop Paul Schulte of Indianapolis and Father Raymond Bosler, editor of *The Criterion,* Indianapolis archdiocesan newspaper; then Msgr. Mark Hurley, at the time a San Francisco archdiocesan priest "on loan" to Stockton, who had been asked by Bishop Hugh Donohue to accompany him; Msgr. Wilfred Paradis, Bishop

Primeau's secretary; and an English priest, Msgr. Peter Whitty. Primeau, an old Roman hand who had directed the Chicago house there for 12 years, was the unofficial leader of the group.

Higgins had little to say publicly about his expectations for the Council. Surprisingly, in view of his own preparatory work, he devoted no Yardstick columns to the Council before it opened (and only one dealing with its first session). However, a draft copy of a letter he prepared for President John F. Kennedy to send to Pope John XXIII on the eve of the Council's opening session provides an insight to his thoughts at the time. "During these three fateful years," the letter read, "millions of my fellow citizens in the United States, including many who do not belong to the Catholic Church, have followed with lively and sympathetic interest the work of the various preparatory commissions appointed by Your Holiness to draw up the agenda for this extraordinarily important Council. They have also read, with particular interest and with genuine admiration for your all-embracing concern for the welfare of humanity, the several inspiring statements issued by Your Holiness on the background and purposes of the Council. In the face of staggering problems which, from the human point of view, seem at times to be almost insoluble, people all over the world have found reason for renewed confidence and courage in the welcome thought that the Fathers of the Council . . .will give special attention to the grave economic and social problems which daily press upon suffering humanity in almost all parts of the world but, more particularly, in the economically underdeveloped nations. It is very heartening to know that the Council, in the words of Your Holiness, will strive to deepen the fellowship and love which are 'the natural needs of man' and 'are imposed on the Christian as rules for his relationship between man and man, and between people and people.' "

Higgins was on the scene when the Council finally opened October 11, 1962. A chatty letter to his parents in LaGrange, one of a series of letters and postcards he wrote home during the Council, provides an unusually personal glimpse of the event:

"You have never seen such confusion in all your life. The Romans are masters at this sort of thing. . .absolute bedlam, but somehow or other everything falls into place five minutes before the deadline. In any event, we have our credentials finally. . .and they are worth their weight in gold. Quinn and I will be able to attend any and all sessions of the Council. The opening of the Council yesterday morning was the most impressive event I have ever witnessed or ever hope to witness. . . .

"Our hotel facilities (Mondial) are perfect. We have one floor to ourselves, plus a common room for our evening bull sessions. It's a very congenial group, which is enlarged almost every evening by visiting priests. You can't walk a block anywhere in Rome without meeting someone you know.

"This morning at the new American college I will be interviewed for a couple of minutes by CBS. My part in the program will be very minor. The headliners will be Cardinal Spellman, Bishop Wright, and other U.S. dignitaries. . . ."

"The first session of the Council will end around December 8. After that, who knows?! My own guess is that the bishops will be called back in the spring for at least three or four months, and possibly again in the fall for the same length of time. It's too early to tell which way the council will go, but with Primeau, Quinn, and Bosler at our hotel, we will certainly get all the rumors. Primeau knows this town inside out.

"Quinn and I had lunch the other day with Cardinal Ottaviani at his home. He is reputed to be a conservative, but I must say that he is one of the simplest and most informed and friendly churchmen I have ever met. We have a standing invitation to lunch with him again very soon. Leave it to John Quinn! John is having a picnic. He speaks Italian a mile a minute."

Higgins continued his work on the lay apostolate commission, a carry-over from the preparatory stage of the Council, and recalls most of it as unexciting and routine. "Aside from that," he said, "we attended every session of the Council. We got to know what was going on, meeting all the bishops, so it became a fascinating thing."

Although the American bishops weren't meeting as a group during the opening session, other national hierarchies were, and positions rapidly took form along liberal-conservative lines on issues such as the liturgy, ecumenical relations, the Church itself. Higgins made his own sentiments clear in a series of postcards and letters home:

October 30: "Thank God for the Germans in the Council. They may be our only hope. In any event, they are our best hope. The German cardinals (including Bea, who lives in Rome) are tops. . . ."

November 10: "The Protestant observers are much impressed

by the freedom of discussion. So am I. The Romans are getting a good scare, for it is perfectly clear that the German-French bloc, the African bloc (and even the Americans) are in the mood to vote for some changes. . . ."

November 13: "Cardinal Spellman is a minority voice on the vernacular. It is my impression that the majority of the American bishops are definitely in favor of the vernacular and will so vote. In any event, the vernacular has won the day. It's only a matter of time. Tomorrow the big fight starts on theology. It promises to be a corker. The German bloc means business and is as well organized as the Kennedy team. The Roman crowd is scared . . .at long last."

November 21: "The conservatives are definitely on the run, at last. Future looks very bright."

The Mondial quickly gained a reputation as the place to get together for lively discussions on Council developments, thanks primarily to Higgins. He invited bishops, theologians and other Council *periti,* newspaper people and visitors from home to share their thoughts on the Council's proceedings. The salon was particularly useful to the American bishops, still struggling to get themselves organized. Without the Mondial's famed common room, they had few gathering places where they could jointly review events, share their reflections, and plan strategies. Many American bishops actively sought out Higgins for guidance on specific votes. His background in international Church affairs gave him a vantage point that many of them lacked, and he happily took the occasions to lobby for the causes in which he was most interested.

In later sessions he would complain good-naturedly that Council decisions were developing too rapidly, but during the first session he seemed on the verge of boredom at times. "The pace of the Council is so slow that many of the participants, including myself, are seriously thinking about going home for a spell," he wrote home at the end of October. Two weeks later he wrote again: "Only the Good Lord can tell how long the Council will last. I would guess a minimum of two years (or about five sessions). I don't intend to come back for all of the sessions. I will concentrate on those topics which interest me the most." (The Council ended with four sessions, in the fall each year between 1962 and 1965. Higgins was present for all four.)

Two letters during that period outlined daily schedules which seemed to refute Higgins's complaints about a slow pace. He said on October 30: "I don't have much free time. We get up at 5:45 AM, go to the Council at 8:15, return to the hotel at 1 PM, have a bull session from 1 to 2, lunch from 2 to 3:30, a short nap, say some prayers, take a walk, another bull session (or meeting), a late dinner, finish our prayers, and then to bed." A month later, on November 25, he described the previous day's schedule as "more or less typical." It included "Mass at 6:30, general Council session 8:30 to 12:30, lunch at 1:15 with Senator and Mrs. Eugene McCarthy, Father (Gustave) Weigel, Father Hans Kung of Germany, and Father Bosler; 4:15 to 5 PM, shopping for new books in field of Catholic social theory; 5 PM, attended (as an observer) a meeting of 300 bishops from commonwealth nations; 6 PM, dinner with Archbishop Lucey at his residence out in the suburbs; 9-11 PM, lively bull session at hotel with American gang. So it goes almost every day. Rome is one big Adult Education Institute for bishops and their advisers."

The first session was inconclusive, a time of testing and probing. Discussing its accomplishments on an ABC television program that December, Higgins spoke not of results (except for the "rather profound" implications of a preliminary vote on the liturgy schema, or draft document) but on directions. He regretted that not enough attention was being given to the religious aspects of the Council, that it was being reported as if it were a political convention (while, it must be noted, his own letters home had made it sound like a battleground). His single dominant impression of the Council's first session, he said, was "as some of the Fathers themselves expressed it, an opening of doors and opening of windows, to try to take a new pastoral ecumenical look at Catholic teaching and Catholic practice (he emphasized the word 'pastoral'.) "But I'd add only this one word of caution—that we are going to be disappointed, I think, if we expect too many immediate measurable results. The process is started. I think it started well, but we've got to be patient."

Higgins and the others in the "American gang" from the Mondial shared the feeling of excitement as they returned to Rome in September 1963 for the opening of the Council's second session. Pope John XXIII had died the previous June, but his successor, Pope Paul VI, whom Higgins had first met as Msgr. Montini many years before, not only quickly confirmed his intention to continue the

Council, but launched the second session with an address of such inspirational quality that Xavier Rynne, the Council's premier chronicler, called it "one of the great moments in Church history." The sentiment was widespread that with the tentative stage of the Council ended, the second session would produce significant results. The American bishops, realizing their error of the previous fall, started to schedule regular caucus-style meetings to familiarize themselves better with Council documents and to discuss voting strategies.

Higgins and his companions found they had run out of room at the Mondial, and he, Quinn, and Hurley (by this time a *peritus* specializing in education matters) found the Villanova, the *pensione* that would serve as their home in Rome for the next three years. Operated by the Sisters of Villanova on the Piazza Ungheria across from the Bellarmino church, it provided the outsized common room that Higgins and company clearly needed to accommodate the ever-growing guest list. Everyone from the Mondial moved to the Villanova except Bishop McNamara, who was ill and remained at home. They joined other Americans there: Msgr. William Baum, the future cardinal who was a Council *peritus* on ecumenical affairs; Bishops Charles Helmsing of Kansas City-St. Joseph, and Marion Forst of Dodge City. In all, some 50 priests and bishops made the Villanova their Council headquarters. One of the best-known residents, invited by Higgins, was Father John Courtney Murray, the eminent Jesuit theologian who had not been present for the Council's first session. New York's Cardinal Spellman appointed him a personal *peritus* to enable him to attend the succeeding sessions, which he did despite frequent and severe bouts with illness.

"The regular list of visitors read like a 'Who's Who at the Council,'" Bishop Hurley recalled in an interview. "The only major theologian I can think of who wasn't there was Karl Rahner, who didn't speak English." Still another was Hans Kung, also present at the Council as a *peritus,* and already at 33 a respected writer on Church reform.

"It was kind of a wild house, I guess," Msgr. Quinn said with a smile. "That was the characteristic given us, I'm sure. We had great discussions. Maybe the ideas might have been a little too wild; we just let the dialogue go on and on."

Higgins himself wrote fondly on his Villanova memories on August 28, 1967, following Father Murray's death: "Villanova was a unique para-conciliar institution and one which deserves at least a passing reference (a favorable reference, I would think) in the footnotes of the Council proceedings. It was an authentic American community in the best sense of the word, a very hospitable community made up of a dozen or so U.S. bishops and *periti* who lived and breathed the Council morning, noon, and night, and went out of their way to provide a congenial atmosphere in which other bishops could gather informally, with or without an invitation, for lively—and sometimes rather noisy—confabs about the progress of the Council.''

The Villanova's reputation as a social center was enhanced notably by the presence of an ice-making machine, one of the few in Rome at the time, which Quinn, designated the group's treasurer by Bishop Primeau, had flown in from Chicago. "It was very beneficial," he said. "It became an important factor in the long dialogues and discussions far into the night."

There were other home-style comforts as well. Through contacts at American Motors—where he had served on a clergy advisory committee for George Romney—and General Motors, Higgins managed to have two cars at the permanent disposal of the Villanova regulars. In addition, Murray had a car and driver of his own, provided, Higgins assumes, through the generosity of a sponsor at home. "Some of the American bishops must have wondered what the devil we were up to," Higgins said. "Every morning they'd be waiting for the bus and we'd wheel away." Primeau, typically, had the last word on the car situation. "For a great labor man," he told Higgins, "you really know how to play around with management."

One of the Villanova's few sour notes developed over the presence of journalists, some of whom, such as Robert B. Kaiser of *Time,* Michael Novak, John Cogley, and Gerard Sherry, were personally close to many of the regular residents.

"The thing became a real institution in Rome," Hurley said. "We wanted to keep it quiet in the sense that we didn't want it to be notorious; everything was off the record. But then we began to get in the press. 'To be anything in Rome is to be at the Villanova,' John Cogley wrote in *Commonweal.* There were other stories, and a lot of talk around Rome, so finally we passed a rule: no more laymen. The reporters kept coming, but we met them downstairs."

Sherry still rankles a bit when the subject comes up, as it did in a 1980 interview. "If George and Ray Bosler and Murray and the rest were to be of any use," he said, "then certainly they ought to be able to sit down and discuss the happenings of the day, the confidences they had and so forth, without journalists being able to pick it up. And the reporters could understand that. But where we hit the ceiling was that at nine o'clock at night, when we wanted to be social with them, there were several people at the Villanova who were saying, in effect, 'Let's not even socialize with them; you never know what might slip.' "

If Higgins and the other Villanova regulars strained press relations with their "no laymen" edict, they more than made up for it, particularly Higgins and Hurley, by their effectiveness in setting up a daily press panel near the beginning of the second session. The Vatican press office continued to hold a briefing for newsmen every day, as it had during the first session, but for reporters trying to make the mysteries of the Council understandable to readers at home, it was largely unsatisfactory. The American bishops decided to follow up the official briefing with a press panel of their own each afternoon. Since it was the only regular forum which could provide them with an intelligent interpretation of the day's key events inside the Council (which was, of course, off limits to outsiders) reporters from all over the world quickly began to flock to the Americans' daily sessions. Paulist Father John Sheerin, editor of *The Catholic World,* served as chairman of the panel, and Higgins, who has a sensitivity to reporters' needs rare outside the profession, became its key contributor. Some of the regular members included Redemptorist Fathers Francis Connell and Bernard Haering, Jesuit Father Gustave Weigel, Msgr. George Shea, Oblate Father John King, Father Frederick McManus, and Father Robert Trisco.

"It was one of the American bishops' great contributions to the Council, I think," Higgins said. "It was a great show every day. Some of the panelists were predictable. Frankie Connell was the mellow, grandfatherly conservative. The press loved him because they could predict what he was going to say. He was friendly. The man from Jersey, George Shea, was the predictable real conservative on dogmatic matters. McManus was the expert on the rules and regulations. He could tell them in great detail what the bylaws were, and why they had proceeded with something in a certain way. They'd bring people in, too. John Murray was always there on religious liberty. There were usually about seven or eight. It was a lot of fun."

"There were some complaints from the bishops that the press

panel was stacked with liberals," Sherry said, "but that wasn't so. They were mostly objective. None of the journalists could have given a complete story to their papers if it hadn't been for the press panel."

They showed their gratitude, Hurley recalls, by picking a mock All-American team from the panel members, placing individuals on the right or left side of the line or backfield according to their theological orientation. (Hurley was designated center, somewhat to his chagrin.) The press corps had no difficulty with the key position, picking Higgins as their quarterback.

Quinn smiled when he was reminded of the incident. "George was a real director, all right," he said. "He was wonderful to the reporters, always at their service. He'd explain things to them, give them background. He took issues and put them in perspective. He and the other press panel members made sure there was time for questioning, so that together they did a great deal to keep the American press informed. And they were grateful. As a result, they gave the Council phenomenal coverage in the papers here at home."

"George Higgins was simply a brilliant interpreter of things for the press," said Sherry. "There were so many times when the press panel would be bogged down, and George would come in and articulate the point in question. He was trusted, too. If there was a problem getting information from the press office, or if people were tight-lipped at the panel, George would be able to calm down the journalists and assure them that there was no censorship going on. He'd intervene anytime there was a gripe about press relations. But I think the main thing he did was to show the bishops that the more information they supplied, the less misinformation would be published in the press. He made the Church more open to the value of communicating with the press. And he convinced people that the Church can't communicate with the secular world if it can't communicate with its own communicators."

In a column written in 1982, as the twentieth anniversary of the Council drew near, Higgins reflected on the wisdom of the Council Fathers, and particularly of the American bishops, in making it easier for the press to report their deliberations and decisions. "After the first session of Vatican II the rule of secrecy was greatly, although not completely, relaxed," he wrote. "As a result, even the least curious began to listen in. Twenty years later they're still listening more attentively than anyone could have imagined."

Higgins was passionately interested in everything going on

at the Council. Like a railbird at a racetrack, one companion said, he knew the jockeys and he knew the mounts. He had a hand in many of the speeches written at the Villanova for delivery by bishops—American, French, and German, mostly—on the Council floor. He gave a presentation at the weekly meetings that the American bishops held at the North American College. He was a first-rate liaison man between the Americans and bishops from other countries, many of whom he had met in connection with international labor meetings.

He missed little that was going on. "As we approach the end of this session of the Council," he wrote home in November 1964, "the pace gets faster and faster. On the average day we go from 6:30 AM until close to midnight. We have been home at our hotel for dinner only twice in two months."

As involved as Higgins was in everything about the Council, though, a few areas interested him more than others — the lay apostolate, for one, that having been the topic he dealt with as a participant in the Council's planning stage. In a Yardstick column for May 11, 1964, he told readers they should not expect the Council to deliver "the final word" on the lay apostolate in its forthcoming document on the topic, advising them that the anticipated document on the Church itself would be much more significant. "We are just beginning to rethink, at the conciliar level, our notion of the Church," he said. "For a long time we have tended to think of the Church much too exclusively in juridical and hierarchical terms. The forthcoming Schema on the Church will help us to redress that balance by highlighting the fact that the Church is the People of God and by emphasizing the fundamental equality of all the members of the People of God not only in the sense that Christians cannot be classified by race, social rank, national origin, etc., but also in the sense that despite the differentiation by functions and ministry, there is no essential difference between those who hold ecclesiastical office and the ordinary members of the faithful, even though, by the very nature of the Church, the priest has functions which the layman cannot fulfill."

Predictably, Higgins was deeply concerned with the fate of Schema 17, which involved social and economic problems (and which wound up incorporated into *Gaudium et Spes, the Pastoral Constitution on the Church in the Modern World,* adopted at the Council's close in 1965). Here again, however, he warned Yardstick readers not to expect the Council to "solve" all the world's major socioeconomic problems.

Writing on January 20, 1964, he said, "The most we have any right to hope for is that this Schema will identify and dramatize the urgency of the principal problems confronting the modern world and will challenge Catholics and all other men of good will to work toward a speedy solution of these problems in the light of sound social principles.

"It seems to me that an ecumenical council should not be expected to work miracles. All of the problems to be discussed in Schema 17 are enormously complicated. The Church, acting through the Council, can help to solve them by analyzing them, with the greatest possible clarity, in the light of Catholic social teaching.

"In the final analysis, however, these problems can only be solved by informed and zealous laymen—laymen who are at once technically competent and adequately instructed in the principles of social ethics and theology and who have a deep and abiding love for the world and are persuaded that their very Christian calling leaves them no choice but to be deeply concerned about the problems with which the world is presently confronted."

Higgins devoted several more columns to the topic during the extended debate on Schema 13 (the major background document for *Gaudium et Spes),* one dealing with its relation to trade unions and another with a then-current European controversy over "the new priests"—that is, liberal clergymen who were accused of playing into the hands of communists. The question of Communism was also at the heart of another Yardstick column on Schema 13, written November 29, 1965, as the debate (and the Council itself) drew to a close. At issue was a petition signed by 450 Council Fathers objecting to a majority decision not to condemn Marxism or communistic atheism by name in its treatment of the subject of atheism. Although he agreed with the majority, Higgins said, he respected the sincerity of the objectors, at the same time lamenting the fact that there were "wild extremists who have predictably jumped on their bandwagon" and were contending that the Council's decision was evidence of "the heresy of neo-modernism."

Many of these extremists, Higgins continued, are cowards: "What they really mean, but are afraid to say, is that Pope Paul— who, after all, could easily get the Council to condemn communism if he so desired—has sold out to neo-modernism or 'progressissimo.'

. . .Thus far, thanks be to God, this sort of heresy-hunting, which could simply be laughed off as a bad joke if it were not so vicious in tone, has been confined to a relatively small group of fanatics. Let us hope and pray that it will not become contagious. God help us all if it ever catches on among ordinary Catholics. The postconciliar Church is going to have enough trouble without being torn asunder by internal hatred and strife. What she will need more than almost anything else for the indefinite future is 'unity in essentials, freedom in those matters which are doubtful, and in all things charity.' "

Higgins continued to stress the pastoral nature of the document in several columns written in the months immediately after the Council closed. On May 16, 1966, he noted that the tone of the constitution derives from its purpose of entering into a dialogue with the modern world, rather than spelling out specific solutions for all its problems. "Faithful to the spirit of Pope John XXIII," he said, "the document refrains from sterile criticism of individuals and institutions and concentrates singlemindedly on its pastoral task of encouraging and motivating men of good will to move not from A to Z but from A to B to C. In taking this approach, the drafters of the document acted very wisely, or so it seems to me."

The same document was also the topic of several talks Higgins gave in the United States after the Council, always in enthusiastic terms. Speaking in Youngstown, Ohio, on March 28, 1966, at a diocesan Vatican Council Review Day, he said the document proved that the Church had abandoned its "way of condemnation" and taken a new stance in the world. That stance, he continued, is to extend to all people "boundless sympathy for their needs and weaknesses and respect for their values."

In all, Higgins was pleased that the Council Fathers had accomplished what they did in the Church in the Modern World. The amount of attention he afforded it, in print and in speaking appearances, is obvious evidence of the importance he attached to the work. However, there were two other Council documents with which he was more closely associated, into which he poured countless hours of behind-the-scenes work—those involving Catholic-Jewish relations *(Nostra Aetate,* the *Declaration on the Relation of the Church to Non-Christian Religions),* and religious liberty *(Dignitatis Humanae,* the *Declaration on Religious Liberty).*

His connection with the Jewish statement began early during

the Council's first session, in thoroughly puzzling circumstances. A young Irish Jesuit priest who identified himself as an emissary of Cardinal Augustin Bea, head of the Secretariat for Christian Unity, called on Higgins at the Mondial with no prior appointment, and immediately began asking the names of American bishops who could be counted on to support a Council declaration on Catholic-Jewish relations. The Jesuit turned out to be Malachi Martin, who later left the priesthood and became the author of several controversial Church-related books. Higgins, who would later describe Martin with a genuine sense of bewilderment as "the most mysterious and intriguing man I've ever met," found the stranger's personality so compelling that they talked for an hour. It was the first of many meetings with Martin in which Higgins (joined by Hurley and Bosler) took part, and one that eventually led, a year later, to a long conversation with Bea himself. Until that point, many of Higgins's companions—and, to a degree, Higgins himself—wondered about the quality of Martin's credentials, but when he and Hurley were escorted to the Brazilian College, where Bea awaited them, they became believers.

"There had been hopes in the beginning," Hurley said, "that there would be schemas on religious liberty and on the Jews, but both were nowhere to be seen at the end of the first session. There was grave suspicion that they would never surface. Bea was very concerned about it. He wanted to know how the American bishops would stand on both questions, what kind of support he could expect. We told him that a number of Americans, perhaps nine out of ten, would be pretty firm on the Jewish document, and that on religious liberty he'd probably get almost 100 per cent. We found it hard to conceive of one bishop voting against it—and remember, we were working with these bishops all the time."

As work on the schema proceeded, Higgins was an intimate participant in its preparation, never as an actual member of the commission or a drafter of the document, but as a liaison between Jewish observers at the Council and the bishops, and as a writer of speeches for several American bishops who supported it on the Council floor. He worked most closely with Joseph Lichten of the Anti-Defamation League of B'nai B'rith, Zaccariah Shuster, who was on the staff of the American Jewish Committee in Paris, and others who traveled frequently to Rome such as Rabbi Marc Tanenbaum. He not only carried their reaction to the document to various bishops, but let them know when he thought their lobbying efforts were going too far, as he did when he squelched an ADL plan to send letters to the bishops, urging support for the schema. He became the press panel's leading spokesman on the document, and in countless private conversations pressed his views on friendly American bishops.

"All during the Council," he wrote reflectively in The Yardstick for October 14, 1968, "I followed with special interest the public as well as the backstage efforts of those who were pushing for a strong declaration on Catholic-Jewish relations and of those, on the other side of the fence, who were trying to prevent the Council from adopting such a statement. It was a nerve-wracking experience, for one could never completely dispel the nagging fear that, in the end, the Declaration on Catholic-Jewish Relations would either be shelved or would be so badly watered down as to make one wish that it had never been brought to the floor in the first place."

However, he noted, "All's well that ends well, or at least ends reasonably well. The final version of the. . .declaration could and should have been much stronger, but, all things considered, it's a good statement and one which marks a great step forward in the tragic history of Catholic-Jewish relations."

Nostra Aetate, the shortest official document to emerge from the Council, was formally published October 28, 1965. As capsulized by Higgins, it repudiated anti-Semitism and the ancient charge of collective Jewish responsibility for the death of Jesus, and called for fraternal dialogue between Catholics and Jews. He took pains to point out that the document was addressed to Catholics, not to Jews, as he did on March 14, 1966: "If Jews mistakenly think that the declaration was addressed to them and was meant—insultingly and condescendingly—to 'absolve' them from responsibility for the Crucifixion, they will understandably be very reluctant to enter into dialogue with Christians. And, by the same token, if Christians fail to understand that the declaration was meant to be a sincere examination of the Christian conscience—which has so much to answer for in this area—they will be ill-prepared for the kind of dialogue which is so strongly recommended in the document." (This column was occasioned by a best-selling satirical record by the Mitchell Trio, on which one song suggested that "Jews can relax and get their first good night's sleep in almost 2,000 years" now that the Council's declaration had absolved them for the crucifixion, an indication, in an offbeat way, that Council activities had indeed been closely followed at home.)

He also emphasized that the document was a first step, a challenge. A year after its promulgation, on November 21, 1966, he wrote a column praising a talk in which Cardinal Spellman assured a group of American Jewish leaders that the Church here would do all it could to implement the spirit as well as the letter of the declaration. Although it could not undo the past, Higgins said, *Nostra Aetate* could help to usher in a new era of mutual knowledge and respect. He continued: "What a proud boast it will be for the United States if we step out in front and set an example for the rest of the world in this regard. Working hand in hand, Christians and Jews together, we have a glorious opportunity to transform the Council's declaration. . .from a lifeless piece of paper into a living document which can literally change the face of the earth."

Higgins's role in the ultimate passage of the Declaration on Religious Liberty was less direct than the one he had played in connection with *Nostra Aetate,* but it was no less essential. The story behind it was one of deep friendship with John Courtney Murray, the principal author of the declaration, and his concern for Murray's well-being during its preparation. At least one close-up observer thinks that Higgins's role spelled the difference between success and failure on the religious liberty question. As Bishop Mark Hurley expressed it:

"Higgins was Murray's mentor. Higgins encouraged him; Higgins advised him. Higgins was his front man. And I heard Murray say that he never would have been able to do the document on religious freedom if he hadn't lived at the Villanova. That was tantamount to saying 'because of Higgins.' "

Higgins backs off from that interpretation, disclaiming any technical role in the document's preparation, conceding that he might have been of value in making contact with various bishops. "But Murray lived with us at Villanova, and he got encouragement there," Higgins said. "He would have been a very unhappy man if he hadn't been living with us because it was a very difficult period for him, healthwise and because of concern over the issues. If he had lived in one of the typical Jesuit houses, he would have gone to his room at nine o'clock and that would have been it. Here he had friends around who took him out to dinner, who admired him and encouraged him."

Higgins drew an appealing picture of Murray at the Villanova in a memorial column (August 28, 1967) shortly after Murray's death: "As one of the permanent, residential members of the original Villanova club, Father Murray, in spite of his heavy workload as a consultant to several of the conciliar commissions, enthusiastically threw himself into the relaxed and rather free-wheeling spirit of the place and was always on hand to welcome our steady flow of guests and to enliven our endless bull sessions with his own brand of sophisticated wit and banter and, when called upon to do so, with his own very perceptive comments on the significance of what was happening down the pike at the Council. Too much of a gentleman, and, by temperament, too sensitive and reserved to take the floor away forcefully from more boisterous conversationalists, he would listen very patiently, especially to his juniors, and would diffidently ask for the floor only when he felt that the group expected him to speak his piece.

"On more formal occasions, when the Americans living at Villanova celebrated a national holiday or some other significant event in the presence of the French, Italian, and Yugoslav contingents who shared our common dining facilities, Father Murray would be delegated by acclamation to speak for all of us and would do so in flawless Latin and with great aplomb. He was at his elegant best on such occasions, and, in spite of his protestations to the contrary, was always delighted to serve as our official spokesman."

Murray, as noted earlier, had not been present at the Council's first session, the victim, apparently, of what Higgins termed "a small but relentless band of heresy hunters both in Washington and Rome." He gladly accepted Cardinal Spellman's invitation to serve as a Council *peritus,* however, and spent the final three sessions as one of the Villanova residents. He assumed the leading role in preparing the religious liberty document—perceived at the Council as a particularly "American" concern—despite the lingering effects of heart disease, and a lung ailment that hospitalized him in Rome during part of the fourth session.

His health the rest of the time was far from robust. He lived in a room on the third floor with Higgins to one side and Hurley on the other. He was painfully ill with colds, Hurley says; he recalls that he and Higgins helped Murray dress from time to time, and on occasion had to rub his chest to relieve the congestion brought on by coughing.

Higgins has gone to some lengths to correct the published and spoken impressions that Murray was something of an outcast, bereft of support from the American bishops. "Murray's real problem was with Rome, not with the Americans," Higgins said. "I've never known of anyone who got the attention that Murray did from the American bishops. At the end of the Council they were falling all over him."

For many years Murray had been the American bishops' chief adviser on church-state relationships, the philosophy of law, and related topics. He wrote extensively on religious freedom, indicating that traditional Church teaching on Church and state, especially that of Leo XIII, was outdated rather than wrong. At the Council he worked in close collaboration with Msgr. Pietro Pavan, a diminutive Italian who taught at the Lateran Seminary, to produce the declaration that encompassed their joint views.

As summarized by Richard McBrien in *Catholicism* (Winston Press, 1980), the *Declaration on Religious Liberty* (in harmony with *Nostra Aetate)* teaches that religious truth is to be found outside the Body of Christ and should be respected wherever it is discovered, and that in no instance is anyone to be coerced to embrace either the Christian or the Catholic faith. "It replaces a too-exclusive understanding of revelation as 'Christian revelation,' as well as the formula, 'Error has no rights,' " McBrien said.

"Murray could prepare all kinds of stuff, but he couldn't get it on the floor," Bishop Primeau noted. "Higgins and myself and others were sort of behind the scenes. Murray picked the broad picture; you'd have to explain it in a series of lectures. It was really cut up into pieces, and we'd talk to the bishops and try to get things together. Higgins did a lot of that."

Hurley recalls Higgins needling Murray about all the backstairs buttonholing that, by political necessity, was going on. "John," Higgins said, "you're a great theologian, but when it comes to politics you're an utter novice."

Higgins followed the debates and other developments avidly, filling his letters home with progress reports. A few samples:

March 18, 1964 (to Bishop Cletus O'Donnell, then an auxiliary in Chicago): "The most encouraging news I heard in Rome is that the chapter on Religious Liberty in the *Schema on Ecumenism* (as the document was originally structured) has not only been retained but has been strengthened considerably, thanks, in large measure, to the forceful intervention of a number of American bishops. By the way, I am reliably informed that the Holy Father is personally promoting the cause of religious liberty. He considers it an absolute must. That's good news.''

September 27, 1964: ''This is the busiest week of the Council for the Americans because of religious liberty and statement on the Jews. Both statements are in good shape.''

September 29, 1964: ''Cardinal Meyer and Cardinal Cushing speak tomorrow. This is *the* big American week.''

On November 22, 1965, two weeks before its formal promulgation, Higgins devoted a full column to the Declaration on Religious Liberty that summed up his enthusiastic feeling for all that it said. While it was true, he noted, that the American bishops had played a key role in its passage, it was important to remember that the ideas the document expressed had widespread support among the Council Fathers, and probably would have been approved even in the first session. (Nevertheless, he continued, it was ''providential'' that the vote was postponed until the final session, thereby giving the document the widest possible consensus.)

With all the support they had, however, Higgins wrote with noticeable satisfaction that it was the American bishops and a leading American theologian who ''made a decisive, perhaps *the* decisive, contribution in Vatican II to the all-important cause of religious liberty. The reason for this is not far to seek. Given the history of the United States and, more specifically, our remarkably successful record in the area of religious freedom, it was to be expected that the American bishops, with the indispensable assistance of a Father Murray, would take the lead on this issue in the Council. Indeed they would have disgraced themselves before the world if they had failed to do so. . . .''

Murray's sudden death in 1967 saddened Higgins deeply. He wrote (August 28, 1967) that the passage of the religious liberty document at the Council, seen as a vindication of Murray's teachings, had given him a visible lift before his final brief illness slowed him down again.

''Those of us,'' he said, ''who lived with him—and suffered with him vicariously all the tortuous ins-and-outs and ups-and-downs of the *Declaration on Religious Liberty*—will always remember him with great affection and esteem, not, in the first instance, as a distinguished theologian, but rather as a witty, delightfully urbane, and warmly sympathetic friend who instinctively went out of his way to make everyone—including, or I should say especially, the domestic servants at Villanova and the younger members of the club—feel perfectly at ease. He was a great priest and a very lovable human being. We miss him very much, especially when we get together, as we did rather sorrowfully in New York City the night before his funeral, to reminisce about the good old days at Villanova. May he rest in peace."

In the autumn of 1965 the good old days at Villanova were drawing to a close and the pace of Council activities built ever faster. Writing home, Higgins mentioned a *Time* magazine article quoting a bishop who said the Council was moving so fast that he felt like a nun who had lost her place in the missal. "Not a bad simile," Higgins said.

He devoted one column after another to Council events, in one of them (October 11) taking John Leo of *Commonweal* to task for his pessimistic report on the makeup of what would become the Bishops' Synod. As a result of what he felt was a disappointment to the progressives among the bishops, Leo said the mood of the Council had turned sour. Among those he cited to make his point was Hans Kung. Higgins challenged him on that and on several other specifics:

"Father Kung, who shares our home-away-from-home at Casa Villanova and regularly takes part in our endless post-mortem bull sessions, is reasonably happy about the new synod. Like the majority of the bishops, he looks upon it as a limited, but nevertheless realistic and very encouraging step in the right direction. It is my impression that the same is true of almost all the other so-called progressive *periti* taking part in the current session of the Council." He concluded the column with a slap at long-distance journalism. Leo, he said, "never should have allowed his personal pessimism to lead him into the trap of pretending to be able to gauge the mood or the temper of the Council Fathers and *periti* from a distance of several thousand miles. When it comes to this kind of reporting, there simply isn't any substitute for good old-fashioned leg work, in Rome."

On October 25 Higgins defended Pope Paul's decision to limit Council discussion of clerical celibacy to written interventions rather than floor addresses. "If there is a need for a thorough study of the problem of celibacy," he wrote, "I would prefer to see it carried out by a post-conciliar commission."

A month before the Council formally ended, in The Yardstick of November 8, Higgins was already beginning to grapple with
following up on the Council, and dealing with all the issues it had
raised. He opened the column in an unusually moody style, noting
that the bishops preparing to leave Rome would probably do so with
mixed emotions, having "reached the saturation point" on the Council's constitutions, decrees, and declarations. He continued:

"On the other hand, most of them, I am sure, will also
experience at least a momentary twinge of sadness and regret at the
thought of leaving Rome. Many of them will never set foot in the
Eternal City again, and while some will have to come back periodically for meetings of the episcopal synod or of postconciliar commissions, it would be safe to predict that none of them will ever again
have the privilege of taking part in an ecumenical council.

"That is not to say that councils have outlived their usefulness
and are a thing of the past, but merely to hazard the guess that there
is not likely to be another one in the lifetime of even the youngest
of the Benjamins in the College of Bishops."

Taking his cue from a Council address delivered by then
Archbishop Michele Pellegrino of Turin, Higgins cited the need for
sound intellectual training for the clergy, respect within the Church
for the intellectual life and the sacred sciences, a "profound and
dynamic renewal of theological learning" combined with a greater
measure of intellectual freedom in the Church. The talk contained
a particular lesson for the Church in America, Higgins said. "It
would seem to be crucially important for the Church in the United
States to do everything within its power to create an atmosphere of
intellectual freedom and of genuine respect for the intellectual life,"
he wrote. "As a matter of fact, it might even be argued that this
is the most important of all postconciliar challenges facing the
Church in the United States."

In The Yardstick for December 20, the first column written
after the Council's conclusion, Higgins agreed with the observation
of a leading eastern prelate, Cardinal Patriarch Maximos V Saigh,
that the effect of Vatican II had been to "put the Church into a
permanent state of dialogue—dialogue with itself for a continuous
renewal; dialogue with our Christian brothers in order to restore the
visible unity of the body of Jesus Christ; dialogue, finally, with
today's world, addressed to every man of good will." (Higgins also
repeated one unidentified observer's remark that after the Council,

the three evangelical vows will be those of poverty, chastity, and dialogue, in place of obedience.)

"Any way you look at it," Higgins wrote, "dialogue is now the order of the day. Short of open rebellion against the letter as well as the spirit of the Council, there is no going back to the time when Catholics, however mistakenly, could regard it as a virtue to stay in their own backyard for fear of being 'contaminated' by the 'dangerous' influences of the world and/or of compromising their own religious principles. To the contrary, Catholics are now expected, in the words of the pastoral *Constitution on the Church in the Modern World,* to engage in 'frank conversation' with all of their contemporaries."

In the same column Higgins repeated the call for "a greater measure of freedom within the Church itself" that he had urged November 8. Unless that problem is solved, he said, "we are not likely to get very far in our dialogue with the modern world."

Higgins turned to the Council for column material on relatively few occasions after 1966. At one point he marveled that interest in the Council was still so high that it could command a nation's attention on an all-night radio talk show; at another he was incredulous that a survey indicated 43 percent of the Catholics in the Worcester Diocese had never heard of the Council. He even took pains to scotch a rumor printed in *The Wanderer* that he was the real Xavier Rynne, the best-selling but still anonymous Vatican II author. Said Higgins, slyly, "The real Xavier Rynne, bless his slippery heart, is still at large and presumably still collecting royalties."

On October 9, 1972, to mark the tenth anniversary of the opening of the Council, Higgins wrote that he perceived a significant turning point in the updating process unleashed by Vatican II. Until then, he said, the emphasis was on institutional and structural reforms in the life of the Church, "probably a necessary first step." But something more spiritual was called for, he added: "I have the impression that there is throughout the Church a growing recognition of the fact that we have yet to plumb the depths of the current crisis in religion; and that since the end of the Council we have tended, by and large, to skirt around this issue by concentrating most of our attention on problems and concerns which, though obviously important in themselves, really don't take us to the heart of the matter. The heart of the matter. . .is to make the 'spiritual life' the Church's major preoccupation.''

On various occasions Higgins has rejected the contention that it was the Council that was responsible for the floodtide of changes in the Church which developed in the postconciliar period, maintaining that the changes would have appeared under any circumstances and that the Council eased their acceptance. As he said in an address at Lewis & Clark College in Portland, Oregon, on April 26, 1981:

"The Council (I am speaking here in general terms and presuming certain qualifications) did not generate the phenomenon of rapid change in the Church but merely coincided with it, validated it, gave it a certain impetus and, even more importantly, a certain theological and pastoral respectability. Rapid change would have come into the Church with or without a Council, but with this all-important difference: In the absence of a Council, it probably would have come largely in protest against the real or alleged inadequacies of Catholic thought and pastoral practice and not in response to an orderly study of theological and biblical sources and a systematic reappraisal of the Church's needs and opportunities. The Council, in other words, was the providential safety valve that made it possible, or so it seemed to many observers, to forestall a disastrous explosion in the life of the Church.''

Father J. Bryan Hehir, a friend of long standing and a man Higgins holds in highest respect, suggests that Higgins matured theologically in a profoundly significant way during the Council; that he overcame a style of theological training—general in that period, Hehir proposes—to expand his horizons after the four autumns in Rome.

Higgins turned the thought down. "That would be true of everybody, everybody who was at the Council," he said. "The Council simply pushed aside the theology we got in our seminary days. Bryan is a much younger man, and overly respectful because of that. Probably what he was saying is that he's surprised that a man of my age was as open to change. But many, many people changed in those four years.''

Higgins, as noted earlier, downplays the significance of the role he played at Vatican II, but those who were part of it feel otherwise—the press people for whom he was a friend and advocate, the Villanova crowd that found him such an engaging catalyst, the bishops who learned from him, and those for whom he wrote; all who were concerned about *Nostra Aetate* and the *Declaration on Religious Liberty,* and know how vital his part was behind the scenes. Whatever his own view about what he did in Rome, he felt that being there was one of the truly memorable experiences in his life. He told readers of his column about it on October 14, 1968:

"October is almost always a glorious month in Washington, and this year, barring an unexpected act of treachery on the part of the weatherman, it promises to break all previous records. And yet, even in Washington, the golden splendor of October is tinged with a note of nostalgic sadness for those who were privileged to attend the four sessions of Vatican Council II. Their hearts are in Rome at this time of the year. For the rest of their lives, come the first touch of autumn, most of them, I suspect, will experience at least a slight twinge of homesickness for the Eternal City and a feeling of bittersweet regret at the thought that, even if they live to be 100, they will probably never again experience anything quite like the thrill of being involved in an ecumenical council."

Above: **In New York,** with Eleanor Roosevelt and Vice President Nixon at the United Nations in 1954. *Left:* **In Virginia,** blessing tools on Labor Day in 1977. *Below:* **In Moscow,** with Russian Orthodox leaders at a conference on world peace in 1972.

In Delano, California at the signing in July 1970 of the contract between the AFL-CIO United Farmworkers and the Table Grape Growers. *Seated, from left:* William L. Kircher, former AFL-CIO Director of Organizations; Larry Itliong, Filipino Farmworker Leader; Cesar Chavez, Director of United Farmworkers Union, AFL-CIO. *Standing, from left:* Ray Oliva, union member; Manuel Uranday; Roger Mahony, bishop of Stockton; Bishop Joseph Donnelly, former chairman of U.S. Bishops' Committee on Farm Labor; Msgr. George Higgins.

Above: **In Gdansk, Poland,** with Lech Walesa in October 1981 at Solidarity Congress. *Right:* **In Gdansk,** with bishop of Gdansk in October 1981. *Below:* **In Gdansk,** concelebrating Eucharist at Solidarity Congress in October 1981. *Far right:* **In Harlan County, Kentucky,** discussing United Mine Workers strike in May 1974.

U.M.W. OF A.
ON STRIKE
Brookside

N.C. PICTURE SERVICE

COURTESY OF GEORGE HIGGINS

Left, top: **In Budapest, Hungary,** with Cardinal Lazlo Lekai, Primate of Hungary, and Geno Baroni on January 6, 1979 on the occasion of returning the Crown of St. Stephen to the Hungarian People. *Left, bottom:* **In Clinton, Iowa,** talking to strikers at Clinton Corn Co. in February 1980. *Above:* **In Washington, D.C.,** delivering invocation on AFL-CIO National Solidarity Day in 1982. *Right:* **In New York** speaking at testimonial dinner hosted by AFL-CIO in his honor in September 1980.

Above: **In Washington, D.C.** in August 1967, conferring with Marvin Braiterman of the Synagogue Council of America *(left)* and Gayraud S. Wilmore, Jr., of the National Council of Churches *(right)* before a Senate Judiciary Committee hearing on constitutional rights. *Below:* **In Bogota, Colombia,** addressing the eighth Congress of the Latin America Confederation of Labor (CLAT) in December 1982.

CHAPTER EIGHT

INTERRACIAL JUSTICE

WHEN ALL THE EVILS OF RACISM BURST UPON THE NATION'S conscience in the Sixties, and the churches, after too many years of silence or ineffective leadership on the issue, urged their members to atone for all the racist sins of the past, George Higgins, predictably, was one of the clearest voices they had to offer. Higgins preached the gospel of interracial justice in his columns and in his talks, in committee work and in his dealings with legislative leaders, and—perhaps most importantly—in his public and private encounters with the labor community. Get your house in order, he repeatedly told his labor friends, or you'll be called to a terrible accounting.

What was noteworthy about Higgins's role in the Sixties is that it had changed little if any from the role he had marked out 20 years earlier. The Higgins who told the 1947 United Auto Workers convention

145

(Atlantic City, November 10) in an opening-session invocation to look on their Negro members as equal brothers in Christ, and to continue their efforts to advance the cause of racial justice, was the same Higgins who used a Labor Day homily in 1964 (September 7, in Washington) to assert that the race issue had put organized labor "on the spot." Even though it was "the most serious problem" facing labor, he said, many labor leaders "have yet to grasp the depth and the passion of the present racial crisis."

He was no trendy liberal on the issue; he deplored the Sixties' growing militancy on race relations and frequently chided young black activists for criticizing the efforts of the pioneer civil rights leaders who had gone before them. For Higgins, the issue of civil rights was one which stood out so starkly as a matter of justice (and for Catholics, a matter of Christian responsibility) that confrontation and debate seemed virtually useless. Above all, he was constant. "On civil rights," says Joseph Rauh of Americans for Democratic Action, "George Higgins was always there."

Regular readers of The Yardstick had known for years just where Higgins stood. An early reference to racial justice appeared on May 29, 1950, when Higgins enthusiastically reviewed a book *(No Postponement)* by Jesuit Father John LaFarge. The book urged Americans to follow the religious principles that were part of their heritage to develop a spiritual work leadership, especially in equality and justice for all racial minorities. It was addressed particularly to Catholics, Higgins noted approvingly. "Catholics, by reason of their faith, have a greater responsibility than others to work for justice in the social order," he wrote. "But if they have a heavier responsibility, they also have a greater source of strength. They have the Mass."

He was in a decidedly feisty mood a few months later, when, on April 30, 1951, at the height of the to-do following President Truman's dismissal of General Douglas MacArthur from command of U.S. troops in Korea, he took on both MacArthur and the Daughters of the American Revolution, who had heard a gloomy talk by the general on the nation's future.

The DAR ("lily-white, of course, and notoriously prejudiced against the Negro") should have been urged to alter its own views on race, immigration, and American ideals, Higgins said. He added: "But what right have we to be telling a general of the army what he should have said to an organization of which his lovely wife is proud to be a member? We beg your pardon, General. But while we were listening to you tell the Congress of the United States about that revolution which at long last is sweeping over Asia, we couldn't help but remember what the Daughters of our Revolution had done to Marian Anderson while you and Mrs. MacArthur were away. [Marian Anderson, the noted contralto, had been forbidden by the DAR to perform at Constitution Hall in Washington because she was Black. The incident took place in 1939, but for many years lived to haunt the organization.]

"'Old soldiers never die.' Maybe not. But what about old prejudices—against the Negro. . .against foreigners. . .against displaced persons? Do these ever die, or do they at least 'pass away'? If not, perhaps the American people ought to start legal proceedings to get back the good name of the Revolution of 1776 which is now being monopolized, as it were, by the Daughters of American . . .Righteousness or Reaction or what have you?"

Higgins ridiculed efforts to tie Black causes to the Communist Party, a favorite right-wing tactic during the late Forties and early Fifties. On May 21, 1951, he lambasted the Foundation for Economic Education for implying that fair employment practices legislation was a communist-inspired proposal. (He quoted a Foundation pamphlet which said that "promoters of the communist ideals have generated chaos and class conflict by generating this phobia about discrimination and persecution. This has led to false claims of rights.") Said Higgins:

"If the Foundation for Economic Freedom is really and truly interested in 'protecting' the American Negro against the wiles of the Communist Party, let it take the initiative in advocating effective remedies against racial discrimination and segregation. . . . It ought to stop distributing insulting little pamphlets on the 'blessings of discrimination.' If the Foundation is really and truly as devoted to the Constitution as it claims to be, surely it ought to be able to understand that the theory of fair employment practices legislation is based on the principles of that great document of human liberty and equality and owes nothing at all to the Communist Manifesto."

As noted earlier, Higgins hounded organized labor on the race issue, telling both its leaders and its rank and file that the cause of working men and women must embrace all workers, Black and White. In quite another way, he pointed out special responsibilities on race to another group with whom he felt especially at home, the Irish.

He took advantage of an invitation to deliver the homily at the 1957 St. Patrick's Day Mass in St. Patrick's Church, Washington, to get that message across, though he did so with some hesitation. In a letter to home on March 15 of that year he confessed that he was worried about how the homily would be received. Still, he said, he had firmly decided that the homily "couldn't be the 'usual line' about the 'glories of the clan'. . . . I've always sounded off about things like that."

At that, Higgins approached his main point with more than a measure of caution. It wasn't until the tenth page of the 11-page sermon that he first mentioned "race relations" as one area of the temporal order "ripe for the Christian harvest." He urged his congregation to greater efforts with a mild rebuke: "Surely the field of race relations is one in which Americans of Irish descent, if only because of their own bitter memory of prejudice and discrimination, should be exercising greater leadership than they have exercised thus far. A competent American historian has recently observed that the Irish are 'today regarded among the most American of Americans.' But he hastens to add—to our embarrassment, if it be true—that 'Some Irish-Americans, forgetful of the antagonisms with which their forebears were confronted a century ago, now look with contempt upon later immigrants and, specifically, on their Negro fellow-citizens whose ancestors were brought to the United States in slavery long before the arrival of the Irish immigrants. To the extent that this criticism is true—if it be true at all—we will have to admit that we are not being completely faithful to the memory of Saint Patrick who lifted us up out of the slavery of the pagan world and that neither are we being faithful to the glorious memory of the Kelleys, Burkes and Sheas who have fought a thousand glorious battles in the name of simple justice and on behalf of human brotherhood."

The admonition is a mild one, by today's standards; yet he delivered it some years before the oratorical excesses of the Sixties, rhetoric which, in time, would lose its shock value as far as most Americans were concerned. As understated as they were, however, Higgins's words had the desired effect, an awakening of concern within the Irish community, and the Church family in general, in matters of racial justice. The homily drew wide attention in the

Catholic press, more than anything else because of the unusual circumstances in which it was delivered.

Higgins repeated the theme a few years later, again attracting wide attention with his remarks, at another St. Patrick's Day Mass in which he linked the Irish even more directly with the Black cause. In the presence of Archbishop Patrick O'Boyle of Washington and Archbishop Egidio Vagnozzi, the apostolic delegate in the United States, Higgins told the congregation at St. Patrick's Church in Washington on March 17, 1965:

"Irish-American Catholics have more reason than almost any other segment of our population to stand up fearlessly for the rights of the disadvantaged minorities if only because of the fact that, not so many years ago, their own forebears were themselves the victims of the worst kind of economic and social discrimination. . . . The same kind of irrational prejudice which victimizes American Negroes in 1965 victimized Irish-Americans in 1865 and for several succeeding decades."

No single incident or series of events shaped Higgins's thinking on racial matters. At some early point in his life—prodded, one imagines, by the liberal tone of the magazine items he read aloud to his father—he perceived the question of Black-White equality as one of simple justice. Everything he would learn thereafter—in the Church, in the classroom, in the social arena—reinforced the notion.

Nor was his interest purely academic. Never a parish priest, he nevertheless had a genuine pastoral interest in all the people with whom he came in contact. That included lower-echelon workers, and over the years in Washington, more often than not that translated into Black.

"Out of everybody I knew at the [Catholic] Conference," Bishop John McCarthy said in an interview, "George was the most pastoral. When maids were burying the 18-year-old boys who'd been shot by the police, George Higgins and I were at the funeral, or George by himself. And when a maid's daughter was getting married at the Antioch Baptist Church, George would be there. I'm not saying that no one else ever went to anything, but George had that real good feel for the role of the priest, especially in moments of sorrow and celebration in peoples' lives."

Higgins was no less enthusiastic in his attempts to live the message of racial equality from the standpoint of the Church as an institution. From his earliest days at the Conference, he supported Fair Employment Practices Code legislation and worked however he could—through his columns and talks and invocations, in personal conversations, in cocktail party-buttonholing—to make Black men and women equal partners in the labor community.

At a time when, tragically, many Catholics looked upon it as a communist-front organization, Higgins championed the National Association for the Advancement of Colored People. He urged his Catholic Yardstick audience on October 9, 1956, to fight challenges which were then under way in some southern states to the NAACP's right to exist, arguing that the organization's objectives were "in complete harmony with Christian social teaching." Not surprisingly, he drew a heavy load of critical letters for his efforts.

"It was and is our firm conviction," he wrote on December 31, 1956, "that to nullify [the NAACP's right to exist], under whatever legal subterfuge, is a clear violation of the natural law and one that should be vigorously opposed as a matter of principle by all right-thinking citizens, regardless of whether or not they agree with the NAACP's admittedly controversial approach to the problem of race relations.

"The spirited reaction of some of our readers to this limited defense of NAACP deserves another column all to itself. Frankly, the reaction was rather disappointing, not because so many of our correspondents disagreed with our conclusions nor that they were critical of the NAACP and its methods, but rather because their criticism of the Association and their disagreement with our conclusions was so fiercely emotional and more often than not was based on prejudiced and discredited sources of information."

With the moral and ethical dimension of the racial question a matter of primary concern, Higgins especially savored his long association with the Leadership Conference on Civil Rights (LCCR). This voluntary and nonpartisan association of more than 100 autonomous national organizations seeks to advance civil rights for all Americans through government action at the national level. Discussing his various assignments over the years as his retirement neared in 1979, Higgins said, "The one that interests me as much as any other and the one that I will sorely miss being associated with when time eventually runs out on me is the LCCR."

With many other early White advocates of Black equality, Higgins was unprepared for the militant mood and the waves of violence which would characterize America's racial strife of the Sixties. In a 1961 column (July 24), for example, he looked back reflectively on John Gunther's *Inside U.S.A.,* a book written 15 years earlier, and contrasted Gunther's description of Detroit at that time with the Detroit of 1961. The author had described Detroit as "the most explosive town in the Western Hemisphere" because of racial tensions and labor-management confrontations.

"Was this a more or less accurate picture of Detroit in the middle Forties?" Higgins asked. "I suppose it was, more or less. But surely it doesn't bear much resemblance to the Detroit of 1961. To be sure, Detroit, like almost every other big industrial city in the United States, is still confronted with a variety of racial, industrial, and economic problems. But these problems are less critical than those of the middle Forties, and a greater effort is being made to solve them. In short, whatever its situation might have been 15 or 20 years ago, Detroit in 1961 is not 'the most explosive town in the Western Hemisphere.' "

Six years later, in the summer of 1967, much of the city was a smoldering ruin, its damage estimated at $150 million. Detroit, like much of the rest of urban America, had become swept up in the violent years.

Unprepared as he might have been for the scope of the militancy which would overtake the Black revolution of the Sixties, Higgins nonetheless took note of the early warnings. On February 4, 1963, he advised White Americans to read James Baldwin's *The Fire Next Time* as an indicator of the mood of many Black Americans.

"It is almost impossible, I suppose," he said, "for white Americans to see the race problem as vividly as Negroes see it or fully to share their wholesome and very understandable impatience with our painfully gradual efforts to eliminate the evil of racism, root and branch, from every sector of American life."

Baldwin's book, he noted, would not make for pleasant reading, but "will do all of us white Americans a lot of spiritual good." He continued: "No other book I can think of is better calculated to impress upon the dominant white majority why the American Negro is so frustrated by our policy of gradualism and so determined to find a comprehensive solution to the race problem right away—not in 1970, not next year, but tomorrow and, if possible, today.''

Higgins hoped against hope that the "comprehensive solution" might lay in the good will of individual Americans and in the legislative process that would translate their desires into the law of the land. In shaping their determination, he argued that the nation's Christian churches had a key role to play, and in his Yardstick column of September 23, 1963, less than a month after the historic, peaceful March on Washington for civil rights, he considered allegations from the Black community that churches had not done their job. Again he quoted from Baldwin, who had written that "whoever wishes to become a truly moral human being. . .must first divorce himself from all the prohibitions, crimes, and hypocrisy of the Christian church.''

It was his impression, Higgins said, that Baldwin ("thanks be to God") spoke only for "a tiny minority of disillusioned American Negroes." He cited with some satisfaction a *Newsweek* poll that showed of all white Americans trusted by Blacks, Roman Catholic priests, many of whom were quietly engaged in Black community ministry, had the highest rating. Higgins conceded that some resentment and criticism of the Church's shortcomings in advancing the cause of racial harmony was understandable. But, he continued:

"In my judgment, (the critics) will be making a serious mistake if they waste too much precious time and energy on sterile and fruitless criticism of the real or alleged failure of the churches and church-related groups to do as much as might have been done in years gone by to advance the cause of civil rights.

"The important thing to bear in mind is that, whatever may have been done or left undone in the past, religious organizations are today more deeply involved than ever before in the struggle for racial justice. And there is every reason to believe that in the months ahead they will play an even more important role in helping to eliminate the scandal of racial justice. For this we can be very grateful, all of us, Negroes and Whites alike.''

Not surprisingly, Higgins was a passionate advocate of the 1964 Civil Rights Act. He sharply took to task right-wing organizations such as the John Birch Society that continued to brand such measures as communist-inspired, and appealed to Catholic members of these organizations to question or discontinue their membership. "If they are as well informed as many of them claim to be about

Catholic social teaching," he wrote on April 13, 1964, "they must have learned by this time that the American bishops have long since come out in favor of comprehensive civil rights legislation as a logical, not to say a necessary application, in our times, of basic Catholic teaching on the equality and dignity of all of God's children, regardless of their racial origin or the color of their skin."

Higgins attentively followed the progress of the bill. As he noted years later, replying to allegations that the NCWC had been silent on the black issue during the Sixties, the conference was actually a prime supporter of and active lobbyist for the Civil Rights Bill. The Social Action Department was indeed involved in the lobbying campaign, but it was Higgins's associate, Father John Cronin, who for the most part carried out most of that assignment. It was an interesting shift for Cronin, whose earlier efforts were largely confined to writing, much of it dealing with the problem of communism. Higgins (August 4, 1975) gave his companion the credit he deserved: "The conference—in the person of Father John Cronin, who was my associate in the Social Action Department—lobbied more persistently and more effectively in favor of the landmark 1964 Civil Rights Bill than it has ever lobbied before or since on any other single issue. The record will show that Father Cronin, working in close cooperation with his Protestant and Jewish counterparts in a then unprecedented ecumenical task force, spent almost all of his time on this issue for a period of many months. . . . There was a general consensus in 1964 that Father Cronin and his associates in the ecumenical task force played a major role in persuading the Congress to adopt the 1964 Civil Rights Act."

On June 22, 1964 Higgins took part in an interfaith outdoor prayer service near the Capitol to give thanks for passage of the Civil Rights Bill. He and the other participants, he wrote in a Yardstick column dated the following week, expressed atonement for the failure of the religious community to address racial injustices earlier and with better effect, and expressed determination to "make up for lost time in the crucial days ahead." He added:

"In summary, they said that the passage of the Civil Rights Bill is not the end but only the beginning of their joint efforts as religious leaders to implement the teaching of their respective churches on the dignity and quality of all men regardless of their racial origin or the color of their skin. . . . It will be up to the churches and church-related organizations and institutions to take the lead in preparing the American people to comply with the Civil Rights law and to go the law one better, so to speak, by voluntarily developing in every community in the United States an atmosphere of interracial harmony.''

One community clearly short of that goal was Selma, Alabama, where officials' efforts to halt a 1965 voter registration drive led by Martin Luther King, Jr. occupied the national conscience for weeks. White northern clergymen were in the forefront of the drive, and their division on the need to have federal troops sent in and their criticism of President Lyndon Johnson for failing to do so, presaged coming divisions over tactics and the generally growing militancy in the civil rights movement.

Higgins sided with the president, who felt that a hasty display of federal force could undermine the long-term effects of the Civil Rights Act and would play into the hands of Alabama Governor George Wallace, who was still pushing a segregationist line. He agreed to take part in a meeting of clergymen with Johnson only after he was assured that the encounter would be held for purposes of counsel rather than protest.

In The Yardstick (March 22, 1965) he chided overzealous critics of the president (''they ought to have enough decency to give the president credit for being sincere and having enough common sense to realize that he might just happen to know at least as much, and conceivably a great deal more, than they do about the ins-and-outs of governmental strategy'') and reported on the ''very constructive'' meeting itself:

''Some clerics have charged that we were taken in by the president, or, as the saying goes, that we were given a 'snow' job. They are entitled to this opinion, but, again, common sense—to say nothing of humility—should have suggested to them the possibility that they might have been mistaken in jumping to such a critical conclusion about a two-hour meeting at which they were not present.''

A measure of order was restored when, several days after a White House meeting with Governor Wallace, President Johnson, rather than sending in federal troops, signed an executive order federalizing the Alabama National Guard.

Selma was one of the first names to appear in the long and tragic litany of place names that would punctuate the history of civil rights as it was written in the Sixties. Another was added a few months later when vicious rioting erupted August 15 in the Watts area of Los Angeles, leaving 35 dead and property damage estimated at $200 million.

Higgins followed the tragic uprising with a column (August 23) in which he was outspokenly critical of the Rev. James Bevel, an aide of Dr. Martin Luther King, Jr., for proclaiming that in the wake of passage of the Civil Rights Act the civil rights movement had in effect ceased to exist, and that it would develop into an "international peace army." Since the Watts riots had taken place within 48 hours of Bevel's "incredible" statement, Higgins said, it might be in order to suggest to Bevel and King that "they bivouac their proposed international peace army in Los Angeles, for at least a few days." Those few days, Higgins said, might convince them that the civil rights movement, properly understood, was really just getting started. If they remain unconvinced, he added, about the existence of a civil rights movement or the need for one, "then the sooner they bow out of the picture, the better it will be for the cause of civil rights in the United States."

The words were harsh, Higgins conceded, but there would be no place in the leadership ranks of the movement for those who see it only in legislative terms. (Harsh indeed, reread in the light of what has since taken place: "If Dr. King and Rev. Bevel would prefer to let somebody else do the hard, grubby, tedious, long-range work that needs to be done to implement the spirit as well as the letter of the civil rights legislation while they go traipsing off at the head of an international peace army, so be it.")

The "Black power" phase of the civil rights revolution exploded into the public consciousness in 1966, stirring Blacks deeply and causing an ever-growing concern on the part of whites who wondered if the movement had already gotten out of hand. Higgins wondered too, particularly if "Black power" thinking was turned against civil rights pioneers such as Roy Wilkins.

On July 11, 1966, he wrote in The Yardstick that the drive for Black power properly understood is unobjectionable, but that when Black power becomes synonymous with Black racism or Black violence, it ought to be condemned.

"Those who hesitate to blow the whistle on Black racists for fear of being condemned as Uncle Toms or lily-livered 'liberals' can take courage from the example of Roy Wilkins, president of the

NAACP, who told the press on July 4 that 'the trouble with Black power is it implies anti-White and we can't have anything to do with it.' Mr. Wilkins said that the term itself was 'a bad choice of words' and explained 'we believe in the legitimate use of power. It ought never to be ethnic or racial,' he added. 'The NAACP, for example, has always been a believer in the unfettered ballot for the Negro. We have counseled him on the use of his ballot for the advancement of his race. Our whole approach is interracial, not antiracial.' Mr. Wilkins is a man of courage and integrity. Some of the Black Power extremists in other segments of the civil rights movement are trying to smear him as an Uncle Tom, but they are bound to fail. Long after they have run out of steam, Roy Wilkins will be remembered and honored as one of the great social reformers of this generation."

The column brought charges that Higgins was out of touch with the Black community and out of sympathy with its legitimate aspirations, and that he was overreacting to press reports about what Black power advocates were really saying. Not at all, Higgins replied in a followup column on September 12, in which he cited "irresponsible" statements by Stokely Carmichael. The young Black spokesman had said at a civil rights rally, "If we don't get the vote, we're going to burn down the city. If we don't get the vote, you aren't going to have no more Washington, D.C." Higgins quoted the Black Washington newsman, William Raspberry, who severely criticized Carmichael in *The Washington Post*. "If I understand Mr. Raspberry correctly," wrote Higgins, "he is saying that if this is what the drive for Black power really means to Mr. Carmichael, he wants no part of it. Neither do I. . . . As a matter of fact, I happen to be in favor of the drive for Black power in the sense in which this term is being used by responsible civil rights leaders. Moreover I share the view of those who say, as Coadjutor Bishop Peter Gerety of Portland, Maine, pointed out in his forthright Labor Day sermon in Washington, that the call for Black power is born of mistrust of the generality of Whites and is an expression of 'deep-seated emotional resentment in the hearts of Black Americans as they face White power.' This is another way of saying that the so-called Negro problem in the United States is really a White problem."

To counter the charge that he was out of touch with the Black community, Higgins concluded the column by quoting the introduction to a new book (*The White Problem in America,* Johnson

Publishing Co.) based on material in a special issue of *Ebony* magazine and declaring his "complete agreement" with it: "For more than a decade through books, magazines, newspapers, TV and radio the White man has been trying to solve the race problem through studying the Negro. We feel that the answer lies in a more thorough study of the man who created the problem. In this issue we, as Negroes, look at the White man today with the hope that our effort will tempt him to look at himself more thoroughly. With a better understanding of himself, we trust that he may then understand us better, and this nation's most vital problem can then be solved."

Questions of militancy and civil disobedience as they applied to the civil rights movement continued to trouble Higgins as the Sixties moved on. In a 1967 column (December 11) dealing primarily with Vietnam, he exploded at reports of the testimony of one civil rights militant who said before a congressional committee that he wouldn't hesitate to shoot Mrs. Lyndon Johnson if he thought it necessary to do so in order to achieve equality for American Blacks. "To mouth this sort of anarchical rhetoric in the name of civil disobedience. . .is to strike at the very heart of the democratic system of government," he said.

On May 19, 1969 he wrote a loving tribute to A. Philip Randolph, the labor leader and "grand old man of the civil rights movement," who had celebrated his 80th birthday two weeks earlier. Noting that Randolph had responded without malice to young Black militants who referred to him disparagingly ("I don't agree with all their methodology, and yet I can understand why they are in this mood of revolt, or resort to violence, for I was a young Black militant myself, the angry young man of my day") Higgins continued:

"These are the words of a wise and tolerant man, a thoroughly decent human being who could teach the younger militants a thing or two if only they would come down from their perch long enough to give him a respectful hearing. He could teach them, for example, that no amount of militant rhetoric can make up for the Black man's lack of effective economic power and that economic power for the great mass of Black Americans, 99 percent of whom are members of the working class, can only be achieved through a coalition of Blacks and liberal Whites working to eradicate poverty among people of all races."

A good portion of that column was reprinted on June 4, 1979, following Randolph's death at the age of 90. Toward the end of the

new entry, Higgins noted that Randolph attached so much importance to the organization of Black workers into bonafide trade unions
because he saw economic reform as an essential prerequisite to the
solution of the "so-called race problem" in the United States.
Younger militants might deride Randolph for that view, Higgins
noted; some of them saw his insistence on a labor-civil rights coalition
as reactionary nonsense. He continued:

"I have the impression, however, that the tide is beginning
to turn in Randolph's direction. In recent years, Black leaders have
increasingly stressed the relationship between civil rights and
economic justice. If their emphasis on this point catches on among
their constituents, Randolph will deserve much of the credit, for it
was he, more than any other single individual, who sold his own
people and the liberal White community on the need for a strong
labor-civil rights coalition. May God reward him for this and for
all of his other contributions to the cause of social justice and human
decency."

His earlier reservations aside, Higgins paid a warm tribute
to Martin Luther King, Jr. in his Yardstick column of April 15, 1968,
a few days after the civil rights leader was assassinated in Memphis.
He did so partly because of all that King had come to symbolize
in the movement, but also because he admired the way King had
developed in his approach to addressing racial ills. His oratory, impassioned as ever, was at the same time less inflammatory; increasingly he called for the same kind of civil rights-labor coalition which
was so closely associated with Randolph.

Accompanied by Bishop McCarthy, then a priest on the Social
Action Department's staff, Higgins took part in the Memphis civil
rights march that followed King's funeral by a day. He wrote of the
mood of despair but added:

"Still and all, one is driven, almost in spite of himself, to
look for signs of meaning and of hope, no matter how faint, wherever
he can find them in the midst of the gloom that has enshrouded this
country since the tragic murder of Dr. King. For my own part, I
think I discerned at least one such sign during our brief visit to Memphis, namely the beginnings at least of a new coalition between the
civil rights movement and some of the more enlightened segments
of the American labor movement."

Noting that it was a labor relations crisis, involving the city's
sanitation workers, that had brought King to Memphis, Higgins

added: "He did so, at the cost of his life, because he was convinced that the time had come for the civil rights movement to turn its attention to the economic root causes of racial justice. Memphis was to have been the first step in his so-called Poor People's Campaign, a preliminary local skirmish, if you will, before he moved on to Washington to launch his highly publicized campaign at the national level. It wasn't too surprising, of course, that Dr. King should have agreed to throw the full weight of his enormous influence and prestige behind the striking sanitation workers of Memphis. These were his people, desperately poor Negroes fighting against almost impossible odds for elementary economic justice. They needed him and, characteristically, he heeded their anguished plea for help even though he must have known that, in coming back to Memphis for a second demonstration, he was putting his own life in jeopardy. His courage and sense of dedication will be forever held in highest honor."

From time to time, Higgins wrote of other coalitions which he felt would work to black advantage. In 1970, for example, at a time when the nation was rediscovering its ethnic roots, he wrote enthusiastically of the work undertaken by Msgr. Geno Baroni of the U.S. Catholic Conference Task Force in developing Black-ethnic coalitions. In his Yardstick column for December 14, 1970, he said, "Few American Catholics have done as much as he has to combat the evil of white racism in this country. Those Blacks and anonymous White liberals who are now saying that, because of his current preoccupation with the ethnic problem, Msgr. Baroni is copping out on the race issue are doing him a great injustice and are seriously misleading their own readers and their own followers. The fact is that Baroni is working night and day to put together viable coalitions of Blacks and ethnic Whites at the local level with a view to making it possible for the two groups to cooperate in solving their common social and economic problems and thereby bridge the potentially dangerous gap which now divides them in so many communities."

The task will be difficult, Higgins noted in a followup column the next week. But he said that Baroni's experience had convinced him it would never happen "until the ethnics themselves become more conscious of their own identity and more convinced of their own ability to reform the system and get off the treadmill on which they are now marking time."

Liberal charges that ethnics were bigoted on the racial issue continued to nettle Higgins over the years, especially since he saw cooperation between the two groups as an obvious mutual benefit. On August 30, 1976, he hailed Father Andrew Greeley's study, *Ethnicity in the United States* (John Wiley & Sons), which concluded that opinion makers continue to circulate charges of racism against ethnics because they misinterpret the superficial information available to them. "My reason for citing Greeley's data," Higgins said, "is that influential writers in the intellectual community, who ought to know better, still say, without evidence or proof, that ethnics as a group are racially bigoted, presumably more than other 'enlightened' segments of our population."

Given his intense interest in migrant labor, it was natural that Higgins would also point to the common interest of Black and Hispanic minorities, although in a June 8, 1970 column he wondered why the Hispanics hadn't seized the day to press their complaints as effectively as had American Blacks. Citing the recently-published work of an expert in the field (Fred H. Schmidt of UCLA), he noted that it was not because Hispanics were not victims of discrimination: "Professor Schmidt doesn't maintain, nor do I, that Spanish-speaking or Spanish-surnamed citizens of the United States, because of the colonial attitudes still prevailing in the Southwest, are worse off than their Black fellow citizens. His statistical evidence. . .does seem to suggest, however, that the plight of the Spanish-surnamed minority in the United States is, in every major respect, just about as bad as that of the Black minority." Schmidt's study, Higgins concluded, "would seem to suggest that the Spanish-speaking people of the Southwest, who, for too many generations, have been our nation's Invisible Minority, are about to move out in front and, at long last, begin to receive the kind and degree of national attention they so richly deserve."

On November 27, 1978 Higgins was unusually enthusiastic about a meeting of Black and Hispanic leaders at which they had agreed to work together rather than compete for pieces of the nation's economic and political pie. "Hallelujah!" Higgins exclaimed. "That's the best news I've heard on the social action front in many a moon." He had feared, he said, that reactionary forces were playing off the two groups against one another, and that they might be headed toward a showdown on the illegal alien problem and on the allocation of high-level federal posts. At the meeting, representatives of leading Black and Hispanic organizations agreed to promote a better understanding of each other's problems, to identify and work for national policy objectives, to encourage registration and voting, and to form a permanent joint committee.

"It was long overdue," Higgins concluded. "The nation's two largest minority groups have everything to lose by fighting each other and everything to gain by working together in a joint committee to advance their common needs and interests."

Yet another alliance on which Higgins focused his interest was that of Black and Jews. As one with a natural friendship with both groups, he worried when ties between the two seemed to be fraying. That happened on two occasions in 1979, first when a Black New York priest, Father Lawrence Lucas, criticized guidelines for Catholic-Jewish relations developed by the Brooklyn Diocese. As background to his distress over the incident, Higgins pointed to the significance of the Black-Jewish coalition:

"Of all the predominantly White religious groups in the United States, the Jewish community has arguably the best record over the years in combating racism. Jewish organizations such as the Anti-Defamation League and the American Jewish Committee were in the forefront of the civil rights struggle long before it became popular in the 1960s. And, proportionately, a higher percentage of Jews were actively involved on all levels of the struggle. The reasons for this are obvious. As victims of racial and religious oppression for centuries, American Jews uniquely are able to understand and empathize with fellow sufferers. As heirs of the biblical prophets whose religion has always oriented them to the living out of God's covenant commands, Jews and Blacks, in many areas, were together excluded from the economic and social mainstream in this country."

For those reasons, Higgins said, manifestations of Black anti-Semitism such as the Lucas article were especially regrettable. He criticized specific points in the piece and chastised Lucas for concluding that "either the Blacks will get their rights or the Jews will." Higgins himself concluded: "Black leaders should. . .be engaged in building coalitions to realize the dreams that all Americans share. Scapegoating the Jewish community as a conveniently vulnerable target on which to vent one's frustration does not even begin to get at the heart of real problems like unemployment and job discrimination. I think the Black leadership in this country should condemn this type of thing for the self-defeating nonsense that it is. And since this particular expression of anti-Semitic propaganda came from a Catholic source, I think the Black Catholic leadership has a special obligation to disown it.''

Later that year Andrew Young's resignation as U.S. Ambassador to the United Nations triggered a number of events that once again threatened the Black-Jewish alliance, notably Young's own stern criticism of the Israeli government, and meetings between the Southern Christian Leadership Conference (SCLC) and the Palestine Liberation Organization. The then-current gasoline shortage was an additional factor; some Blacks concluded that their self-interest should be steering them in a pro-Arab direction. As it was expressed by Walter Fauntroy, the District of Columbia delegate in Congress, ''As the gas lines and unemployment lines lengthen. . .it is us (Blacks) who will be the first fired, the last hired and the most harsh hit economically.''

Higgins was deeply troubled by the events of the day.

''To cut the Black community away from its longest and strongest ally in the struggle for equality at a time of crisis is, in the long range view, self-defeating,'' he wrote on August 27. ''Before going down the road of legitimizing the use of terrorism as a political tactic, the heirs of Martin Luther King, Jr.'s doctrine of nonviolence might well want to reflect on who, ultimately, will be the beneficiaries of a split in the Black-Jewish coalition. It is a common historical practice for two minority groups to be pitted against each other so that those who hold power can siphon off unrest. If Blacks and Jews get together to compare notes, some interesting results might be forthcoming.

''In the meantime, it is important for the two communities to learn more about each other. Few non-Jews in this country fully understand the depth of Jewish spiritual dependence on the survival of Israel. Jews, equally, need to understand how this support of Israel is perceived in the non-Jewish community. If Blacks feel that Jews have placed their traditional commitment to civil rights in a subordinate relationship to internal 'Jewish' issues, tension and distrust will be inevitable. Jews need to communicate to Blacks their support, not only for civil rights but for the Third World causes, especially in Africa, with which Blacks identify.

''The Black and Jewish agendas in this country are interdependent. No minority can make it alone. Minorities cannot allow their self-interest to be played off against each other. That way, everybody loses.''

Higgins dealt thoughtfully and perceptively over the years with the problems connected with the fight for racial justice as they affected the rest of society, practical matters such as busing and preferential job treatment, and further-ranging concerns as well: a fragmented society that seemed to see its component parts drifting more and more apart—Black and White, rich and poor, city and suburb.

Higgins himself was decidely cool toward the use of court-enforced busing to integrate public schools, a point he made clear in a Yardstick column on April 19, 1976. Writing in the wake of violent antibusing demonstrations in Boston, he said: ''There is obviously room for honest disagreement among men and women of good will over the issue of court-enforced busing. I, for one, tend to agree with those who say that it is not the best way to go about integrating the public school system in the major cities of the United States. The fact that a good number of Black leaders are themselves dubious about the effectiveness of busing and that others have publicly opposed it must also be taken into account. . . . Whatever of that, however, dissident whites cannot be permitted to take the law into their own hands. . . .''

But he warned that opposition to busing must be carefully expressed: ''Many spokesmen for (the ethnic movement) have taken a strong stand against busing for reasons which I find rather convincing. I have the uneasy feeling, however, that in putting forth their reasoned arguments against busing, they may unwittingly be providing aid and comfort to some of their more rabid followers. . . .''

His antibusing disposition aside, however, Higgins vigorously opposed plans to restrict busing by limiting court jurisdiction. He hit out at the Ford administration's antibusing program on July 5, 1976, after joining 15 other civil rights leaders (on behalf of the Leadership Conference on Civil Rights) in a meeting with the president to discuss the measure. *''The Washington Post,''* he said, ''.it the nail on the head when it said in an editorial on busing that the administration's plan to hamstring the courts is both 'misguided and mischievous.' It gives aid and comfort to those who are opposed to busing for the wrong reasons and encourages resistance—even violent resistance—to future court orders.''

His words were even stronger three years later (July 30, 1979) when he attacked the Mottl antibusing amendment then before Congress. "It represents the most serious attempt made thus far by a congressman or senator to nullify the Supreme Court's 1954 landmark civil rights decision in Brown v. Board of Education," he said. Passage of the amendment, he claimed, would effectively nullify the 14th Amendment, and it was for that reason that many organizations interested in civil rights, including the U.S. Catholic Conference, were vigorously opposed to it. And many people not in favor of busing nevertheless opposed the amendment, he said, on constitutional grounds. He glumly concluded: "It represents the worst possible way of dealing with the busing controversy, regardless of one's views on that volatile issue."

Higgins wrestled with the delicate problem of preferential minority hiring and layoff exemptions in a column on March 3, 1975. He politely took issue with columnist Carl Rowan, who argued against seniority as a determining factor in layoff priorities in favor of "sexual, racial and ethnic justice." He quoted Rowan: "That is the only way to break a circle that is not only vicious but destructive of everything the nation stands for."

All well and good, Higgins responded, but what if the employee with seniority happens also to be Black, or female (as many are, for example, in the United Auto Workers)? "Does Mr. Rowan believe that 'sexual, racial and ethnic justice' should take precedence over the seniority of these veteran members of the UAW, or would he put them in a separate category and bump only those senior UAW members who happen to be white, male Caucasians?"

Rowan, Higgins concluded, had oversimplified the seniority issue. "He is correct in saying that union seniority provisions create a real problem when they conflict with the rights of minority workers who have been grossly discriminated against for generations both in terms of hiring and firing. But it is easier to raise this problem— and easier to wax rhetorical about it—than it is to solve it. To abolish the seniority system, far from solving the problem, would only make matters worse and over the long haul would be a great disservice to minority workers themselves."

Higgins considered the city-suburban gap in a two-part column series on March 17-24, 1969. He weighed the arguments of those who lamented the disengagement of much of the church community from the inner city against other observers (including, again, Greeley) who defend suburban Christianity. Greeley, for one, is extremely critical, Higgins said, "of what he calls the 'inner city mentality,' which he says attaches some special virtue to being poor or being Black and tends to equate the priestly or religious apostolate with an assignment to the inner city."

But conceding some element of the "antipathy" toward the city and city dwellers that critics of suburbia say exists there, Higgins said, "the problem we face. . .is to prevent the development of a house divided, a metropolitan community split by invisible political boundaries into the city dwellers and the suburbanites, the haves and the have-nots, the Whites and the non-Whites—into 'us' and 'them'. . . . We have to break a vicious circle. Riots in the inner cities intensify the suburban fear of the ghetto dweller and make a racially integrated housing program much harder to secure. Yet the more we build walls around the inner city, the more we pen up explosive forces that will erupt in violence. . . . Violence is often a form of blind protest, a desperate attempt to call attention to an intolerable situation. In the short run we must use every measure to keep or restore law and order. But the time is past for stop-gap palliatives rushed out each spring in the effort to head off the disorders of the so-called long, hot summer. Now is the time to rebuild America physically, economically, morally and spiritually. This challenge must be met, whatever the cost."

The same divisions were the subject of a Yardstick column later that year, on June 23, when Higgins commented on a piece about the white working class written by Pete Hamill for *New York* magazine. Higgins concludes: "The point is. . .that it is power and position, not prejudice that lie at the true heart of the division between Blacks and Whites (and very often, between various groups of Whites as well). This being the case, piecemeal remedies aimed exclusively at raising the standards of disadvantaged Blacks will not resolve our national crisis. We will have to look for much more radical remedies designed to expand and redistribute the national economic pie so that all of our citizens, regardless of color, can share more equitably in the wealth of the nation."

The 1968 Kerner Report, the Report of the National Advisory Commission on Civil Disorders, had attempted to analyze some of these same questions. Looking back on it two years later on March 23, 1970, Higgins said that for all the attention that accompanied its release, the Kerner Report "never really caught on."

In fact, he added, it could be argued that it was counter-productive; that instead of winning over the public to the cause of interracial justice, it turned off many people and made it easier for them to rationalize their indifference to Blacks. A major reason, Higgins suggested, was the report's most widely-publicized conclusion that "White racism is essentially responsible for the explosive mixture which has been accumulating in our cities since the end of World War II." The statement might be substantially correct, Higgins said, but many people never got beyond that one widely resented sentence. As a result, many felt they were unfairly accused of a sin they were not conscious of having committed.

Higgins praised a follow-up document to the Kerner Report, Anthony Downs's *Racism in America and How to Combat It,* issued by the U.S. Civil Rights Commission. He singled out one of Downs's recommendations for dealing with racism, one that would provide benefits to Whites as well as for non-White minority groups in federal aid programs, so that it would be in the Whites' self-interest to support them.

"What Mr. Downs is telling us," said Higgins, "is that we cannot expect to eliminate the evil effects of White racism at bargain rates, or, to change the metaphor, that we cannot hope to have our cake and eat it too. That's admittedly a hard saying, but unless the more affluent citizens of the United States can learn to swallow it gracefully, there is no hope of our being able to solve the urban-racial crisis which, on all the available evidence, threatens to destroy our society."

Over the years, Higgins repeatedly returned to two key points in connection with problems of racial injustice: the need for unions to avoid any taints of racism, and the need for the Church to continue teaching and preaching on the issue.

Labor's record, he said in a conversation in 1982, remains spotty; on a national level unions have performed well but many problems continue to exist locally. Nor is that likely to change significantly, he added; local unions are not always that easy for a national organization to control. Still, Blacks have benefitted enormously from union membership. Not only are Black workers who are union members higher paid than their non-union fellow Blacks;

within union ranks there is less of a wage gap between Whites and Blacks as there is on the outside.

In the same conversation, Higgins was asked if the Church had met the challenge of the Sixties on the race issue.

"No," he replied, "but neither did anyone else in the White community. However, I think it did an outstanding job on civil rights legislation. On that point I'd agree with Hubert Humphrey, who said in his autobiography that without the leadership of the churches, the civil rights legislation of that decade would never have been passed."

Higgins has pointed to the necessity of continued Church teaching on racism on many occasions, as he did in a November 12, 1979 column praising two bishops for issuing pastoral letters on the subject, and noting that some observers had asked if they were really necessary.

"Some real progress has been made over the last several decades in the area of civil rights," he wrote. "Laws have been changed. Schools, lunch counters, and buses have been integrated in many parts of our society. Increasing numbers of Blacks and Browns have gained access to professional careers and better paying jobs. On the whole, despite the recent resurgence of the Ku Klux Klan, racism does not surface in the blatant way it did in earlier decades.

"But as a society we have little cause for relief or self-congratulation in terms of social progress for racial minorities. A closer look may reveal that while racism has been channeled to less obvious, more subtle avenues, its grip retains a strong hold on many Americans. While the gains achieved by some Blacks and Browns have been widely acclaimed and celebrated, the continued sufferings of the many have been widely ignored and forgotten."

Higgins cited the main problem areas: low-level jobs, unemployment, income, educational opportunities, housing. He continued: ". . .Statistics do not constitute a definite analysis of our progress or lack thereof in achieving racial equality. They do, however, give cause for serious reflection and for a healthy sense of skepticism in the face of those who say we have done too much for Black and Brown America. Racism, in new forms, is still with us. Indeed, in an atmosphere of narrowing economic horizons for our entire society, the threat exists that racial minorities will be forced to an even greater extent to bear the brunt of the economic squeeze.

Seen in this light, the recent bishops' statements on racism are a welcome sign of concern. I hope they signal a broader effort by the Church and its leaders to renew and strengthen the movement for racial justice."

Speaking informally in 1982, Higgins thought his own approach to the racial question had undergone little significant change. He might temper his strong reaction to the Black militancy of the Sixties, he said, but time had proved to his satisfaction that the Black power approach had reached a dead end. "The Black power advocates simply burned themselves out," he said. "It showed that people have to stay for the long haul."

What about the civil rights movement itself, he was asked. In view of all the continuing racial ills, had it failed to do the job that was needed?

"I agree with Bayard Rustin, who comes from an old socialist tradition," Higgins said. "First, that we have to keep united; second, that the race problem isn't going to be solved until there's a full employment. That's where our efforts should be. The problem can't be addressed in Black-White terms, but only with a strong coalition. The movement hasn't failed; the economy has failed.

"It's been said before, but it bears repeating: the movement only did part of the job. It gave everyone the right to order a meal where they wanted to eat; the trouble was that it couldn't give them the money to pay for it. There's still a lot of work to be done."

CHAPTER NINE

THE ISSUES AT HOME

OVER THE YEARS, GEORGE HIGGINS HAS WRITTEN ABOUT a complex variety of domestic issues, ranging from the Welfare State to welfare rights, from Moral Rearmament to the Moral Majority. For each issue on which he staked out a position, he drew on a background that combined a clear understanding of the Church's social doctrine and a sure knowledge of economic forces, fusing them into a broad vision of an ideal society in which labor, management, and the state would join forces to serve the common good of the people.

If the vision was idealized rather than simply ideal, Higgins has never been deterred from pursuing it. His guides were the great social encyclicals and the landmark 1919 bishops' program, as noted in an earlier chapter, and the teaching of mentors such as Msgr. Ryan and Father McGowan.

Much of the vision found its expression in the program known as the Industry Council Plan, a topic on which Higgins wrote no fewer than 30 separate Yardstick columns during the Fifties. He became one of the best-known advocates of the plan, which had its roots in Pope Pius XI's 1931 encyclical, *Quadragesimo Anno.*

The program, he explained in a column on April 24, 1950, "is based upon the principle that an organized economic society is as natural and as necessary as an organized political society." Quoting Pius, he said this would be one in which "men have their place, not according to the position each has in the labor market but according to the respective social functions which each performs."

This meant, Higgins continued, that all the people engaged in a given industry or profession, workers and employers alike, are intended by nature to cooperate with one another for the good of their own industry and for the entire economy. Nature intends them to organize for this purpose, forming self-governing associations which would regulate economic life according to the requirements of social justice. Each industry forms a separate organization (an "industry council"); the various industry councils then work cooperatively with each other and with the government to advance the common good.

"It is very important to emphasize," he added, "that this. . . is not a distinctively Catholic program, but rather one which is based upon the natural law—upon the nature of man and the nature of society—and therefore one which ought to recommend itself to all right-thinking Americans."

In another early column (January 24, 1949) he championed the Industry Council Plan (ICP) as "the only realistic alternative" to the excesses of economic life condemned by the American bishops: perpetual economic conflict on one hand, excessive governmental intervention on the other.

Communists, he said, "get jittery" when the Industry Council Plan is favorably mentioned. "The philosophy of the Industry Council program is the Christian philosophy of organized cooperation for the general economic welfare, the very opposite of the communist philosophy of the inevitability of the class struggle. Is it any wonder, then, that *The Daily Worker* doesn't look with favor upon such a program or upon its distinguished sponsors? Not at all."

Less understandable, Higgins said, was the reluctance of

American industry to get behind the Industry Council Plan. By not doing so, he said, they were playing into the communists' hands.

Higgins was impatient with critics who saw tinges of fascism in the ICP, or those who blindly identified it as a Catholic program. He was somewhat more receptive to those who complained that the ICP was too vague and too theoretical to be put into practice, conceding (in a Yardstick column on June 8, 1953) that "gradualism. . . is the only practical approach to the establishment of the ICP in the United States." In the same column, however, he pointed to one successfully operating organization that he characterized as "the most significant example of an industry council in any part of the American economy": the Millinery Stabilization Commission. The commission, formed in 1936, included three members, none of whom was part of the millinery industry or one of its unions. Working with a Joint Advisory Board from the industry and a staff of 14, it sought to maintain equitable standards of labor and fair commercial practices in the millinery industry, "with a view to promoting the common welfare of the industry and the public good."

"To the best of our knowledge," Higgins concluded, "the agreement (which created the commission) is the most perfect example in the United States of a realistic attempt to put the principles of the Industry Council Plan into practice. It would be difficult to exaggerate its importance as a working model for unions and employers' associations in other industries. Theorists and practitioners alike will find it worthy of their careful study and sympathetic consideration as a practical application of a theory which is too often discussed in a vacuum."

The strong right arm of the ICP was the Association of Catholic Trade Unionists (ACTU), an organization with which Higgins forged exceptionally close ties. In a column (January 31, 1949) defending ACTU against an attack—conservatives of the day, and especially non-Catholic conservatives, often professed to see in ACTU a Catholic plot to take over the American labor movement—Higgins defined the organization as a friend of labor, "and a very loyal friend at that."

Later that year (November 28, December 5) he reprinted in The Yardstick excerpts from a talk he delivered to the Detroit ACTU chapter, in which he described the organization in more detail: "ACTU is neither a political pressure group within the trade union movement nor a negatively anticommunist organization. ACTU is an organization of practicing Catholics who are proud to belong to bonafide American unions and who wish to do a better job of permeating economic and industrial life with the principles of Christ. They are Catholic laymen who believe that in Christ alone is the salvation not only of the individual but of society as well. They have banded together in an organization to help one another to act upon their belief as intelligently and as effectively as possible.''

Its most important accomplishment in its few years of existence had been to popularize the philosophy of the Industry Council Plan, Higgins said—which, he continued, rather than individualism or socialism, ''can save the soul of the American economic system and lead us gradually, with the help of God, into a new era of social justice.''

ACTU had made other valuable contributions, Higgins continued, especially in advancing Church teaching on the necessity of trade unionism, and in its vocal support for racial equality in the union movement. But the work of establishing the Industry Council Plan was clearly its first priority, and Higgins had some characteristically pointed hints on how to deal with critics:

''If a misguided industrialist, Catholic or non-Catholic, tells you that the Industry Council Plan is socialistic, tell him politely that you are proud to be in the company of such distinguished 'socialists' as Pope Pius XI. If a socialist tells you that you are reactionary, don't take it too seriously; for, again, you are in perfectly good company, in the company of men like Philip Murray and other labor leaders who have given their lives to the cause of labor and of social justice. And if a communist accuses you of being a fascist, say a little prayer for him.''

However, the ICP as Higgins envisaged it would fade into the background before many years had passed. True, in 1954, (The Yardstick, August 9) he would write—on the basis of new publications in the fields of labor economics, political science, industrial sociology and social ethics—that ''the Industry Council Plan is here to stay.'' But only three years later, on June 17, 1957, he was forced to agree with an unidentified office visitor, he wrote, who concluded that Catholic theorists and social actionists were no longer enthused about the ICP. ''It was his impression, he said, that during the past four or five years very little has been written about the subject by Catholic academicians and that one hardly ever hears it mentioned any more at public meetings or forums under Catholic auspices,''

Higgins wrote. "The record will show, I think, that our visitor's analysis of the situation is substantially accurate. . . . His theory is. . .that it's hard for people to get excited about the long-range reconstruction of economic life when things are going reasonably well for the majority of the population. He probably has something there."

That did not mean, to Higgins's way of thinking, that the ICP should still not be pursued. As the seventieth anniversary of *Rerum Novarum* and the 30th anniversary of *Quadragesimo Anno* approached in 1961, he wrote (May 1) of their common bond and of the need for a reorganized society with the ICP as one of its key elements. Legislation and organization ("of farmers, employers and professional people") would be esssential, he wrote, implementing the central principle of the two encyclicals: "that ownership and work are both individual and social in character and therefore must be made to serve the interests not only of individuals but of society as well." He continued: "What is needed, if we are to avoid the dictatorship of wealth on the one hand or the dictatorship of government on the other, is an overall reconstruction of the social order along the lines of the so-called Industry Council system."

Under that name, however, it continued to drop from public view, and from public discussion. The Yardstick itself served to illustrate the point; from 30 columns during the Fifties in which the ICP was the central topic, the total dropped to one, cited in the paragraph above, in the following decade. There were none past that point. Higgins addressed the loss of interest in the ICP in an article prepared for *Chicago Studies* ("Issues of Justice and Peace") in 1981, attributing it at least in part to the more flexible approach endorsed, to achieve the same goals, by Pope John XXIII in *Mater et Magistra.*

"It would appear to be partially correct," Higgins wrote, "to say that Pope John XXIII was less interested than was Pius XI in the so-called Industry Council Plan. Pope John's approach to the problem of social reconstruction and his terminology were less theoretical—more flexible, if you will—than that of Pope Pius XI. But it would be a serious mistake to conclude that Pope John was any less interested than was Pius XI in the basic principles of social reconstruction underlying the so-called Industry Council Plan. The basic principles of social reconstruction outlined in *Mater et Magistra* are the same as those which are to be found in Pius XI's encyclical *Quadragesimo Anno. . . .*"

One way of moving in the direction of the ICP, he added, would be to develop a system of co-management or co-determination. While organized labor had shown little interest in that approach, he said, the economic crisis of the Eighties brought a limited form of co-determination to the auto industry when the United Auto Workers agreed to make drastic wage concessions in negotiating its contract with the Chrysler Corporation, in return for a seat on Chrysler's board of directors and a compensatory share in any future Chrysler profits.

"It's too early to tell," Higgins wrote, "whether or not other U.S. unions will follow the UAW's lead in demanding profit-sharing and co-management as a quid pro quo when asked to make similar concessions. My guess is that they will, if it means keeping their employers in business.

"Despite the unions' traditional lack of interest in profit-sharing and co-determination, hard-headed pragmatism will compel them to try this approach. Union members will not and should not be expected to approve drastic concessions to corporations which are unwilling, in return, to make equitable concessions of their own."

Virtually every Yardstick column of the early Fifties was related to labor or economics, and in that vein Higgins dealt with topics such as the Taft-Hartley Act, the welfare state ("for better or for worse, the United States, like almost every other industrial country in the world, is committed to a far-reaching program of welfare legislation, a program which is sometimes confused with socialism, but which, as a matter of fact, is supported by many enlightened employers as a necessary bulwark of the system of private enterprise"—March 19, 1951), anti-trust legislation and the capitalistic system itself. Excesses of the latter, he warned repeatedly, were no less dangerous to the health of the American economy than the evils of communism.

He did not write excessively about Senator Joseph McCarthy or what came to be known as McCarthyism, one of the sensations of the period, but dealt in a number of ways with anticommunism in general, as often as not relating the subject to the labor movement. On November 12, 1951, for example, he conceded that charges that some American labor unions needed to purge themselves of communists, charges heard since the end of World War II, had some validity. He hailed the CIO for expelling a number of communist-dominated affiliates, particularly the United Electrical Workers (UE), but lambasted employers who continued to "play footsy" (his phrase) with that organization, thereby hindering the work of the strongly anticommunist International Union of Electricians-CIO. "This is hypocrisy at its worst," Higgins fumed. "Undoubtedly it would be castigated as such by almost every newspaper editor and radio commentator in the United States if the offending party were a union instead of a promiment corporation."

In a 1982 conversation Higgins explained that he had not written or spoken about McCarthyism to a great degree because the subject fell more into the lap of his associate, Father John Cronin, whose primary responsibilities within the NCWC included dealing with the communist problem. The conference did not take a specific position on McCarthyism, Higgins said, but he recalls a general impression that even among those who would have supported the ends that Senator McCarthy had in mind, he was seen as a "buccaneer" or a "bumbler."

Higgins's only direct treatment of the McCarthy phenomenon appeared early in the Wisconsin senator's years of national prominence. On June 5, 1950, while the country was transfixed by McCarthy's charges of communist infiltration in the government, Higgins reminded his readers that on the communist issue, "there is a world of difference between intelligent caution and vigilance on one hand and a 'fixation' on the other."

If Higgins's discussion of McCarthyism would turn out to be infrequent, there was no mistaking his position. "The time has come," he said, "to expose the insulting myth, which is being circulated even by some Catholics, perhaps for political reasons, that American Catholics as a group are behind the McCarthy investigation and that, because they are Catholics, they are necessarily committed to Louis Budenz." (Budenz, a former managing editor of the communist newspaper, *The Daily Worker,* had renounced communism in 1945 and returned to the Catholic Church. He supported McCarthy's charges that Owen Lattimore, a Far East adviser during the 1940s, was a communist, although in 1947 he had told a State Department security officer that he was unable to link Lattimore to the party.) Catholics, Higgins continued, are free to make up their own minds about the McCarthy charges, about the Senate investigation convened to examine them, and about the propriety of Budenz's testifying and his credibility as a witness. But again, his personal position was clearly stated: "Many Catholics, including the present writer, have concluded that the investigation has degenerated into a fiasco, which in the long run will do the country much more harm than good; they have concluded, too, that it represents the worst possible way of accomplishing its announced objective, namely, safeguarding national security. Other Catholics, to be sure, have concluded differently and are therefore siding with McCarthy in the current controversy. So be it. But let it not be said any longer, either by friends or enemies of the Church, that Catholics are unitedly and, as it were, necessarily behind McCarthy. They are not."

As for Budenz, Higgins said he wished that since the witness was invariably identified as a Catholic "he might make it clear to the American people that the anticommunism of the Catholic Church goes hand in hand with a radical program of social justice which is not being honored too faithfully, either in principle or practice, by some of the 'patriots' who applaud him most enthusiastically as an all-star witness against communism. We may be altogether wrong, but we sometimes have the feeling that Bundenz is being 'used.' "

In a 1952 column (June 9), Higgins dealt somewhat more sympathetically with another noted ex-communist turned witness, Whittaker Chambers, agreeing with some literary critics who had called Chambers's autobiography a minor classic. However, Higgins said, his literary competence did not make him an authority on the New Deal (which Chambers called "a great socialist revolution") or the great tradition of social teaching of the churches.

The collapse of McCarthyism following 1954 hearings in the Senate and a formal vote of censure by that body did not signal an end to the virulent brand of anticommunism that had accompanied it. On April 3, 1961, Higgins lamented the continuing efforts of extremists who fought the communist menace by fair means or foul. Some, he said, were characterizing President Eisenhower, then only weeks out of office, and John Foster Dulles, the late Secretary of State, as communists. "The fact that these distinguished public servants and many other honorable Americans are being subjected to this kind of character assassination is enough to make a decent man sick to his stomach," Higgins said.

In the same column Higgins took issue with the Cardinal Mindszenty Foundation of St. Louis, which had described as a "pernicious liberal" anyone "who enthusiastically endorses all welfare legislation though it threatens to stifle individual incentive and paves the way to statism and socialism.''

Said Higgins: ''I take this to mean, in context, that all welfare legislation is being condemned as a deliberate effort to advance the cause of communism in the United States. Does this make any sense at all from the point of view of Catholic social teaching? I think not. And the fact that it emanates from an organization which, on its own authority and for its own purposes, has appropriated the venerable name of Cardinal Mindszenty makes it all the more regrettable. The good cardinal deserves better than this. . . .''

Earlier chapters traced Higgins's involvement in three major areas of concern during the Sixties: in Rome, the Second Vatican Council, and at home, the progress of civil rights, and the growth of the farm labor movement. A number of other domestic issues occupied him as well. Although some were broad in scope—the National Association of Manufacturers, for example, continued to come under Higgins's critical eye—most were family or work-oriented. They included the question of birth control; the women's movement, then in its early stages; a minimum wage and the guaranteed annual wage; and the overall topic of poverty, to which he devoted five separate columns in 1964 and 1965.

Higgins and many other people in the nation were focusing on poverty, of course, because President Johnson, sworn into office November 22, 1963, was determined to make war on poverty a priority concern of his administration. He said so directly in his first State of the Union address in January 1964, a fact that Higgins applauded in a column dated February 3. In the same article he commented favorably on a Georgetown University seminar on poverty in the midst of plenty, a seminar that pointed out the moral nature of the poverty problem, and warned that only an intensively activist approach would even begin to solve it. One facet of the problem, he said, was the ever-widening gap between the rock-bottom poor and the rest of American society:

''Take the case of average suburbanite, for example. He and his family are not well-to-do by any means. On the contrary, they have to watch their budget to make ends meet. But they are not poor and, because they live in suburbia, they seldom, if ever, personally come into contact with poverty in the raw. They know, of course, that there are tens of thousands of poor people in the inner city, many of them disadvantaged Negroes, but, for all practical purposes, these poor people might just as well be living in India or Guatemala for all that most of us know about them from firsthand experience.''

Although he was exaggerating, Higgins continued, those Americans who are not poor need to surmount the geographical and psychological barriers that separate them from those who are. "Unless and until this is done," he said, "the problem of poverty. . . will be a fashionable conversation piece at university seminars and even at sophisticated cocktail parties, but very little will be done about it, in spite of the best efforts of the administration to keep the issue alive.''

A few weeks later, on March 16, he returned to the subject, expanding on a statement on poverty issued by the NCWC's Social Action Department, the department he then headed. While the department was indeed concerned with remedial services of the type proposed by the administration's war on poverty, the forces for which were then just being mobilized, there were deeper, more underlying concerns that needed to be addressed. Chief among them was work itself. "Avoiding job discrimination is but one step," he wrote, quoting from the department's statement. "It is equally vital to be sure that work is available and that the poor are educated and trained to do useful work.''

He went on to comment:

"This, it seems to me, is our number one economic problem at the present time, and unless and until it is faced up to realistically, I can see no real hope of solving the problem of poverty, no matter what we do for the poor in terms of remedial services and no matter how hard we try to retrain the unemployed or to help them, in other ways, to help themselves. . . . In developing our anti-poverty program, we ought to put major emphasis on basic economic reforms, not to the neglect or the exclusion of social reform and additional remedial services for the poor, but as the necessary prerequisites for their long-range effectiveness.

"To be more explicit, and to bring this discussion down to earth, I think that while the administration has made a remarkably good start in its current campaign against poverty, it is still fighting a series of more or less uncoordinated skirmishes and has yet to declare all-out war against the real enemy, whose name is unemployment.''

Higgins returned to the general topic of poverty several more times in the Sixties, once (May 9, 1966) to defend R. Sargent Shriver—the director of the Office of Economic Opportunity (OEO), which administered the government's antipoverty program—from a pair of widely disparate attacks. He regretted the verbal abuse Shriver had taken while attempting to address a convention of the Citizens' Crusade Against Poverty, during the course of which a group took over the microphones, shouting Shriver down and accusing him and the OEO of "pussyfooting." The near-assault on Shriver was alarming, Higgins said, but might be beneficial "if it helps us to understand a little more clearly the nature and the extent of the crisis we are facing in the country."

He was far less patient with another Shriver critic, Saul Alinsky, the community organizer, whose comments about OEO Higgins termed "savagely critical and ridiculously intemperate." In talks and magazine pieces, Alinsky had steadily referred to the OEO as a political pork barrel and boondoggle. "The poverty program," he wrote in an article in *Harpers,* "is a prize piece of political pork barrel, and a feeding trough for the welfare industry surrounded by sanctimonious, hypocritical, phony, moralistic crap."

"This is a cheap form of demagoguery," Higgins shot back, "and I suspect that Alinsky knows it is. Saul is a great organizer and a great actor, but I think the time has come for his friends, and I am one of them, to tell him point-blank that he is beginning to act like an old-time vaudeville ham who will say almost anything, no matter how embarrassingly silly, just to get a laugh from the galleries. Well, there is nothing funny at all about getting a laugh at the expense of Sargent Shriver and the OEO. . . . It is a form of sick humor, very sick indeed."

What was perhaps Higgins's most thoughtful and compelling column about poverty was written (June 24, 1968) on the eve of the Poor People's March on Washington, and in it he addressed the spiritual roots of the problem.

He recalled that as Moses and his followers were about to enter the Promised Land Moses said there would still be no lack of poor. In dealing with a brother who has fallen on lean days, Moses advised: "Do not steal thy heart and shut thy purse against him; be generous to his poverty." When Jesus came to earth to perfect and fulfill the law of the Old Covenant, Higgins said, he told his followers to deal with the least of his brethren as they would with him.

"Perhaps never before in the history of mankind has this teaching been so timely and of such crucial importance as it is today in the United States," Higgins said. "Poverty was in those days, and in many parts of the world still is, the perennial and almost irremediable lot of all but the favored few." That poverty exists in the United States in the midst of plenty is doubly regrettable, Higgins said. "There is less excuse today," he added, "for the continuation of widespread poverty and infinitely less excuse on our own part for steeling our hearts and shutting our purses against its unfortunate victims."

The first obligation of Americans, he said, was to realize the number of poor and their plight, a realization "very slow in coming" but speeded by demonstrations such as the Poor Peoples' March. The fact that the scope of the problem was becoming recognized and that remedial programs were under way was welcome, Higgins said, but a "purely impersonal" interest in the poor would be inadequate in dealing with their plight. "Much more is demanded of all of us," he said. "We are called upon to perform the corporal and spiritual works of mercy on a person-to-person basis and to do so with profound respect for the dignity and the sensibilities of those whom we are privileged to serve in the name of the Lord. We will most certainly fail to meet this challenge effectively if we think of the poor and the underprivileged only as so many digits in a cold statistical abstract and fail to see them in all their dignity as the favorite children of God. . . . This is our common responsibility and not merely an elective, so to speak, for the few. None of us, in other words, is free to look the other way or to stand on the sidelines as a passive spectator. We are all called upon to become personally involved in helping the poor to help themselves."

Birth control, while a subject of personal concern to many Catholics, was one which Higgins rarely discussed in The Yardstick. On the rare occasions when he did, it generally centered around a social program, or, as on July 9, 1956, when it came up in relationship to a union matter.

At the time he objected specifically to an endorsement of the Planned Parenthood League by a union official, who also recommended that the Planned Parenthood program be incorporated into the social service program of the American labor movement. Higgins objected first of all on the theoretical level: "His endorsement of birth control as a solution to the population problem is utterly reactionary from the point of view of economics, and potentially harmful to the cause of international peace. Moreover, it runs directly counter to the traditional economic program of the American labor movement. The American labor movement has consistently taken the optimistic position that a properly organized economic system can provide an adequate living for all of God's children, and has consistently talked in terms of an expanding economy geared to meet the needs of an expanding population."

Secondly, Higgins warned, the official's proposal would result in nothing less than a civil war within the labor movement, "which, if it lasted long enough, could tear the movement apart." He explained: "American workers don't want the labor movement meddling in their personal or family affairs, least of all if this meddling involves a violation of their religious beliefs. If worse came to worst, many of them would disaffiliate rather than permit even a portion of their union dues to be misappropriated as a subsidy for an organized program of birth control. Let us hope that a word to the wise will be sufficient to put an end to this controversy once and for all. If not, we are heading for a showdown which could conceivably do more harm to the American labor movement than any other battle in which it has ever been engaged."

Years later, in a series of three columns beginning September 13, 1965, Higgins took to task those who would have used federal funds to support family planning programs, or who would have made family planning an integral part of federal antipoverty programs. Debate on the question, he said, should not be thought of as merely a Catholic issue, even though Catholics were most vocal in their opposition. "The fact is," he said, "that many non-Catholics also have serious reservations about the direct intervention of the federal government in the field of family planning. This is so not because they are necessarily opposed, on moral grounds, to artificial birth control as such, but simply because they feel that family planning is a profoundly personal matter and one which lies outside the competence of the government."

He saw the consolidation of birth control into the antipoverty program as an insult to the poor and especially to Blacks.

"Let's face it," he argued. "Negroes constitute the biggest single group of poor people in the United States. By and large, they are wretchedly poor because we, the White people of this country, made them poor in the first place and have kept them poor for many generations. What are they to think if we now turn around and tell them from our comfortable middle-class ivory towers that the solution to their problem (which is really our problem) is to limit the size of their families or, in other words, that the solution to the so-called Negro problem (which is largely a White problem) is to cut down on the number of Negroes in the United States?''

Higgins concluded the series on a gloomy note, citing a Planned Parenthood report to back his contention that some people were interested not only in providing birth control information to the poor, but actively encouraging them to limit the size of their families. The report called on the American business community to help check population growth because such a program would lead to rising profits, safer investments, a break on spiraling taxes for support of welfare services, more prosperous markets abroad, a more prosperous and productive population at home, and greater individual and corporate freedom.

The determination of the report's authors to cut population for profit motives "speaks very poorly for their sense of values," Higgins said. From there he noted a rising interest in compulsory sterilization programs for the poor as a means of trimming welfare taxes. "How widespread is this crassly materialistic point of view?" he asked. "I really don't know, but I do know that a substantial number of states have already enacted sterilization laws applicable to certain categories of their citizens. The Chinese communists may have something when they say that Western culture is doomed.''

The subject of birth control rarely appeared in a Higgins column after that date. There were two passing references in 1968 to *Humanae Vitae*, Pope Paul's encyclical on human life published in July of that year. On September 9, arguing against intra-Church divisions along liberal–conservative, "good guy–bad guy" lines, he commented: "The current controversy over the encyclical on birth control will undoubtedly aggravate the situation, but even before the encyclical was published the lines had begun to harden." On November 25 he noted with interest the number of questions on birth control directed to the press panel at the conclusion of the annual U.S. bishops' meeting, following issuance of their pastoral letter on human life. "This was perfectly understandable, of course, from the reporters' point of view," he wrote. "Nevertheless I cannot help but regret that the second section of the bishops' pastoral. . . got lost in the shuffle, so to speak, with the result that the average newspaper reader. . . may never catch up with what the bishops had to say in their pastoral about selective conscientious objection, selective service, nuclear deterrence, foreign aid, and a number of related issues.''

A final reference to birth control appeared in The Yardstick for October 13, 1980, when Higgins lavishly praised Archbishop John R. Quinn of San Francisco for his "measured, forthright" address at the 1980 Synod of Bishops, in which the archbishop warned of a severe pastoral problem regarding Catholic teaching against artificial contraception. Quinn, emphasizing that he personally adheres to the Church's teaching, cited statistics showing that 80 percent of American Catholic women used contraceptives, and that only 29 percent of U.S. priests considered artificial birth control intrinsically wrong. For such reasons, he said, the Church should "create a new context" for its teaching on birth control, going beyond the three existing choices of "silence, repetition of past formulations, or dissent." He called for a new round of dialogue on the issue, including those who dissented but were nonetheless loyal to the Church.

The address, said Higgins, "was among the most significant statements made by any U.S. bishop either at Vatican Council II or at any synod since the Council. It was an example of pastoral initiative and leadership at its best."

He continued:

"In speaking to this issue with such deep pastoral concern and with such refreshing honesty and frankness, the archbishop was doing what bishops are supposed to do at a synod but are often inhibited from doing for fear, presumably, of appearing to be mavericks or, in some cases, for fear of appearing to be disloyal to the Holy See. Such fears, if given into by any significant number of bishops, would nullify the purpose of a synod and in fact make a mockery of the institution.

"It is true that the synod, at its present stage of development, is only a consultative or advisory body and is not authorized to make decisions binding on the Church. But it cannot fulfill its advisory role unless the bishops are prepared to speak their minds openly and to communicate their pastoral concerns and pastoral insights, without fear or favor, to the Church at large.

"Archbishop Quinn went to the current synod prepared, after extensive consultation in the United States, to do just that. He did it superbly well."

George Higgins's views on the role of women in the working force have changed remarkably little over the years.

As long ago as 1953, in a Yardstick column dated April 13, he was arguing for equal pay and equal opportunity for women in industry, but arguing at the same time against an attitude that would deliberately encourage young mothers to enter the labor market when there was no economic necessity involved.

The issue arose during discussion of a resolution on women in industry at a national convention of the United Auto Workers. As Higgins explained it: "There was no disagreement about the general purpose of the resolution: to guarantee a policy of equal opportunity for men and women workers in the auto industry, or, to put it negatively, to eliminate discrimination against women workers in wages, hiring, promotion, training opportunities, and seniority." There was serious opposition, he continued, to a section of the resolution which would have supported legislation to permit working married women to deduct expenses related to going to work, including nursery costs for preschoolers.

The rank-and-file delegates were concerned about that section, Higgins said. "They were perfectly willing to make adequate provision for the special needs of widows and other mothers of young children who are required by economic necessity to enter the labor market in order to support their dependents. On the other hand, they were very much opposed, and rightly so, to any resolution which would lead to the further disintegration of family life in the United States by deliberately encouraging married women with young children to enter the labor market when there is no economic necessity in their doing so."

A column on September 26, 1955 paid tribute to prominent Catholic women in the labor-social action field, especially Linna Bresette, who had retired a few years earlier as field secretary of the Catholic Conference on Industrial Problems. In that role, he said, she "did as much as any other single American of our generation to promote the social teaching of the Church."

Whatever his early support for equality of opportunity in the labor field, Higgins in 1961 was not quite ready for what had become 20 years later an acceptable if not widespread phenomenon, the working wife whose husband stays home to tend the house. On July 31 of that year, he took issue with a UAW economist, Lewis Carliner, whose predictions along those lines had been reported in *The Washington Post*.

"I think my friend Mr. Carliner was way off base when, in the course of prophesying that it will be Mama who pays while Papa keeps house, he went on to say at a recent meeting in Washington that this is the theory behind the drive for 'equal pay for equal (or comparable) work,' " Higgins wrote. "American trade unionists in general and the members of the UAW in particular vigorously support the drive for equal pay for equal work. But I simply refuse to believe that their understanding of the purpose of this drive is the same as Mr. Carliner's. . . . I am confident that they would not agree with him when he suggests that community thinking be conditioned to accept a voluntary switch in the traditional roles of husband and wife, so that disapproval would not fall on a father who preferred to keep the house. On the contrary, I think their attitude would be that there are too many mothers working at the present time—some out of necessity, some by personal choice—and that the sooner this trend can be reversed, the better it will be for everybody concerned. . . . Perhaps I am being too dogmatic. . . . It's posssible—God help us all—that the American labor movement wants to reverse the traditional pattern of family in the United States, but I doubt it."

Higgins turned to the question of women's rights with increasing frequency in the late Sixties and early Seventies, as what became known as the women's liberation movement and the campaign for the Equal Rights Amendment gained momentum.

With a touch of flippancy that one assumes might not have been totally appreciated, Higgins endorsed (April 22, 1968) charges of ecclesiastical antifeminism leveled by Mary Daly in her book, *The Church and the Second Sex*. He wrote: "We men are generally inclined to take this curious state of affairs for granted, or worse than that, to laugh about it as though it were a big joke. So women are not treated equally in the Church—so what? It was always thus, at every level of ecclesiastical administration, and always will be— or so we seem to think, if indeed we ever stop to think about the matter at all. All of which merely goes to show that we really aren't as smart as we think we are. Either that or we haven't been listening very carefully to what the distaff side has been trying to tell us for lo these many years. What they have been trying to tell us, politely and in modulated tones, is that the game is all over, fellows, Since we have refused to give them a decent hearing some of them now are beginning to shout, metaphorically speaking, and, under the circumstances, who am I, as a mere male, to say that they are out of order?''

In general, Higgins agreed with Dr. Daly's main points. He called ecclesiastical antifeminism ''a silly and sad tradition which goes all the way back to St. Paul and the early Fathers of the Church and is still very much alive.'' But he concluded: ''By way of a postscript, let me add that better men than I (I beg your pardon—I meant to say men and women) will have to decide whether or not Professor Daly is on the right track when she says that the acid test of the Church's sincerity on this matter will be her willingness to admit women to sacred orders. Miss Daly makes much of this point. I almost said 'too much,' but I lost my nerve when I thought of what she might do to me in her next article or book on the alleged conceit of celibate males.''

He came down negatively in his first specific comment on the Equal Rights Amendment, taking a jab at its liberal supporters for turning ''elitist'' on the issue.

''On the face of it,'' he said, ''this proposed Equal Rights Amendment seems to make perfectly good sense and to be long overdue, but, for reasons which ought to be well known to its supporters, it is open to serious criticism from the point of view of social justice. Incidentally, if this be treason, Women's Lib will have to make the most of it.''

The problem with the ERA, Higgins explained, was that it would have negatively affected working-class women by doing away with legislation that supplied them with sorely-needed additional benefits. He quoted Myra Wolfgang, a long-time trade union leader working with women who then headed the Coalition for Women's Advancement, to support his point. She had noted, for example, that the ERA would have canceled out legislation such as a California state minimum wage guarantee for women, which gave them a 35-cent-an-hour edge in the state's farms and orchards. ''That's quite a price,'' she had written, ''for working women to pay in behalf of a mythical equality that professional women are supposed to attain through an Equal Rights Amendment.''

Higgins concluded: "That's telling it like it really is. Cheers for Myra Wolfgang. She knows more about the problems and needs of rank and file working women than all the liberal proponents of the Equal Rights Amendment put together."

Two columns early in 1974 had praise for various Church documents as they related to the modern role of women.

On January 28, Higgins praised Pope John XXIII, who, in *Pacem in Terris* had written approvingly of the changing status of women in society. He also quoted extensively from the Second Vatican Council's *Pastoral Constitution on the Church in the Modern World,* which had called for an end to discrimination of all kinds. It specifically condemned the denial of rights that were fundamental and personal: "Such is the case of a woman who is denied the right and freedom to choose a husband, to embrace a state of life, or to acquire an education or cultural benefits equal to those recognized for men."

"That's a pretty good statement, don't you think," Higgins asked, "coming as it did from a group of 2,500 celibate males who, because of their previous cultural conditioning, might have been expected to take a somewhat more stand-pat position with reference to the role of women in the modern world?"

On April 1 he enthusiastically summarized Pope Paul's apostolic exhortation, *Marialis Cultus* (Marian Devotion), in which the pope said that the gains made by women in terms of equality and co-responsibility had not lessened Mary's exemplary role in the life of the Church.

"Pope Paul," he said, "wants us not to gasp with amazement at the virtues of the Blessed Mother, but to imitate her life of faith, hope and charity in terms of today's problems, challenges and aspirations. She is, for him, the perfect model of the disciple of the Lord 'who builds up the earthly and temporal city while being a diligent pilgrim towards the heavenly and eternal city, the disciple who works for that justice which sets free the oppressed and for that charity which assists the needy. . . .'

"While Pope Paul, in emphasizing this point, probably doesn't go as far as some people in the women's lib movement might have wanted him to go, his apostolic letter does represent a significant step in the direction in which the more realistic leaders of the movement are trying to lead us."

Finally, Higgins devoted three 1976 columns to the women's

rights issue, the first two (January 26 and February 2) forming a series in which he pleaded for dialogue and understanding. In the first, he warned that it would be a serious mistake for the U.S. Church or the Holy See to underestimate the importance of the women's liberation movement, "or to try to defuse it with superficial and token changes." It would be a tragedy, he continued, if the Church ignored the legitimate demands of women for equal treatment in the Church and in society. "But it is almost bound to happen, unless the hierarchy (and the Roman Curia) are prepared to listen more attentively than the Church has ever listened in the past to the women's demands for equal rights—including the right to ordination." The second column criticized the movement itself for its elitist image, and called on its representatives to listen more attentively to working women and housewives.

Somewhere along the line, Higgins adapted his views on the ERA—as did many activist liberals with the labor community. With them, Higgins switched from criticism of the amendment to open support, with the understanding that provisions be made to protect the interests of the working woman.

That was one of the key points he made in a June 5, 1982 talk at the College of New Rochelle, a major address on women in society and the Church in which he incorporated many points he had discussed in his columns. He also took the occasion to hit out at the Reagan administration for proposing that all mothers in the welfare program be required to search for work, regardless of the age of their children. "In a country as wealthy as ours," he said, "it's worse than wrong, it's barbaric. If feminists fail to protest this move and demand that the administration reverse itself, they will forfeit much of their hard-won credibility."

Higgins also challenged his audience, almost all of whom were women, on the purpose to which an achieved equality would be put: "Equality for what—for what purpose and to what end? Surely not as an end in itself, but rather to enable and empower women to play a more effective role in shaping public policy in defense of women's rights, and especially the rights of the poor and underprivileged."

Higgins's February 2, 1976 column was titled "What's Wrong with Women's Lib?" He gave one particularly clear answer: "Equating women's lib with abortion on demand should cease immediately."

The reference to abortion, along with several columns he devoted specifically to that subject, is interesting in light of later criticism that he was "soft" on abortion or, in the contention of one conservative columnist, that Higgins "has never shown, so far as I know, any interest in the abortion issue."

He had touched on the issue earlier, but began to write extensively about abortion, right-to-life groups and their rights and responsibilities, and related topics following the January 22, 1973 decision of the U.S. Supreme Court which, in effect, made abortion legal.

Shortly after the decision, on February 19, 1973, he not only severely criticized the decision itself—"a disaster from every conceivable point of view"—but also strongly disagreed with an old friend, Rabbi Balfour Brickner of the Union of American Hebrew Congregations, who objected to public criticism of the court because of its abortion ruling.

"What he seems to be saying," Higgins commented, "is that once the Supreme Court has ruled on any given issue, the people of the United States should forever hold their peace. In other words, he seems to be suggesting that the Supreme Court is the final and binding arbiter of social morality. . . . He will simply have to reconcile himself to the fact that, whether he likes it or not, critics of the court's decision on the abortion issue have absolutely no intention whatsoever of heeding his unsolicited (I almost said insulting) advice on this matter. There is no way that he or anyone else can possibly shame or frighten them into 'urging acceptance of this new law (*sic*).' They are going to do everything they possibly can to neutralize its bad effects and, hopefully, at some point to get it reversed."

Two years later, on February 3, 1975, he chided liberals for not getting involved in the campaign to end abortion and for making it seem to be a "Catholic" issue. In the same column he defended the pro-life movement against charges it was interested only in abortion and was silent on other issues—gun control, the world food crisis, and the like. He strongly endorsed statements by the bishops in general and Archbishop Quinn in particular in yet another column (May 8, 1978), which called on voters to examine the record of candidates on a wide range of issues, and which emphasized that respect for human life must be comprehensive.

On December 17, 1979, after Sean Morton Downey ended his quest for the Democratic presidential nomination as a pro-life candidate with a bitter attack on the American bishops, Higgins rebutted the criticism. He added: "In differing with Downey, I do not suggest that abortion is not an important issue. It is crucially important, and we need a strong pro-life movement in this nation to keep the issue squarely before us. That movement has the right and the responsibility to focus its energies on the abortion issue. It is quite another thing, however, for any interest group to urge that candidates be elected or defeated exclusively on the basis of its particular issue. The cause of justice is not well served by that kind of tunnel vision."

In the heat of the 1980 campaign, Higgins pointedly called on the press to show some consistency if it felt the need to criticize clerics for entering the political arena. He noted that although Boston's Cardinal Humberto Medeiros had received much attention, and no small amount of criticism, for calling on voters to defeat a candidate in a congressional primary election because of his position favoring abortion, relatively little interest had been shown when Bishop Leo Maher of San Diego urged voters in his diocese to reject another congressional candidate, a Catholic, who was also a member of the Ku Klux Klan.

"I agree churchmen should rarely, if ever, endorse or oppose candidates by name," Higgins said. "But this is a prudential judgment, not an absolute constitutional principle."

The alternate gains and setbacks which the pro-life movement experienced over the years had a number of effects. Some of its workers became discouraged and dropped out. Many other sympathizers followed the bishops' advice and widened their sights, incorporating their battle against abortion with other life concerns. Many who remained active in the right-to-life campaign redoubled their efforts, becoming in the process less willing to see room for compromise, and less understanding of those who did. They frequently joined forces with ultraconservative political movements, the so-called New Right, or "Moral Majority." Catholics identified as liberal on social issues, such as George Higgins, were more and more targets of criticism.

In Higgins's case, part of the criticism stemmed from a not-so-private dispute within the bishops' conference during the 1976 Ford-Carter campaign (which will be discussed in this chapter's concluding section). Part of it was more generalized, as was the case with that offered by James Hitchcock, the St. Louis University history professor whose column regularly appears in *The National Catholic Register.*

In a column written late in 1979, Hitchcock took issue with Catholics who disagreed with the thesis that a strong level of anti-Catholic sentiment continued to exist in the United States. It flourished, he contended, partly because it served the interests of some within the Church who have made common cause "with those who dislike the institution from the outside." Secular politics, and especially the political ramifications of the abortion issue, had a lot to do with it, he said, adding: "Msgr. Higgins has never, so far as I know, shown any particular concern about the abortion issue. . . ."

An interesting exchange of letters followed. Higgins provided a sample of his comments on the abortion question, but Hitchcock said they were not sufficiently numerous or recent, thereby justifying his original charge. (He also said that on his first personal encounter with Higgins, in 1975, his one-time boyhood hero "seemed rather like a pompous monsignor." Higgins replied: "It is good for a man's humility to be told, in a letter dated on his birthday, that he came through to at least one participant in the St. Paul Bicentennial Hearings as a 'pompous monsignor.' God knows it's humiliating enough these days to be known as a monsignor of any kind without being thought of as a pompous one at that. I intend to work on this matter very prayerfully during my annual retreat. . . .")

In recent years, Higgins has focused attention increasingly on the growing entanglement of pro-life organizations with right-wing political groups, warning Catholic pro-life advocates in particular of the risks involved in such alliances.

An article in *America* ("The Prolife Movement and the New Right," September 13, 1980) summarizes his views on the matter, including the Church's identification with pro-life causes and its leadership role:

"This deep involvement. . .flows naturally from the Church's traditional teaching on human dignity and the sanctity of human life. Abortion is not simply a 'Catholic' issue, or even a religious issue, a point that pro-life activists have strenuously and correctly emphasized. Nevertheless, it cannot be denied that the Catholic Church has a special role and responsibility that, in part, is thrust upon the Church by those outside the Catholic community who regard the protection of the right-to-life as an especially important Catholic concern. This public identification of the Church with the

right-to-life cause not only imposes an obligation on the Catholic
community but also offers an opportunity to provide leadership and
counsel in the overall effort to engender respect for human life.
Because of this unique role of the Church it is all the more important
for Catholics to scrutinize the relationship of the prolife movement
to the political ideology and strategy of the New Right.''

Higgins commended the Church's "official position" on
respect for life, which, he noted, treats abortion as one issue that
is viewed in the context of the respect-life principle. "Unfortunately," he said, "there are many in the pro-life movement who
do not share the bishops' broad application of the pro-life principle. Instead, they apply the principle selectively—to the unborn child,
but not to prisoners on death row, nor to the poverty-stricken family
in the inner city, nor to the starving child in the Sahel.''

The Church, Higgins said, must make clear the distinctions
of organizations under the pro-life heading, particularly in connection with the New Right. He identified the latter as "a loose coalition of extreme conservative organizations that focus on emotional
'social issues' and employ highly sophisticated fund-raising techniques to finance their activities." The New Right, he said, is "against
pornography, the Equal Rights Amendment, abortion, gun control,
gay rights, feminism, the Panama Canal Treaties, SALT II, and most
government regulations in the field of economics. It favors prayer
in public schools, capital punishment, and increased military
spending.''

Given that mix, Higgins continued, right-to-life had become
increasingly identified as a right-wing issue lumped together with
other issues that almost without exception contradicted official
Church positions: "capital punishment, disarmament, gun control,
national health insurance, welfare reform, foreign aid, inflation, full
employment, and agricultural policy are a few examples in point.''

The notion of a "Christian republic" where "far-right ideo-
logues" would determine what constitutes Christianity "is disturbing
in and of itself," Higgins wrote. "Connecting the right-to-life movement to a political effort to establish some sort of state-mandated
political orthodoxy dominated by the right wing should be unthink-
able to anyone seriously hoping to enact the Human Life Amendment
and build a genuine broad base respect-for-life movement." He was
not suggesting a conspiracy, Higgins said; "rather what I am posing is the possibility that in a subtle and sophisticated ay parts of

the pro-life movement are being used as a vehicle to promote a much broader right-wing agenda.''

The article brought a rejoinder from Dr. J.C. Wilke, president of the National Right-to-Life Committee, who declared that the NRLC and its 51 affiliate right-to-life organizations were not part of the New Right.

Nevertheless, some elements of the right-to-life movement enjoyed their association with the New Right, a state of affairs with which Higgins found no quarrel, "so long as they are aware of what they are doing." However, he continued:

"I would hope that they seriously consider the way in which the Church applies the sanctity-of-life principle not only to the issue of abortion but also to the full range of social justice issues. In addition, I would hope that pro-life Catholics seriously consider the possibility that in collaborating with the right wing on abortion they risk defeat of the overall social justice agenda. Many of the issues on this agenda are an integral part of our concern for the sanctity of human life and are intimately tied, morally and practically, to our opposition to abortion."

The relationship of the Church to the government, to politics, and to American society at large has occupied George Higgins in one way or another over the years.

There was no more fierce defender of the Church than Higgins when blatant attacks were leveled years ago by Paul Blanshard and other professional anti-Catholics of the day. In more recent years, however, he has taken issue with Catholic organizations, such as the Catholic League for Religious and Civil Rights, over certain claims of anti-Catholicism, particularly as they related to political or labor incidents.

A case in point was his criticism of a 1974 talk by Jesuit Father Virgil Blum, the League's director, in which Father Blum described most Catholics as "politically simplistic," adding, "Therefore the Democratic Party and the AFL-CIO can 'twist a broken bone into the flesh' of Catholics without loss of votes."

Presumably, Higgins said, the statement meant the AFL-CIO's position against aid to parochial schools reflected a spirit of anti-Catholicism, an interpretation that Higgins found astonishing, given the number of Catholics at the top level of the organization.

"It's one thing to disagree with the AFL-CIO on aid to parochial schools or any other public issue," Higgins wrote, "but something else again to accuse its leadership, without a shred of verifiable evidence, of being anti-Catholic. This kind of off-the-cuff rhetoric tends to suggest that the people in charge of the Catholic League for Religious and Civil Rights may be suffering from a bit of a Catholic inferiority complex. I hope I am wrong, but in any event, I have no intention of associating myself with the League until it comes up with a more precise definition of what it means by anti-Catholicism and shows a greater willingness to dialogue with the 'opposition' on controversial public issues before raising the specter of religious bigotry."

That column was dated November 11. Two weeks later he devoted the bulk of the Yardstick to a reply in which Father Blum denied accusing the AFL-CIO leadership of being anti-Catholic. The League, Blum continued, was devoted to serving the Church and members of the Catholic community and merited the support of individual Catholics. To the extent that Higgins's criticism had undermined confidence in the organization, he said, it would be less able to meet its assignment.

Higgins apologized for the misinterpretation, but made it clear that providing as much space as he did to Blum's reply was not to be seen as an endorsement for the League. "While I have the highest regard for Father Blum and for many of his associates," he said, "I am not at all sure at this stage that I completely agree with the League's approach to the so-called Catholic issue in American public life."

In 1978 Higgins expressed similar reservations about another organization, the National Committee of Catholic Laymen, which set out, among other things, to refute what it saw as "a new wave of anti-Catholicism in America." While the issue must be faced, Higgins wrote, he confessed he was unsure of the degree to which anti-Catholicism was a factor in American life. "I have not found it to be quite so extensive as some of those who have written about it would have us believe," he said.

In successive columns (October 9 and October 16) Higgins dealt with two aspects of the problem. The first column took issue with a booklet written for the NCCL by James Hitchcock which, in Higgins's view, criticized interfaith dialogue. "It is significant," wrote Higgins, "that Hitchcock invariably puts quotation marks around the word dialogue, as though to suggest there is something fishy about it. Indeed, at one point, he shows his hand rather openly by referring to the dialogue, in what are obviously meant to be uncomplimentary terms, as 'that blessed liberal ritual.' Moreover, he repeatedly challenges American Catholics to be 'militant' and 'aggressive' in the way they carry on the dialogue." Instead of that, Higgins suggested Catholics follow the guidelines for dialogue set down by Pope Paul VI in his first encyclical, *Ecclesiam Suam,* with courtesy, understanding, and good will. "It's obvious that dialogue, as Pope Paul was at pains to emphasize, involves a certain amount of risk," Higgins said. "But that's no excuse for refusing to engage in dialogue and certainly no excuse for belittling its importance."

The second column tackled an intriguing facet of the "anti-Catholicism" question—the contention, stated directly or merely implied, that American Jews are not targeted for discrimination the way Catholics are because they have enough backbone to mount a counterattack. Said Higgins:

"More often than not, this comparison is made to look like a compliment to the Jewish community. I seriously doubt that American Jews, by and large, see it as such. I think they tend to see it, and with good reason, as a roundabout way of exaggerating, however innocently or inadvertently, the extent of Jewish power or influence in the United States. They would feel this to be a gross underestimation of the extent of anti-Semitism in what is still, at least in name, a predominantly Christian country. Jewish people have had long experience with this kind of reverse flattery. They don't like it. They are frightened by it for reasons that anyone the least bit familiar with their tragic history will readily understand. I strongly recommend, therefore, that those who are writing about anti-Catholicism leave the Jews out of it."

Higgins fired a final salvo on the topic—again, with Hitchcock drawing the fire—on October 22, 1979, over American press treatment of Pope John Paul II. Yes, Higgins said, stories dealing with the pope's remarks on sexuality might have been, in the main, poorly reported. But on the other hand, the press handling of the pope's trip to America was almost reverential, and overwhelmingly sympathetic. "That being the case," he said, "I would hope that those who maintain that anti-Catholicism is a problem of major proportion in the United States will take another look at their cards."

It would be impossible, he concluded, to "ignore or underestimate the changing mood of the country as dramatically exemplified by the unbelievably warm reception given the pope, not only by the media but by the American people as a whole."

The abortion question was a key element in divisions within the Catholic community during the 1976 presidential campaign between Jimmy Carter and Gerald Ford, and in few places were they as pronounced, and, at times, as bitter, as in the staff house of the U.S. Catholic Conference.

The Carter forces kept pressing for a meeting with top-level representatives of the bishops. They knew that much of the Democratic platform was already in harmony with the Church's social positions, and were confident that their stand on abortion, which said, in effect, that Carter was against abortion but not against what was now seen as a constitutional right, would be understood if a dialogue with the bishops could be arranged.

They were wrong. A committee which included Cardinal Joseph Bernardin (then president of the NCCB-USCC), the late Bishop James Rausch (then the general secretary), the late Cardinal Terence Cooke of New York (chairman of the bishops' pro-life activities committee), and others, pronounced the Carter position on abortion as unsatisfactory. Shortly thereafter, the bishops met with Ford, and used the word "acceptable" to describe his position on abortion.

The effect was electric. No matter how much the bishops attempted to discuss other issues important in the campaign, and no matter how much they insisted their characterization of the Ford position did not constitute an endorsement, the media kept returning to two points: the bishops were talking about abortion, and they liked Ford.

"Never once did we support a particular candidate although we were accused of doing this, at least indirectly," Cardinal Bernardin said in a 1980 interview. "While the specific subject in this instance was abortion, we always went out of our way to mention all the other issues that needed to be addressed. But it was the media and others who slanted these things. It was never our intention to get involved in anything that might be perceived as partisan politics, and I resisted the meetings as long as I could. All we wanted to do was to state our position on all the issues. But there was great pressure from the candidates themselves to dialogue. I know it would be difficult to keep everything in correct perspective.''

What followed was a period which Bernardin described as ''one of the most difficult of my life.'' National media focused unrelentingly on the bishops, and on Bernardin as their president; within the Church community a wave of angry reaction arose from liberal and social activist elements. The staff house was badly divided over the situation and those who were unhappy with the bishops' handling of it made no secret of it. No one was more unhappy than Higgins, and on the day the bishops met with Ford, according to a priest-friend who had dinner with him that evening, he was furious. The dinner occasion was a serious one; the two priests met with a Catholic university president to discuss a proposal to present a somewhat controversial Middle East figure with an honorary degree. But throughout the dinner, Higgins's mind was obviously on what had happened earlier that day. He changed the subject over and over again to what the bishops had done—in terms that were anything but complimentary.

Despite his anger, Higgins refrained from taking part in any organized protest of the bishops' action, or—as what he refers to as ''cocktail party rumors'' had it—from spearheading, behind the scenes, a move to ''get'' the bishops for what he saw as a major blunder.

''My only exchange with Archbishop Bernardin on this was a personal letter in which I wondered if we were getting in a little deep,'' Higgins said in an interview. ''I suggested that if he had the time it might be nice to sit down with the staff and chew this around. And I got a nice letter back from him. Other rumors were going around, and the stories are still repeated, that staff people were laying down demands; that there were going to be widespread resignations by people in the building. Well, I certainly wasn't thinking of anything like that, and I don't know any people who were.''

Within the staff house, though, the arguments raged on, primarily between Higgins and Msgr. James McHugh, the Newark archdiocesan priest who was then the USCC's pro-life activities director.

As bitter as the combat was, the principals' recollection of the period is refreshingly benign.

''We're very good friends,'' Higgins said, ''and to this day if Jimmy comes to town I'm the first one he comes to visit. But we had a terrible knock-down, drag-out fight over this. Man-to-man fighting. McHugh is the sort of fellow you can fight with, and the next morning that's the end of it."

"We went at it," McHugh agreed in a 1982 interview, "but it was all good fun. We would've argued about something else if it weren't for that; maybe first confession before first communion. But there were absolutely no lingering bad feelings."

Higgins, of course, thought the bishops were wrong to get involved in the campaign in the first place. McHugh felt that the meetings with the candidates were not a good idea, but that once they had taken place, and once the abortion issue had surfaced as it had, the subject should be addressed squarely.

"That's where the tension existed," McHugh said. "Once it was out there in the open, people should be questioned in a fair way so that we'd get an accurate response. And once having gotten it, it should be fairly represented. Not in the sense of saying that if someone doesn't agree with us, he's antilife; nothing like that. But the issue was important. I disagreed that it should be just one of 15 issues; it transcended others because of its magnitude and its timeliness."

The bitterness of the ongoing squabble was especially distressing to Bishop Rausch. As general secretary of the conference he was ultimately responsible for harmony within the house, and he did as much as he could to act as a moderating influence. Higgins liked Rausch, profoundly respected him, in fact, but, as one table guest recalled, had a way of needling him when the discussion seemed to be going the wrong way. "That's very interesting, Jim," he would say. "Would you pass the butter?"

Rausch himself recalled the atmosphere at the time, and one night in particular, in a long, relaxed interview in his Phoenix office a year before his sudden and untimely death in 1981:

"George was very upset with the activities of the executive committee of the conference during that period, and with Msgr. McHugh. It became a regular topic of conversation around the table in the recreation room downstairs, *ad nauseam*. I was caught in the situation of being on the executive committee, and this thing got to be terribly uncomfortable.

"One night we were sitting around, right before the elections, and the thing was going around again. I tried to interrupt George a couple of times, which was not easy to do, because George was going to be heard. I finally stood up and said, 'George, shut up. I have something to say.' I said, 'It's time that we stopped discussing this issue. It's tearing us apart. If we want to discuss this down at work, fine. But let's get it off the agenda in this house, because bitterness and hatred are developing.'

"George was rather stunned that I was that direct, and I had pointed my finger at him and said that I meant him. And at that moment I got a telephone call. When I left the room, George's reaction was that I didn't have the guts to face what he might have said to me in return, or that I was so angry that I was stomping out. I took care of the phone call—and, incidentally, it was from Jimmy Carter—and I walked back to the room and said, 'That's that. There'll be no more about what I just said.' And we sat and talked for another hour.

"That's the way I felt about George. I could be honest with the man anytime, and tell him exactly how I felt, and he would respect that. But he sure as heck was not going to agree if he had a point of disagreement. He knew that night that the discussion had gone too far in the house, and that ended it. He's an older man than I—I don't know how many years older—but his taking it the way that he did really impressed me. Here, I thought, is one heck of a man."

The discussion, indeed, was over at that point. But its memory lingered on. It surfaced again two years later when the leadership of the bishops' conference tried to get Higgins to agree to an early retirement, an incident described in the final chapter.

The election of 1976 was barely over when a four-part series of Yardstick columns appeared, beginning on December 6, which outlined Higgins's historical perspective on the role of the Catholic Church in the United States in relation to the political order. The series, which summarized a paper he had presented on November 30 in Munich under the auspices of the Bavarian Catholic Academy, began with an account of the leadership displayed by Bishop John Carroll, the nation's first Catholic bishop, and continued through the Church's immigrant period, the gradual growth of Catholic political influence, and the development of the National Catholic Welfare Conference and its interests in social reform.

In the past, he said, American Catholics exercised caution

about political and social change and concentrated on family virtues, personal strengths, and the rights of the Church as an institution. That was changing, he continued, particularly since the Second Vatican Council; quoting Father John Courtney Murray, he added: "The time has come for Catholics to move beyond the issue of religious freedom and church-state separation so as to 'get to the deeper issue of the effective presence of the Church in the world today.' "

Higgins continued: "In the aftermath of the Second Vatican Council, U.S. Catholics and the institutional Church here have gone far beyond explaining that their religion does not conflict with Americanism, far beyond simply defending the Catholic faith and the rights of the Church in the public order. The institutional Church is now fully prepared to dissent, not from the American political system, but, when necessary, from the prevailing political ethos and specific governmental programs. The old charge that the Church in the United States was uncritically committed to the American ethos is no longer valid or, in any event, not as valid as it appeared to be until a few generations ago."

He developed the point as he described the structure of the NCCB and the USCC and their political function: "It is important to emphasize that the conference does not confuse the mission of the Church with that of government, but rather sees its ministry as advocating the critical values of human rights and social justice. It is equally important to emphasize that the bishops who administer the conference do not seek the formation of a confessional or sectarian voting bloc, do not endorse political parties or candidates, and do not attempt to instruct people on how they should vote." To illustrate the point further, he quoted from the statement issued by the bishops only a few weeks earlier at the height of the misunderstanding of their expression of views regarding abortion and its effect on the presidential election: "As bishops we have a duty to make clear the moral and religious dimensions of secular issues, to point to God's word as an authentic norm for social and political life, and to make clear the practical requirements which spiritual and moral values impose upon efforts to achieve a more just social order. At the same time, we are not supporting religious bloc voting nor are we instructing people for whom to vote. Rather, we urge that citizens make this decision for themselves in an informed and conscientious manner, in light of candidates' positions on the issues as well as their personal qualifications."

Higgins's own post-election analysis, which had appeared in the Yardstick for November 22, concluded that American Catholics had followed the bishops' advice. The media's preoccupation with abortion as an election issue was a mistake, he said: "Granted that Catholics, as a group, are (to their everlasting credit) more united on the abortion issue than other identifiable groups in American society, the pundits should have known . . .that Catholics are not and probably never had been one-issue voters and that they do not vote as a monolithic religious bloc." He concluded:

"Catholic voters of both parties followed the bishops' advice. They examined the candidates on the full range of issues and, for better or worse, voted accordingly. In doing so they demonstrated again that there is no such thing as a 'consistent Catholic vote.' . . . It is impossible to understand why this should have taken the pundits by surprise. It was as predictable as the rising and the setting of the sun."

CHAPTER TEN

"MUTUAL KNOWLEDGE AND RESPECT"

BISHOP JOHN MCCARTHY IS NOT THE FIRST OBSERVER TO have commented on George Higgins's versatility, but he did it affectionately and with perception in the course of a long and rambling interview at his home in Houston.

"George is a great generalist," he said. "Good generalists are in adequate supply, but the great ones are hard to come by. Take something like dogmatic theology, for instance. I would guess that in dogmatic theology, for instance, George is as good as maybe all but 15 or 20 other men in the country. But those other men, that's all they do! Ecumenism? George is as well known in the area of ecumenism as anybody in the country, but those others, that's all they do! In Jewish-Christian relations, George is currently the only identifiable, national Roman Catholic with deep, deep ties to the

Jewish community. And the labor movement. . .well, everybody knows about that.''

In November 1979 Higgins was honored for one of those special interests (with McCarthy and a score of other long-time friends looking on) when he received the Religion in American Life award for his contributions to interfaith relations.

"Vision and courage have long made Msgr. George Higgins one of the most admired members of the Catholic community in the United States,'' said Rabbi Joseph B. Glaser, RIAL chairman, in presenting the award. He added that Higgins "is a role model for every clergyman in America. He reflects honor not only on his own Church but on all religion in American life.''

On a more personal note, he added: "There are some people for whom I have respect, others admiration, others affection. I relate to George on all three levels. He has been at times controversial, but I am reminded of something a famous rabbi said in another time: a rabbi without controversy in his congregation is not exactly a rabbi; a rabbi afraid of controversy is not exactly a man. He's not only an example to people, but also an example to fellow clergy. The name of George Higgins is known throughout the clerical world. As far as movements or organizations or statements are concerned, I have a simple test: If George is in, I stamp it kosher.''

The sentiments were similar a few weeks later when Higgins was honored with a black-tie "pre-retirement dinner'' hosted by Arthur Goldberg in the Israeli Room of the Kennedy Center. The former justice seemed to be presiding over a family party, lingering over the introductory remarks, calling on all 60 guests to introduce themselves, one by one; thanking the guest of honor, with obvious affection, for all he had done in many fields, including the improvement of relations between Catholics and Jews.

Higgins responded in kind. After a bow to the host and hostess ("Dorothy and Arthur are the best friends I have had during my own 40 years in Washington''), he spoke of the bright promise for Catholic-Jewish relations brought about by the Second Vatican Council and, quoting the late Cardinal Augustin Bea, noted that Christians and Jews live by substantially the same faith in the God of Abraham, of Isaac and Jacob, and shape their lives according to the same divine wisdom.

Then, in a sentence, he summed up the reason that for so many years he has passionately worked to bring about happy and harmonious relations between people of different faiths:

"It is our common call as Jews and Christians to make known the name of the one God among all nations of the earth in every age, and jointly to serve the cause of peace and justice among the peoples of the earth."

The main thrust of Higgins's ecumenical concern over the years has been directed toward Jews rather than toward other Christians for a variety of reasons, chief among them the fact that in the course of his day-to-day work with labor and economic affairs he came into contact with Jews far more often than he did with Protestants. He recalls that he had a fair amount of contact with the National Council of Churches in the Forties when a staff man, Cameron Hall, represented the NCC at labor gatherings, but that no close working ties developed until the 1960s, when the NCC became heavily involved in the civil rights struggle, and, to a slightly lesser degree, the farm labor movement. He respected those ministers such as the Rev. Chris Hartmire who made the farm workers a special cause, but only if they had done their homework, and if they were in for the long haul. There was no discrimination involved here; it was the same test he applied to Catholic or Jewish clergy or lay people attracted to the cause of farm labor.

There was a general reserve to Catholic-Protestant relations when Higgins first came to Washington, a time when extremists such as Paul Blanshard were able to command attention and even respect, no matter how strident their tone. Higgins relished the prospect of jousting with Blanshard, so much so that in dealing with others who distorted Catholic teaching in attacking the Church, he was given to using "Blanshard-like" to describe their activities. Thus, in the Yardstick for March 3, 1952, he dealt with Conrad Henry Moehlman: "His article in *The Christian Century,* to put it very bluntly, is a rather sophisticated variation on the Blanshard theme: communism is bad, but Catholicism is just as bad and perhaps in the long run even worse. It is the old confidence game all over again: head I win, tails you lose." In 1953 he gave a generally favorable review to a six-volume work entitled *The Ethics and Economics of Society,* prepared by the Department of the Church and Economic Life of the Federal Council of (Protestant) Churches, but lashed out at sections he felt were anti-Catholic. One in particular was that by

Frank Knight, a University of Chicago economist. "Professor Knight, to put it very plainly," wrote Higgins (April 20, 1953), "is almost a professional iconoclast in his attitude toward organized religion in general and an incurable wiseacre in his attitude towards the Catholic Church in particular. Whenever he jumps over the traces of technical economics and wanders brashly into the field of theology (which is inexcusably often) he carries on like an imitation Paul Blanshard in academic cap and gown. . . . The Federal Council, to be sure, officially—and very sincerely, I am certain—disclaims any responsibility for any of the statements or conclusions of the various contributors to this series of volumes. Well and good. The fact remains, however, that the Federal Council wouldn't dream of sponsoring expressions of anti-Semitism under any circumstances whatsoever, with or without an official disclaimer of responsibility."

Blanshard himself came under Higgins's fire on a number of occasions, mostly in the Fifties and early Sixties. An unrelenting critic of things Catholic, Blanshard was obsessed with the concept of "Catholic power." He rarely missed an opportunity to denounce the Church, for anything from its body of teaching to its feared influence on legislators. Capable spokesmen such as Higgins who responded to him did their best to make it clear that Blanshard's scattershot attacks did not represent a Catholic-Protestant division (although, they might have noted more privately, it was regrettable that those in the Protestant mainstream put up with Blanshard so quietly).

Blanshard particularly nettled Higgins with an attack on the social encyclicals of Leo XIII and Pius XI, *Rerum Novarum* and *Quadragesimo Anno*. Bolstering his own convictions about the encyclicals with quotations from labor leaders William Green and Philip Murray, Higgins wrote (May 28, 1951): "The time has come for all fair-minded Americans, non-Catholics as well as Catholics, to stand up and publicly repudiate the prejudices of a former clergyman whose gospel of secularism is just as much opposed to orthodox Protestantism as it is to Roman Catholicism. . . . I am perfectly sure that Protestant social action organizations, all of which pass judgment on a hundred and one so-called secular matters from bingo to socialism, do not agree with Blanshard's thesis on the function of the Church in the social and economic order. I think they ought to stand up and say so as forcefully as possible. I do not expect them to disagree with Blanshard on the question of papal infallibility or any other specifically Catholic dogma, but I do think it reasonable to expect them to repudiate Blanshard's philosophy of secularism in the social and economic order. This isn't a Catholic-Protestant controversy. It's a controversy between pure and simple secularism on the one hand, and religion on the other. And secularism, as our Protestant colleagues in the field of social action would undoubtedly agree, prepares the way for totalitarianism, which even Mr. Blanshard fears almost as much as he fears the Catholic Church. Almost as much—but not quite.''

Despite Blanshard's virulent anti-Catholicism and despite Higgins's spirited rejoiners to his insults, a certain civility developed in their relationship over the years. Blanshard went so far as to consult Higgins for a book he was writing on religion and politics, but after the book *(God and Man in Washington)* appeared, he might have regretted the decision. Higgins commented in The Yardstick (February 8, 1960):

"I remember telling Mr. Blanshard during our very cordial, very frank but very inconclusive conversation several months ago that, in my opinion, he has made a substitute or an *ersatz* religion out of democracy and that this, rather than his fear of the alleged power of the 'dictatorial' American hierarchy, is the real reason he is so obsessively critical of the Catholic Church. . . . I find it absolutely impossible to reconcile (his) innocent statement of purpose with his monotonous criticism of Catholic teaching on divorce, contraception, mixed marriages, education and censorship.''

More or less inevitably, Blanshard produced a book on the Second Vatican Council *(Paul Blanshard on Vatican II),* and by the time it appeared in 1966, the mellowing process was continuing. Not only had Blanshard been to the Council and received press credentials as a freelance journalist, but had been treated, he reported, with "complete friendliness. . .and the greatest possible generosity.'' His opinion of the Church had changed favorably "to the extent that the Catholic Church has changed,'' he wrote, but added that he was unhappy as ever with manifestations of what he saw as clerical autocracy.

"That's a fair summary of his new book on the Council,'' Higgins wrote (October 17, 1966). "The book is a curious and very uneven mixture of the old and the new Paul Blanshard. The new Blanshard is unexpectedly but not consistently mellow; the old Blanshard is still just as savagely critical of the Church as he ever was in his salad days, and for precisely the same reasons.''

By 1973, when Blanshard was 80, Higgins was mellowing a good bit himself—but only up to a point. The occasion was the publication of Blanshard's autobiography, *Personal and Controversial,* and Higgins gave it a lengthy review in his column of April 16. "I wish him health and happiness in his declining years," he wrote of Blanshard. "In the course of reading his autobiography I even had the feeling at times that I owed him a personal apology for having been so severe in my criticism of his several books on Catholic issues. Much as I like him as a person, and respect the sincerity of his convictions, honesty compels me to say that apologies are not in order.'' He lists a series of anti-Catholic statements in the book, including one that labels the Church "still the baldest, most unashamed, most absolute dictatorship in the world," and concludes, "I suppose it was this one statement, more than anything else, that made me change my mind about apologizing to Blanshard."

Higgins reprinted most of that column February 11, 1980, just after Blanshard had died at 87, ironically enough, as he pointed out, in a Catholic hospital.

Higgins has written sparingly on the specific topic of Catholic-Protestant relations over the years. More than once he has referred to himself as a "rank amateur" in the field of ecumenism. In 1972 (May 29) he took issue with a Catholic writer who argued against Catholic membership in the National Council of Churches because of, in the writer's words, the NCC's "dangerous predilection for politics." Said Higgins: "To raise the question is one thing. It's something else again, however, to argue across the board, as one's major premise, that the churches should concentrate exclusively on individual responsibility and should not be concerned about the application of religious principles in the social and political order."

On March 1, 1971 he quoted approvingly from an article by Rabbi Marc Tanenbaum of the American Jewish Committee entitled, "Is Christian Ecumenism a Threat to the Jews?" Tanenbaum's answer was yes, and Higgins made it clear that he agreed with him.

"I fully agree with Tanenbaum," he wrote, "that the interfaith programs in the field of social action should always include representatives of the Jewish faith on an equal footing with their Catholic and Protestant counterparts. As Tanenbaum points out, there is no reason in the world why Catholics and Protestants who decide to do their 'Christian thing' jointly or ecumenically in areas of common social concern cannot work constructively with Jewish leaders on a peer-to-peer basis. As a matter of fact, I happen to feel so strongly about this matter that I have long since made up my mind that I will never, under any circumstances, enter into an interfaith social action program which does not provide for equal Jewish representation."

As favorably disposed as he surely is to the improvement of relations between members of all faiths, and to the end, for once and all, of the old ghetto mentality which isolated Catholics for so long from Protestants as well as Jews, the overall issue of Catholic-Protestant relations has never been a priority item on George Higgins's agenda. Catholic-Jewish relations, of course, are something else again.

"I really don't know how it started," he said in a 1980 interview. "It wasn't from having close Jewish friends when I was growing up; there was only one Jewish family in town. My father, of course, was very open. There was never any prejudice toward Jews expressed in the house. Just the opposite, in fact, and in that sense I suppose you'd say that my father was pro-Jewish. But gradually I did a lot of reading on Catholic-Jewish relations, and then I got to dealing with Jews in the labor field, in the government, and then from time to time with the various Jewish organizations.

"I've been fascinated by the common interests that Jews share with Catholics, and I've wondered from time to time about charges of anti-Semitism in the Catholic community. Are American Catholics more anti-Semitic or less anti-Semitic than others? I think most studies would show less. On a whole range of issues Catholics tend to be more sympathetic to Jews than are non-Catholics. Which is what I would expect, not for theological reasons, but because of the geographical and ethnic concerns. Jews and Catholics have common enemies, or common problems at least. We're both outsiders in the Protestant community. We had to fight our way up the ladder. We've worked together in unions and other things. There's undoubtedly a lot of anti-Semitism in the Catholic community, but everything I've read would seem to indicate that it isn't as bad as some people think."

The interest might have been long standing, but the subject of Catholic-Jewish relations was one which Higgins did not address in The Yardstick until the mid-Sixties, when the spotlight was focusing on the Vatican Council.

On January 25, 1965, when *Nostra Aetate,* the Council document on Catholic-Jewish relations, had not yet been approved, he took sharp issue with Patriarch Maximos IV Saigh of Antioch, the leading spokesman for Catholics of the Melkite rite "and one of the most imposing figures in the Council," who had issued a communique about what was then the draft document. He endorsed the patriarch's criticism of the Arab press, which had attacked the tenor of the document, but had trouble with his explanation.

Patriarch Maximos had pointed out that the projected Council document was religious rather than political in nature, spurred by a spirit of humanity, justice, and sympathy in the wake of the Holocaust. Fine, Higgins said, but what about the patriarch's other comments:

• That a "stain of shame" remains on the forehead of the Jewish people. "It is difficult to know precisely what this statement means in theological terms, but, in any event, it does not reflect the spirit or the tone of the Council's declaration and most certainly would have been overwhelmingly rejected by the Fathers if it had been put to a vote on the floor of the Council."

• That because of their propaganda skills, Jews exploit the least word said to serve their political interests. "Jews all over the world will legitimately resent this accusation. . . . For my own part, having followed the debate on the Council's declaration very closely, I can only report that I have yet to find the slightest evidence that the Jews of this country are exploiting the declaration for political purposes."

• That American bishops were likely to vote for the document out of a sense of pity and because of Jewish commercial interests in the United States. "The latter part of this statement is demonstrably unfair to the American bishops and, however unintentionally, is calculated, I am afraid, to fan the flames of anti-Semitism, a monstrous evil which, in all its forms, is solemnly condemned in the Council's declaration on Christian-Jewish relations."

When the document itself was formally promulgated on October 28, Higgins rejoiced in a Yardstick column (November 1) at its passing, confessing that Middle East political interests and the theological opposition of "a handful of theologians and Council Fathers" had made it a cliff-hanger until the last minute.

He called *Nostra Aetate* "a blessed landmark in that all-too-tragic history of Catholic-Jewish relations," one that could not undo all the harm of the past but could usher in an era of mutual knowledge and respect. He continued:

"If our Jewish neighbors and friends will bear in mind that this is the long-range purpose of the declaration, perhaps they will find it easier to live with the fact that, from their point of view, it is not a perfect document. The fact remains, however, that, in spite of its imperfections, which are just as disappointing to this writer and to many of the Council Fathers as they are to our Jewish friends, it is, on the whole, a very good declaration and one which, to repeat, holds out great promise for the future.

"This promise will only be fulfilled, however, if Catholics, too, bear in mind that the solemn promulgation of the documents on October 28 was not the end of the story, but only the beginning. It will be up to us to take the lead, humbly and penitently, in fostering 'mutual knowledge and respect' and in looking for opportunities to engage in fraternal dialogue with our Jewish fellow citizens."

The following year (May 2, 1966) he deplored the findings of a survey by Charles Y. Glock and Rodney Stark of the University of California Survey Research Center that showed that of Americans with anti-Semitic attitudes, 25 percent had a religious basis for their prejudice, and another 20 percent had the same religious basis "at least in part." The Glock-Stark findings, published under the title "Christian Beliefs and Anti-Semitism," were mentioned frequently in later columns, particularly after the ultra-conservative John Birch Society criticized the study. Birch officials said the survey presumably meant that the more time Catholics and Protestants spent in church, the stronger would their anti-Semitic feelings become. That brought a sharp rejoinder from the Anti-Defamation League (ADL) of B'nai B'rith, which Higgins endorsed (June 20): "It is important to note that Glock and Stark do not maintain that there is an inexorable causal relationship between Christian beliefs and anti-Semitism. They merely say that their sociological studies indicate that for many Christians the relationship exists. Their book, as they clearly state in the introduction, 'is not to be read as an indictment of religion.' Moreover, they readily admit that the good will and serious concern of most Christian leaders has already been demonstrated. . . The Birchites have no business spreading false impressions about the Glock-Stark study. And to imply that this study is a diatribe against church-going certainly does that."

Echoes of the Vatican Council, and particularly its declaration on Jews, continued to play a major role in Higgins's activities and his writings involving Catholic-Jewish relations.

One of the direct results of the declaration was the formation of the Subcommittee on Catholic-Jewish Relations of the Bishops' Committee on Ecumenism and Interreligious Affairs. The chairman was Bishop Francis Leipzig of Baker, Oregon, who persuaded Higgins to sign on as secretary pro-tem at the behest of a mutual friend, Msgr. Vincent A. Yzermans.

Leipzig's designation to head the committee had puzzled Higgins somewhat—"I think he had five Jewish families in his whole diocese," he said with a smile—but it proved to be a good appointment.

"It was a providential thing," Higgins said in an interview. "His home diocese was fairly small, so his duties there weren't that heavy. He liked to travel, he liked Jews, and he was interested. That was the key thing. But he didn't have any staff, so when Art Yzermans asked me to help, I said I'd be glad to do whatever I could. I helped him get started with the paperwork, organized a few meetings, that kind of thing. We got off to a good start, and my association with Bishop Leipzig was great from that point on."

He wrote at length about his hopes for the committee in a column entitled "A Providential Opportunity," which appeared November 21, 1966. It followed an unprecedented ceremony at the Catholic University of America at which leaders of the American Jewish Committee extended their appreciation to the U.S. bishops for their leadership role in seeing the Council declaration through to its final approval. Cardinal Francis Spellman of New York, speaking at the program on behalf of the bishops, pledged their determination to carry out the spirit of the document by fostering stronger and more extensive bonds of mutual understanding, a process which Higgins saw brought to life in the Catholic-Jewish committee.

From time to time, he pointed out, Christian-Jewish dialogues had taken place on social and civic issues of mutual interest, but the coming together of Catholics and Jews to discuss biblical and theological matters would be unique. Citing the Council's call for a new era of "mutual knowledge and respect," he concluded:

"What a proud boast it will be for the United States if we step out in front and set an example for the rest of the world in this regard. Working hand in hand, Christians and Jews together, we have a glorious opportunity to transform the Council's Declaration on the Jewish People from a lifeless piece of paper into a living document which can literally change the face of the earth. May God give us the wisdom and the courage to take advantage of this providential opportunity without further delay."

Soon it became apparent that a full-time executive secretary was needed, and the selection of Father Edward Flannery of Seton Hall University—a Providence diocesan priest known even at the time for his outspoken views against anti-Semitism—pleased Higgins immensely. He liked the choice because it signaled to outsiders, particularly the Jewish community, that the bishops were serious about the committee and meant it to have an effect. He feels as enthusiastically about Dr. Eugene Fisher, who succeeded Flannery in 1976.

"I think it's one of the best commentaries you can make about this conference," Higgins said. "Right from the start the official line has been to take a strong position and hire strong staff people. They could easily get around by picking somebody who'd keep quiet, but to their great credit they didn't."

Even after Flannery took over formal reins of the office, Higgins continued to do what he could, principally helping Flannery produce statements on behalf of the bishops, and then steering them through to approval. At roughly the same time, he addressed a number of topics involving Catholic-Jewish relations in The Yardstick—the reappearance, in English, of a viciously anti-Semitic book entitled *The Plot Against the Church,* which had been distributed, in Italian, to the bishops attending the Council (March 6, 1967); the emergence of a small but influential group of Jews speaking out in behalf of some form of government support for children in parochial or other church-related schools (February 27, 1967).

On December 4, 1967, six months after that year's Israeli-Arab war, he welcomed what he saw as a softening of the attitude of many Jewish Americans who had bitterly criticized the "silence" of the Christian churches at the height of the Middle East crisis. Some had gone as far as to say that any future attempts at dialogue between Jew and Christian would be meaningless.

"My own instincts told me at the time that the situation wasn't really as bad as all that and the crisis in Christian-Jewish relations, however unpleasant it proved to be in the short run, would probably do more good than harm over the long haul," Higgins said. "If nothing else, I thought, it would help to clear the air and, hopefully, would also help to move the dialogue to a new plane."

The published views of a number of his Jewish friends—Rabbis Arthur Hertzberg, Marc Tanenbaum, and Balfour Brickner, and Dr. Joseph Lichten of the Anti-Defamation League—tended to support his position, Higgins noted, adding:

"The willingness of so many distinguished Jewish leaders to begin the dialogue anew and hopefully to pursue it in even greater depth as time goes on is a most encouraging development. In view of what happened last summer, they might have been tempted to cut their losses, so to speak, and to withdraw from the dialogue until further notice. Instead, they have again extended the hand of friendship to their Christian colleagues. I admire them for doing so, and I think I can assure them, without fear of contradiction, that their opposite numbers in the Catholic community are equally ready and anxious to take up where we left off last summer and to make up for lost time as rapidly as possible. Rabbi Hertzberg warns us that we may find at first that the dialogue will now be 'less agreeable.' So be it. I am inclined to agree with him, however, that it will also be 'more open. . .and more constructive.' "

In a column a year later, on November 4, 1968, he agreed with a report in which Flannery had expressed guarded optimism about the state of the dialogue. With all their limitations, he said, Americans had made at least as much progress as people from any other country, and probably a little more, in the field. But, he added, that isn't saying much: "Given the fact that approximately half of all the Jews in the world live in the United States and given the numerical strength of the Church in this country, we ought to be away out in front and miles ahead of any other nation."

He lamented the fact that Jewish organizations were doing much more than Catholic groups to initiate the dialogue process. "Some Jews resent this very much," he wrote, "and I can't say that I blame them at all. They feel that Catholics should take the leadership in promoting the dialogue or, stating it negatively, that Jewish agencies shouldn't be put in the position of having to plead with Catholics to join them in dialogue. I thoroughly agree with them in this regard."

But Higgins strongly disagreed with a Jewish critic of the dialogue on another point. In a book Dr. Judd Teller had complained that in the dialogue process Catholics expect Jews to give up "deepseated principles" on parochial school aid and other public policy matters.

"I think I know almost all of the American Catholics who are promoting the dialogue," Higgins wrote, "and I am confident that they are not expecting a quid pro quo from the Jewish community. On the contrary, I think they would unanimously reject and repudiate any attempt to misuse the dialogue as a means of persuading or cajoling or subtly pressuring Jews to abandon their own convictions on matters of public policy as the price of continued Catholic participation in the dialogue."

Higgins took issue with another Jewish critic of the dialogue in The Yardstick for January 26, 1970, responding sharply to a book in which Howard Singer had expressed contempt for leaders of major Jewish organizations, "because of their alleged indifference to Jewish needs and Jewish survival and, more specifically, because of their eagerness to enter into dialogue with the Christian community."

Despite misstatements about Christian churches and despite Singer's conclusions, Higgins urged his audience to read the book, to learn why some Jews oppose the dialogue, and why they mistrust Christians.

"Mr. Singer's basic complaint is that too many Christians have learned nothing from Auschwitz," Higgins concluded. "I would like to think that he is exaggerating. Indeed I am sure he is. The fact remains, however, that all of us in the Christian community still have much more to learn from Auschwitz. . . . I promise Mr. Singer that I, for one, will listen to him very carefully if he will agree to get involved in the dialogue. I would only ask him to lower his voice a bit so that both parties to the dialogue will be able to hear themselves think and get on with the discussion."

Two weeks later Higgins tackled one of the most sensitive, and frequently discussed, issues involved in Catholic-Jewish conversations: the real or alleged failure of Pope Pius XII to speak out effectively against the mass murder of Jews in Nazi Germany. He agreed with a British historian, Eric John, who had said that a papal pronouncement would have had little effect on Germany's rulers as long as local bishops, parish priests, and individual Catholics did nothing themselves. Theologically speaking, Higgins said, those who think the Church functions like a disciplined army, through a clear chain of command starting at the Vatican, are wrong. He concluded:

"Obviously, of course, the presence or lack of lay initiative can never dispense ecclesiastical authorities fr m playing their own proper role in expounding the moral law. . .(but) we tend to expect too much of the authorities and too little of ourselves. Incidentally, this gives us the very comforting advantage of being able to put the blame on others and to excuse ourselves, sometimes rather pharisaically, when things go wrong. . . .

"The moral of all this is that, with regard to the specific case we have been talking about, putting all the blame on Pius XII for what went wrong in Germany simply won't wash. . . . The German people can't pass the buck to Pius XII any more than we Americans can salve our consciences by making a scapegoat out of a series of U.S. presidents for what went wrong in this country in the field of race relations generations ago and is still very wrong even in the year 1970."

Higgins has made three trips to Israel, one of which he referred to in a Yardstick column on February 7, 1979:

"I had gone to Israel," he said, "with an open and sympathetic mind, determined to try to understand, as well as any Christian can, what the new state means theologically to the Jewish people, but since I had taken with me only a meager knowledge of Judaism as a living reality, I was less than adequately prepared to grapple with that central question. Unfortunately, I brought back from Israel what I had taken with me to Israel—a superficial understanding of the Jewish attachment to the 'land' which God had sworn to Abraham, Isaac and Jacob that he would give to their descendants. My visit to Israel was highly instructive, even in this regard, for it brought home to me in a very personal way my obligation as a Christian to try to make up for lost time in my study of the theology of 'the people and the land.' "

In that regard, he commented favorably on a book by Father Flannery's long-time associate at Seton Hall, Msgr. John M. Oesterreicher, which examined that relationship. The theologians should indeed be concerned about the living reality of the state of Israel, Oesterreicher had written, not on specific political questions, but the survival and well-being of the nation. Higgins quoted Oesterreicher enthusiastically: "I cannot see how the renewal of the land could be anything to the theologian but a wonder of love and vitality, how the reborn state could be anything but a sign of God's concern for his people," and praised both Oesterreicher and Flannery for their contributions to Catholic-Jewish understanding.

"Their followers, alas, are not as numerous as one would hope," he concluded, "but the tide of Catholic opinion is beginning to turn their way."

That was not the case with Jesuit Father Joseph Ryan, speaking in Washington later that year under the auspices of the Middle East Affairs Council, when he charged that ecumenical relations between Christians and Jews in the United States had suffered from Jewish insistence on support for Israel as proof that Christians are not anti-Semitic. "As Americans," he had said, "we are culturally prejudiced, ignorant of the Middle East, made mute by fear of anti-Semitism (from within or without), and acutely sensitive to Jewish pressures."

"That's a gratuitous insult to those American Catholics who are working in the field of Catholic-Jewish relations," Higgins wrote in his December 11 column, "and an even greater insult to their Jewish friends and colleagues." Ryan, he said, had the reputation of being one of the most vocal of the pro-Arab, anti-Israeli propagandists operating in the United States. "In my judgment," he continued, "he is doing a great disservice to the cause of Catholic-Jewish relations in this country by injecting his own political views into the ecumenical dialogue and, even worse, by trying—none too adroitly, I might add—to play the Vatican off against American Catholics." He defended the record of Flannery's committee in this regard and took aim at another of Ryan's charges: "To say that the Church in this country doesn't deal with Arabs for fear of offending American Jews is to falsify the record. The Office for Ecumenical and Interreligious Affairs. . .would welcome a continuing dialogue with Arab Moslems. The fact is, however, that while there are several million Jews in the United States, there are relatively few Arab Moslems. . . ."

Then, a final shot: "Father Ryan is billed on the lecture circuit as an expert in the field of Arab culture. So be it. If that's his last, I think he ought to stick to it and stop meddling in the field of Catholic-Jewish relations in this country. His knowledge of the latter subject is extremely limited. . .and his point of view is notoriously one-sided, so much so, in fact, that to my certain knowledge he has lost all credibility with the Jewish community in the United States. This being the case, the less he says about Catholic-Jewish relations in the American context the better it will be for all concerned."

(He was only slightly easier on an old friend, Father Andrew Greeley, when Greeley wrote a piece for *The New York Times* charging "a strong and powerful anti-Catholic feeling" within the American Jewish community. In his column for July 26, 1976, Higgins responded: "I disagree in large measure with Father Greeley. . . .I say this with diffidence, for he claims to have 'empirical evidence' to support his allegations. I have never seen this evidence and I doubt that it is either as extensive or reliable as he makes it out to be. Father Greeley also says his criticism of the Jewish community is borne out by 'the impressions of many Catholics.' I wouldn't know about that. Speaking as one whose contact with the Jewish community has been extensive during the past 25 years, I can simply report that I have a substantially different impression. . . ." Interestingly, the column was withdrawn from publication, one of the few times that happened, and replaced by a substitute. As Higgins recalls the circumstances, he and Greeley talked over their differences on the matter and decided that since general interest in the issue was already declining, another column might serve no purpose other than to keep the argument going.)

Higgins strongly endorsed a set of guidelines on Catholic-Jewish relations issued in January 1975 by the Vatican's then-new Commission on Relations with Judaism. The guidelines, intended to implement the Vatican Council's declaration, reaffirmed the Church's condemnation of anti-Semitism and urged the elimination of all forms of discrimination against Jews that might be present in the life of the Church. They also called for dialogue, cited the joint biblical and theological heritage of Catholics and Jews, and emphasized common elements of liturgical life.

Jewish reaction, however, was somewhat mixed. The International Jewish Committee on Interreligious Consultations gave a cautious endorsement to the guidelines but regretted their failure to mention Israel or to answer the questions as to whether Jews were seen as requiring conversion to Christianity.

"I agree with the committee on the question of Israel," Higgins wrote on January 13. "I wish that the Vatican commission, in calling upon Catholics 'to learn by what essential traits the Jews define themselves in the light of their own religious experience,' had openly declared that this admonition, in the words of the Jewish statement of response, 'requires an acknowledgment of the central role of peoplehood in Jewish religious thought and of the consequent religious character of the historic attachment of the Jewish people to the land of Israel. . . .'

"While I fully agree with the authors of the Jewish statement of response on this particular issue, I think they may be unduly alarmed about the so-called 'conversion' issue. The Vatican has already strongly denied that it had any intent of proselytizing in the 'fraternal talks' between Catholics and Jews advocated in the guidelines. I think our Jewish friends would be well advised to take the Vatican at its word in this regard. On the other hand, given the tragic history of Catholic-Jewish relations, I can readily understand why the Jewish people are so concerned about the conversion issue."

Proselytism was the main topic of another Yardstick column, on July 24, 1978, which had been inspired by an article (in *Our Sunday Visitor)* in which Maryknoll Father Albert Nevins had deplored past Christian excesses in this regard.

"While it would be fatal to become entrapped in the guilt of the past," Higgins responded, "we cannot pretend it never happened or that its effects are no longer with us." He mentioned the Vatican's 1975 statement, as well as the followup declaration issued by the American bishops in November 1975, which outlined "the harm done to the Church by the process of 'de-Judaization' in which we Christians sought to deny the Judaic roots of our tradition." The call to fulfill God's plan for both church and synagogue contained in the bishops' statement, Higgins said, "implies that not all theological issues between us are resolved." What Catholics can learn from Jews, he said, can be accomplished only through honest dialogue. He concluded the column with a clear statement of his views on the subject of proselytism:

"One side of a dialogue cannot approach the other with a hidden intention of suing the dialogue to convert. We need to dialogue with Jews, not only to discern who they are, but also to ask their help, as our parent religion, in working out our own self-understanding.

"Many sacred mysteries need to be discussed. What is the

content of the biblical promises? What do we do now that we have finally come to admit the truth St. Paul proclaims in Romans 9-11 that the Jewish covenant with God remains valid on its own terms? How can we work together for common goals?

"While no one would wish to turn away the sincere Jewish convert, or in any way dilute our essential Christian belief in Jesus as the Risen Lord, our stance as a community should be that of working together with Judaism toward common witness to the one God, Father of us all, in the face of rampant secularism and relativism. We need to develop, together, structures in society capable of bringing about the kingdom of justice and peace in which we both believe.

"Evangelization and dialogue are thus compatible if one takes a broad, deep view of the history of salvation. We have had 2,000 years of conversionary effort, and the Jews are still there. Perhaps God is trying to tell us something."

George Higgins has been a personal witness to many of the developments in Catholic-Jewish relations in recent years, certainly the most dramatic ones. He discussed some of them in a reflective column on July 31, 1978, marking the fiftieth anniversary of the formation of the National Conference of Christians and Jews.

"There is something uniquely American about the success story of Jewish-Christian relations over the last 50 years," he wrote. "For the NCCJ did not come out of a vacuum, nor has it flourished in a vacuum. . . . While the various religious organizations were officially 'ghettoized' each in its own little enclave of triumphalism in those narrow days before Vatican Council II, Americans were busily discovering each other in the factories and political parties.

"Catholics and Jews were perhaps especially involved in this 'pre-dialogue' activity. Both were immigrant groups and highly urbanized as communities. The beginnings of the labor movement in this country are largely the fruit of a Catholic-Jewish coalition that came together out of common hurts and desperate needs. Without articulating the interfaith implications of their actions, Catholics and Jews joined (one might say they were almost forced) together into coalitions to achieve the social and political goals that neither community could have won on its own.

"Here, as in so many other ways, the Church has learned its theology from the grass roots up. In America, the coalitions and compromises, recognition of mutual agenda and shared priorities came first. Only later did the official dialogue begin. But when it began, in the late 1950s and 1960s, it had here (as it did not have in Europe, or anywhere else for that matter) a solid base upon which to build. The network of personal and programmatic relationships, developed over the years through the hard knocks of American coalition politics, gives the Jewish-Christian dialogue in this country a style and a depth among the people nowhere else, perhaps, achievable.

"This fact, of realistic and self-aware group activity on all levels of the religious communities involved, is perhaps America's greatest contribution to the interfaith movement in the world today. And NCCJ stands as a fitting symbol of that contribution."

On June 23, 1980 Higgins wrote of a "new maturity" in Christian-Jewish relations after attending an international meeting on that subject in Dallas. He listed some sensitive areas of discussion: the controversial Middle East policy of the National Council of Churches, the continuing role of Judaism in God's plan of salvation, and Christian attempts to convert the Jews, Christian theology and the state of Israel. Frankness and honesty had characterized the exchanges, Higgins said. It was only dialogue with the Jewish community that could enable Christians to grapple effectively with that range of issues.

Dialogue and understanding. "Mutual knowledge and respect." The two phrases have formed the heart of George Higgins's attitude toward the Jewish community from the start. Few things have grieved him as much as the persistence of anti-Semitism, as he explained at length in a column on March 1, 1971:

"There is no question about the fact that there is still a lot of subtle, and sometimes not so subtle, anti-Semitism in this country. This means, to put it bluntly, that a lot of U.S. Christians, including a fair share of Roman Catholics, are still indulging in an ugly form of prejudice which can in no way be reconciled with the faith which they espouse and, indeed, runs completely counter to that faith. This is a sad commentary on the state of Christian belief and Christian practice in a country in which one out of every 30 citizens is a Jew.

"It need hardly be said that the Christian community as a whole has a serious obligation to try to correct this tragic situation by every means at its disposal. In the case of the Catholic community, a number of constructive programs are now under way, but, if the truth be told, we have hardly come to grips with a problem which has been with us for centuries, has very deep cultural roots, and is much more serious, I suspect, than most of us would like to admit.

"The very fact that our response to Vatican II's Declaration on Catholic-Jewish Relations has been so spotty and, on the whole, so inadequate may help to explain why so many American Jews, despite the progress the Jewish community has made both in terms of economic and professional success and in terms of social and political acceptance, are still haunted by the fear of anti-Semitism.

"In the light of all this, we Christians in general and we Catholics in particular would be well advised to start listening more carefully to what responsible Jewish spokesmen are trying to tell us, from their point of view, concerning the state of Christian-Jewish relations in this country."

The dialogue goes on, due in no small way to Higgins's patient efforts to make sure that it does, an appreciation shared by participants, Christian and Jewish alike.

At a Catholic-Jewish colloquium in March 1982, in the parish house of St. Patrick's Cathedral in New York, in which Higgins spoke of "courtesy, esteem, and goodness" as the rules of dialogue, Rabbi Balfour Brickner made that point as he referred to the "exemplary" state of Catholic-Jewish relations, despite all the differences between the faiths.

"George G. Higgins has helped to create that climate for the past three decades," Brickner said. "In fact, there was a tie even before the formal Catholic-Jewish relations began. That was because George Higgins was there."

CHAPTER ELEVEN

JUSTICE AND PEACE: THE INTERNATIONAL VIEW

IN FEBRUARY 1983, TWO-AND-A-HALF YEARS AFTER HIS retirement, George Higgins left on an extended trip that would take him to Hong Kong, the Philippines, and a few other Far East points. Several weeks earlier he attended a labor federation meeting in Colombia, his third Latin American journey in the space of a few months. Not long before that he attended the first national congress of Solidarity, the short-lived Polish labor union, in Gdansk, extending a hand of fellowship on behalf of American labor and the Catholic social movement in the United States.

In short, neither age nor retirement had dimmed Higgins's long-standing interest in the international scene, or his determination to be personally a part of the events overseas which concerned him most.

For the most part (but not exclusively, it should be noted) they were labor-related, continuing a pattern that began with his first trip overseas. As reported in an earlier chapter, that was a three-month visit to Germany in 1949 under the auspices of the religious affairs branch of the U.S. Military Government there. The specific purpose of the trip called for Higgins to survey social action initiatives in the labor field in Germany, although Higgins took advantage of the occasion to make side trips to Italy, Switzerland, France, Ireland, Great Britain, Denmark, and Sweden, acquainting himself with the social action movements in those countries. On his return he told an NC News Service interviewer that the German labor movement had made great strides since the end of World War II, changing from the prewar pattern of division (along either Christian or socialistic lines) into a unified force with greater strength than it could muster before. "It is something new for Germany," he said. "The one big problem for its success is whether they can continue to work together, concentrating on trade union problems and keeping out of political or religious differences. Personally, I hope the single movement will continue and I believe that if it does, it will speed Germany's economic recovery."

Nonetheless, Higgins staked out a strong rationale for European Christian labor unions, and for their right to exist, in a series of four columns beginning on January 16, 1950. At issue was their entry into the then-new International Confederation of Free Trade Unions, and the demands on the part of some, notably the socialists, that Christian unions which were admitted to membership surrender their confessional affiliation.

"We are not making out a case," Higgins concluded the series, "for or against the desirability of Christian trade unions (whether Protestant, Catholic, or non-sectarian) at this stage of Europe's economic, political, social, and religious development. We are merely making a case for their right to exist and for their right to be members of the new world federation of labor without being asked to commit organizational suicide as the price of admission. We are making a case for freedom of association. Having attempted to make that case, we again express the hope that the Christian unions will see fit to join the new international federation. . . . We again express the hope that socialist and Christian trade unionists and trade unions will learn to work together for the welfare of European labor and for the peace and prosperity of the continent."

Through the years, Higgins's primary interest on the international labor front has been the ILO, the International Labor Organization, or as it was first known, the International Labor Office. Formed in 1919 as an integral part of the League of Nations, the ILO has sought to guarantee human rights in general and the basic rights of workers in particular through a coalition of labor, management, and government representatives. In 1946 it became one of the specialized agencies of the United Nations and over the years has adopted a series of position papers—or conventions, as it refers to them—covering basic work interests such as working hours, safety regulations, and fair wages, as well as more generalized concerns including the freedom of worker and employer association, freedom from forced labor, and freedom from discrimination in employment. Through its World Employment Program it has attempted to insure the availability of such vital universal needs as food, shelter, health care and education. It has also provided technical assistance to many Third World nations with a variety of job training programs.

The ILO's record in these areas occasioned a warm tribute from Pope John XXIII in his 1961 encyclical, *Mater et Magistra.* "We are happy," the pope wrote, "to express our heartfelt appreciation of the International Labor Organization which for decades has been making its effective and precious contribution to the establishment in the world of a socioeconomic order marked by justice and humanity and one in which the lawful demands of the workers are recognized and defended." Pope John Paul II voiced similar expressions during a 1982 visit to ILO headquarters in Geneva, continuing a pattern of Vatican support that has existed since the organization was founded.

In the United States, the ILO has had few more faithful supporters, or more vigorous defenders, than George Higgins. The first of many Yardstick references to the ILO appeared on November 6, 1950, when Higgins defended the organization after a Swiss economist of the "decentralist" school suggested it could be phased out if mankind were to return to small-scale manufacturing and self-sufficient farming operations. This would be preferable, he said, to continuous large-scale organizing as a means of combating the evils and excesses of society. This approach, of course, was directly opposed to Higgins's own.

"The ILO is deeply interested in all of these specific remedies," he wrote. "It is primarily interested, however, in something exceedingly more important and far-reaching in its final results: the encouragement of collaboration in the economic and social field between free, strong, and independent organizations of employers and workers. . . . Its primary emphasis is on the freedom of association and on the all-important role of self-governing economic organizations collaborating with one another in behalf of social justice. . . . Long live the ILO.''

More often than not, Higgins was defending the ILO against American critics rather than those from overseas. This was especially so from the mid-Fifties on, when there was mounting pressure from some American interests to force the nation's withdrawal from the international organization.

It came first from extreme conservatives and isolationists who charged that the ILO "conventions" could be used under the treaty power of the federal government as a means of bypassing Congress and invading the rights of the various states. Nonsense, answered Higgins in a February 25, 1952 column, as he pointed out that even if that were the goal of ILO backers, a treaty would still require two-thirds approval by the Senate.

In the same column, he dealt with a more deep-seated objection: the charge that the ILO was "socialistic." It came from William McGrath, the adviser to the American Employer Delegate to the ILO, and in it he claimed that American labor and government delegates were at least sympathetic to socialistic philosophy. Since the list of American delegates included George Meany and other equally respected citizens, Higgins rang in with a predictably outspoken defense:

"As one who happens to know all of them personally, I cannot believe that Mr. McGrath really means what he is saying when he accused them of going down the line of state socialism. I presume he is just a little emotional, either that, or he hasn't the foggiest notion of what state socialism really is; in which case he hasn't any business representing the United States in any capacity whatsoever at international conferences. The United States has enough trouble on its hands already without the added embarrassment of being represented abroad by people who apparently don't know the difference between *Das Kapital* and *Quadragesimo Anno*.''

The Eisenhower administration came under even more pressure (again, with McGrath spearheading the attack) to withdraw from the ILO when the Soviet Union was admitted to membership in 1955;

Higgins attributed the decision not to do so to a man (as noted earlier) for whom he had the deepest respect and admiration.

"The fact that the administration has been able to withstand this kind of anti-ILO pressure," he wrote on January 14, 1957, "is largely due to the statesmanship of Secretary of Labor James P. Mitchell, a man of extraordinary ability and personal integrity. Mr. Mitchell, who himself comes from the ranks of management and has ready access to its councils, has taken every advantage of every possible opportunity to defend the ILO against the relentless and exaggerated criticism of Mr. McGrath and to demonstrate the advantages of continued U.S. participation in the ILO in spite of its admitted imperfections and in spite of the fact that the Soviet Union is now a voting member of the organization."

Grumbling about the political direction of the ILO persisted in conservative American political circles throughout the Sixties, but it was not until 1975, in the wake of newer and somewhat more credible criticisms, that an actual break with the organization began to emerge as a genuine possibility. In November 1975, with President Ford in office, Secretary of State Henry Kissinger served formal notice of America's intention to withdraw—"presumably," Higgins wrote in a column dated May 24, 1976, at the urging of the American labor movement and our employer delegates. Kissinger had listed four areas of primary concern: the erosion of tripartite (labor, management, government) representation in the ILO, the organization's allegedly selective concern for human rights, its alleged disregard of due process, and its increasing politicization.

Higgins's defense was measured. He understood and sympathized with Kissinger's objections, he said, and although he opposed withdrawal he thought they merited serious consideration. The admission of the Palestine Liberation Organization, the incident that triggered the crisis, was "a serious mistake," he added. Nonetheless, he said, the United States should pay its ILO dues for 1975 (the House had failed to appropriate the necessary funds) rather than stand accused of "financial blackmail," and, citing Meany's defense of the ILO during an earlier dispute over membership, pointed out the need to stand firm against totalitarianism in world forums.

"Meany was right," he concluded. "We have everything to lose and nothing to gain by adopting an isolationist policy."

America did finally break with the ILO under President

Carter, who, pointing to the same objections voiced by Ford, ended the country's 43-year association with the organization in 1977. Higgins was "ambivalent" about the decision, he later said, aware that the criticisms were not without merit. But when the president announced on February 13, 1980 that the United States was renewing its membership because "a majority of ILO members, governments, workers and employers, have successfully joined together to return the ILO to its original purpose," Higgins approved wholeheartedly.

"I am delighted that the president has come to this conclusion," he wrote on March 3. "The ILO, whatever its failures or limitations, deserves our full support. Its potential for helping to lay the indispensable economic foundation for a just and lasting peace can hardly be overestimated. For this reason, the Holy See and Catholic social action organizations throughout the world have always strongly supported the organization." To illustrate the last sentence, he quoted from a talk given by Cardinal (then Archbishop) Patrick O' Boyle nearly 30 years before at a meeting of the Catholic Association for International Peace, a talk, incidentally, that he had a strong hand in drafting:

"The ILO is not a perfect agency, but in these days when cynicism is such a common temptation for the best of men it is well to bear in mind that the ILO, by reason of its many accomplishments in the field of international labor legislation, is a living proof of the fact that it is possible for the nations of the world to cooperate with one another on behalf of the international common good—an effective antidote to the enervating virus of defeatism and despair."

The Catholic Association for International Peace (CAIP) was part of the network which linked together social actionists of the Fifties; it was no surprise that it would have been interested in a healthy and effective ILO. Established in 1926 (by Msgr. Ryan and Father McGowan, among others) to promote Christian principles of justice on an international level, the organization maintained a small but active membership until the late Sixties, when it faded from public view.

Influential far beyond its numbers for most of its lifetime, CAIP nevertheless had a persistent problem with membership and finances, concerns over which Higgins, a firm friend, worried publicly in The Yardstick.

"Many reasons can be advanced for CAIP's failure to attract a larger membership," he wrote on November 9, 1953. "Perhaps the principal one has been a lack of adequate publicity and promotion which, in turn, can be traced back in a vicious circle to a lack of sufficient members. A secondary reason is that CAIP, wisely or unwisely, has specialized thus far in producing scholarly studies and reports rather than so-called popular pamphlets." He hoped, he said frankly, that the column would attract more members to CAIP.

Higgins made the same pitch four years later, on December 2, 1957, ticking off some CAIP activities ("It has publicized and emphasized the pronouncements of the popes and of the American bishops on international peace, and has made particular efforts to encourage college students to make a serious study of Christian principles and their application to world problems") and urging his readers to join up.

CAIP members found themselves disagreeing within their own ranks on American involvement in Vietnam— and related issues, such as selective conscientious objection, the subject of a special CAIP seminar in 1967. Writing about the seminar on November 13 of that year, Higgins said while he had not changed his personal views (he still favored the concept of selective conscientious objection) it had succeeded in showing him some of the complexities of the issue. "I am now more conscious than ever before," he said, "that many Catholic and Protestant experts disagree with me in this regard. Consequently I am not prepared to urge that my point of view be adopted, at this stage of the game, as the 'official' Catholic point of view. What is needed at the moment is not an official statement that would tend to foreclose the debate on the pros and cons of SCO, but rather a wide open, free-wheeling discussion of the issues involved in this debate which, far from having run its course, is really just getting started."

Indeed, it was getting started, and the division it would occasion, on selective conscientious objection itself, and on the broader issues of war and peace that surfaced during the Vietnam years, helped to signal the end for CAIP.

An organization that had been noted for its generally unified approach to international matters, it found the Vietnam-related debates hard to contend with on an internal basis. For the most part, its members took a conservative position in backing the Johnson administration's military decisions, a stance that separated the organization from the increasingly influential peace movement.

There were administrative considerations as well. For years CAIP had relied on Higgins's Social Action Department within the NCWC to tend to the meeting notices, minutes, and other paperwork which held it together. ("It wasn't much," Higgins recalled. "We serviced CAIP in a hand-me-down, bargain-basement way. But it did serve to keep things going.") However, part of the conference's reorganization called for the establishment of the Office for International Justice and Peace, with Higgins being shifted (in title only, as noted earlier) to the directorship of the Division on Urban Life. That meant that any CAIP paperwork would logically be the responsibility of the new justice and peace office. Its first director, Msgr. Marvin Bordelon, preferred to set his own agenda, and CAIP was left to shift for itself.

Both the organization and its members were aging, and Higgins suspects it might not have endured even if the conference's reorganization hadn't caused a record-keeping problem. Eventually it simply ran out of steam. From its ranks, however, came many men and women who would help to shape the great debate over Vietnam within American Catholic circles as in the country at large.

Higgins's own position on the Vietnam war followed a path not unlike that taken by many other Americans: early support for the nation's policy, a gradual realization of the scope of the horror that Vietnam had become, and then a call for an end to the bloodshed.

His early support unquestionably was influenced by his friendship with and admiration for President Johnson, a man he genuinely believed had compassion for the poor and an interest in the welfare of humanity around the globe. Those sentiments were reflected in his first column on Vietnam, on April 16, 1965. In it he took issue not only with the vocal band of American clergymen even then speaking out against U.S. involvement, but also with Cardinal Stefan Wyszinski. The Polish primate had strongly criticized American bombing of Vietnamese targets as a sign of what he called the tendency in the modern world to "solve all problems by means of death." That was a low blow, Higgins said, "a serious misreading of U.S. policy." He continued:

"For better or worse, our government is carrying on limited warfare in Vietnam because it is convinced, rightly or wrongly, that this is the only way to bring about the kind of negotiated peace which will meet the minimum requirement of justice. It goes without saying, of course, that President Johnson and his advisers are not infallible. Their policies with regard to Vietnam may be mistaken, but, by the same token, Cardinal Wyszysnki's unfavorable interpretation of their intentions is, in my opinion, very wide of the mark. . . . In the absence of proof to the contrary, I am prepared to believe that we are in Vietnam not because we are arbitrarily determined to pursue our own 'doubtful reasons of state' [as the cardinal had alleged] but because the people of that beleaguered nation want us to be there.''

Then Higgins took on the American clergymen, noting the recent appearance of a full-page ad in *The New York Times* calling on the president to end the Vietnam war at once.

''At the risk of appearing to be a heartless warmonger, I am frank to say that this form of clerical 'witnessing' leaves me unimpressed,'' he wrote. ''For one thing, it seems to assume that clergymen, who are not privy to all of the facts about the crisis in Vietnam, are nececessarily better equipped than the president to interpret the will of God in the field of international relations. Moreover, it reveals an alarming degree of *naivete* with regard to the frightening complexities of international relations.''

By putting their call for multinational peace talks in ''patronizingly clerical'' terms, Higgins said, the clergymen were insulting the president and his advisers, especially since the other nations involved had already refused to attend such a conference. He continued:

''Are they required by the demands of our 'Judaeo-Christian faith' to withdraw our troops immediately, regardless of the consequences, as so many of their clerical critics have urged them to do? I think not. I am not suggesting that the top officials of our government are necessarily better interpreters of the moral law in the field of international relations than are their clerical advisers and critics. I do think, however, that clerics who feel called upon to criticize our foreign policy 'in the name of God' ought to be prepared to talk in terms of viable or realistic alternatives. To talk, as many of them are doing at the present time, in terms of absolutely black-and-white distinctions between good and evil is, in my opinion, a very unsophisticated and potentially harmful form of clericalism.''

Two weeks later, responding to a suggestion that clergy take a lead role in the world peace movement (a suggestion advanced by

Father Francois Houtart, the Belgian sociologist), Higgins sounded a cautionary note. The call had been well taken, he said, "but, in my judgment, the clergy will do more harm than good if they overplay their hand in the field of international relations or if they assume that, simply by reason of their calling, they are experts in this field."

That in turn led to a fuller explanation of the points he had made two weeks previously, since the column, he confessed, had been "widely misunderstood."

"I merely said," he wrote, "and should now like to repeat, that criticism of U.S. foreign policy, from whatever source, should be based on an adequate knowledge of the facts and, equally important, should be stated in terms of viable or realistic alternatives and not in oversimplified terms of an absolute black-and-white distinction between good and evil. . . . Presumably [the drafters of the statement] are honestly convinced that they are speaking in the name of God and that the Johnson administration, by contrast, is obstinately going against God's will. They are obviously entitled to this opinion and certainly should not be barred from expressing it. But neither should they expect to be immune from honest criticism just because they happen to be wearing the cloth."

He noted that another group of clergymen, "some of whom are personal friends of mine," were planning a vigil at the Pentagon, adding: "Presumably the purpose of this vigil is to get people thinking about the moral issues involved in the tragic Vietnam crisis. But, whatever its original purpose, it will almost inevitably take on the character of an anti-administration protest meeting. Even at the risk of being accused of playing the administration's game, I must say again that I am not greatly impressed by this kind of clerical witnessing."

Higgins's criticism of anti-Vietnam clerics took on a decidedly personal tone a few weeks later, on July 12, when he strongly disagreed with Dr. Martin Luther King, Jr.'s announced plan to launch a series of peace rallies along the lines of those he had organized for civil rights. Commented Higgins:

"In my judgment, Dr. King will do a great disservice to his own reputation as well as to the cause of civil rights, which he has served so effectively, if he rashly decides to go ahead with this ill-conceived plan. He is a man of many parts, but he isn't Superman—and, more to the point, he isn't President of the United States or commander-in-chief of the armed forces. He has demonstrated almost charismatic gifts of leadership in the struggle for racial equality, but the gods have made him mad if he really thinks that these gifts can be transferred automatically to the field of international relations. Perhaps the time has come for his friends and supporters to remind him, with great respect, that if success can spoil a Rock Hudson *(sic),* it can just as easily spoil a Martin Luther King, Jr.''

Higgins repeated some of the points he had made in criticizing the other clergymen: that Johnson's critics were oversimplifying the issues involved, and that all parties, including the clergy, had a right to address the moral questions which the issues posed. But he said of King: "Does he have a right to try to foreclose the debate, on a matter which is certainly very debatable from the moral point of view, by resorting systematically to high-powered tactics deliberately calculated to force the president's hand? I think not—and if he is foolish enough to try to short-circuit the democratic process in such a demagogic manner, I sincerely hope and confidently expect that he will be repudiated by the American people.''

Early in 1966, in columns dated February 7 and February 28, Higgins had an exchange with fellow-columnist Donald McDonald over the wisdom of clergymen criticizing the government for its Vietnam policies. McDonald's rejoinder took a curious personal line. Since Washington is "a moral quagmire," he said, anyone who had lived there as long as Higgins would "have a way of rationalizing and justifying morally questionable American actions in a way they would never do under other, more reflective circumstances.''

"Empty rhetoric," Higgins replied, that was "almost insulting." Then he challenged McDonald: "Is it a fact, as clearly implied by Mr. McDonald, that the administration is in the habit of bringing pressure to bear upon American bishops to silence those priests who are critical of U.S. policy in Vietnam and that the bishops are giving in to this alleged pressure? In my judgment, this is not a fact, and, as an 'old Washingtonian,' I am conceited enough to think that my sources of information on a matter of this type are better than Mr. McDonald's.''

For the first time, however, Higgins quietly hinted at a reservation himself on the overall Vietnam issue. After repeating the point, expressed on several earlier occasions, that he doubted the moral questions about Vietnam could be easily and absolutely resolved, he added parenthetically: "I am referring, of course, to our overall policy in Vietnam and not to any excesses which our government may have been guilty of in carrying out this policy."

Higgins's own questioning process continued, and he found an opening to express the questions that November, during the annual bishops' meeting in Washington. Cardinal Lawrence Shehan of Baltimore excused himself from one of the sessions to visit with Higgins and Father John Cronin in their office, declaring that because of the urgency of both issues, the bishops shouldn't leave Washington without issuing statements on the racial question or on Vietnam. Would Cronin and Higgins, he wondered, help him get something together?

Cronin began working on the race declaration, and Higgins finished a draft of a Vietnam statement within a few hours. It eventually underwent a number of changes, but substantially it said what Higgins thought it should: that the bishops were not qualified to make definitive judgments about the morality of the overall American position, and that the questions involved were serious enough to warrant a legitimate national debate.

Higgins commented on the statement in a column dated November 28, referring to the moral difficulties of the situation and the need to review them constantly, and not at all to a defense of the American policy.

The bishops, he said, "know that their fellow citizens differ among themselves over the moral issues involved in this tragic conflict. They do not claim to be able to settle or resolve all of these issues authoritatively in the name of the Church. For my own part, I do not think that they can reasonably be expected to do so in the fulfillment of their pastoral office. Their pastoral task at the moment is not to try to determine authoritatively, in the name of the Church, whether or not our nation's involvement in Vietnam is morally justified under present circumstances. It is clearly their duty, however, to insist that this issue and all of the related moral issues involved in the Vietnamese crisis be kept under constant moral scrutiny. This duty they have fulfilled in their recent statement on peace. They have reminded us that we are all obliged in conscience to keep testing and refining our judgment—not only about the war itself but also about the means which are being used in the war— against the norms of morality."

Those are obligations we cannot transfer to government

officials, Higgins added, although, he said, we should pray for those "who bear the awesome responsibility of making life-and-death decisions, by the day and by the hour, about our national policy with regard to the Vietnamese crisis."

A month later, on December 26, he emphatically defended the right of selective conscientious objection as one in harmony with traditional Catholic teaching. He also lamented the fact that many Catholics regarded conscientious objectors with disdain or even disgust. "Let's hope that the number of such misguided superpatriots will rapidly decrease in the wake of the Vatican Council's passionate plea for peace," he said. "We do not have to agree with the conscientious objectors in our midst, but, at the very least we ought to respect their sincerity and their dedication to the truth as they happen to see it." To do otherwise, he added, "is to betray a lamentable ignorance of what Christianity is all about."

In the same column, he pointedly noted that the American bishops had not issued a "binding moral judgment" when they stated that "in the light of the facts as they are known to us, it is reasonable to argue that our presence in Vietnam is justified." The fact was, Higgins said, that the bishops had explicitly added that there were serious divisions among Americans over Vietnam, and that they did not claim the ability to resolve them authoritatively.

The role of the clergy and religious institutions in addressing the Vietnam problem continued to occupy Higgins during 1967. A March 13 column explained at length why he had declined an invitation to sign an "Open Letter on Vietnam" which was to be published in a number of Catholic periodicals. "I just don't like being asked to sign public statements of this kind when I haven't been consulted in advance about their content and phraseology," he said by way of introduction. In the column he reprinted his reply to those who had invited his signature, in which he had said that while he shared their concern over Vietnam, he'd rather express it in his own words. He hoped that those who did not sign would not be seen as standing in disagreement with papal statements about Vietnam: "This type of criticism, however well-intentioned, can easily degenerate into a crude form of blackmail," he concluded. "Be that as it may, I honestly think we could do with a little less pressure and a little more freedom in this matter of 'witnessing' to our respective points of view on controversial issues."

On July 24, 1967 he suggested a major ecumenical conference

to address the question of the role of the churches and syna-
gogues in the face of the Vietnam crisis. "To say that they must do
more than they are currently doing to resolve this crisis is one thing,"
Higgins said. "But to spell this out in detail is something else
again. . . . There are few problems more difficult to settle."

An old friend, Paulist Father John Sheerin, crossed editorial
swords with Higgins the following year, after Higgins had seconded
(February 26, 1968) Father Hans Kung's suggestion that while the
Church should be in the world, its priests should not involve
themselves in partisan politics. In his own column, also distributed
by NC News Service and carried in the diocesan press, Sheerin said
that Higgins should have been focusing attention on "the greatest
single moral problem of our time, the Vietnam War."

In return, Higgins said that Sheerin and he were arguing at
cross purposes: "He wants all Christians, including bishops and
priests, to focus moral attention on the war in Vietnam. So do I.
But I don't think it would be wise for clergymen to get involved in
partisan politics, starting at the precinct level, or to become activists
in the two major parties."

Higgins curiously underplayed his observations about Vietnam following a trip to the Far East in 1969. In a column dated
December 29, one which seems to represent a major turning point
for him on the Vietnam issue, he spent most of three typewritten
pages commenting on foreign travel in general (unlike Cardinal
Newman, whose views on the subject he cited, he couldn't get enough
of it) and on the efficiency of the Japanese. He directed his few
Vietnam-related observations along broad lines related to the
American presence in the Far East as a whole:

"My one overriding impression of the trip is that the so-called
American presence throughout the Far East—and not only in
Vietnam—is much too great and is more widely resented than I had
been led to believe. Every time I saw an American military installa-
tion, and you keep stumbling over them all the time in the Far East,
I couldn't help but ask myself how I would have reacted, as an
American, and how the people of the Far East would react if these
were Soviet instead of American installations.

"I think I would have reacted very badly. In saying this, I
am not suggesting that the United States can or should pull out of
the Far East completely and retreat into a kind of neo-isolationism,
nor do I think that the majority of the people in the Far East would

want us to do so. On the other hand, clearly aside from the issue of Vietnam, there must be a limit to the extent to which we can or should get involved in the Pacific area, and I wonder if we haven't already exceeded that limit."

On May 3, 1971 Higgins wrote that he had mixed reaction to a Holy Week editorial which had appeared jointly in *Commonweal, The National Catholic Reporter, The Christian Century,* and *Christianity and Crisis,* and which accused the United States of "repeating the crucifixion of Christ" through its policies in Southeast Asia.

"I agree with the overall thrust of this composite editorial and, needless to add, prayerfully hope that it will have the desired effect," he said. "On the other hand, I am frank to state, not in a critical vein, but simply for purposes of discussion, that I have certain queasy reservations about the highly theologized and moralistic rhetoric of the editorial and about some of its political overtones."

Specifically, Higgins wondered why the editorial had been overly critical of only Presidents Nixon and Johnson, and not of Presidents Kennedy and Eisenhower, since the roots of the problem extended that far back. Those thoughts were advanced not to make a villain of Kennedy, Higgins explained: "To the contrary, they are meant to suggest that perhaps the time has come for all of us to stop looking for villains, and, more specifically, to stop judging other people's inner motives. Indeed I would even be prepared to argue that our penchant for judging individuals, and judging them very harshly, is one of the less attractive and more worrisome signs of the troubled times in which we live."

Along those lines, he concluded the column with a none-too-gentle swipe at Jesuit Father Daniel Berrigan, who had made much, in an interview, over Johnson's visit to a church before ordering the bombing of North Vietnam to begin. The experience, Berrigan said, had enabled Johnson to return "clothed in a kind of divine approval for the murder of people in cities. . . ."

"That's a terrible cruel thing to say about any individual, even a wartime president, and how I wish, for his own sake and for our sake as well, that Father Berrigan hadn't said it," Higgins responded. "Criticism, even brutal criticism, of a given president and his public policies is one thing. Presuming to judge his motives and pretending to know what prayer means to him in the deepest recesses of his heart and soul is something else again. I think we had better leave that to God.''

The final Yardstick column devoted to Vietnam appeared on October 16, 1972, and in it Higgins had clearly come a long way from the all but unqualified support he had expressed for America's Vietnamese policy seven years earlier. He urged those planning the following year's Respect Life Program (the first of which had just been held) to address the Vietnam war more specifically and ''condemn it as severely and as pointedly as we have always condemned abortion.''

''There is certainly nothing vague or theoretical,'' he said, ''about the killing that has been going on in Vietnam for more years than most of us like to remember and unfortunately is still going on. . . .''

He quoted a *Wall Street Journal* report which said that if America proportionately lost as much of its population as had Vietnam in the war, our nation would have had two million dead and six million homeless—''a staggering figure,'' Higgins said. He added:

''So far as this writer is concerned, there is enough information in that one sentence to warrant the conclusion that the war in Vietnam is an evil of almost incalculable proportions. Please God, it will have come to a merciful end before we enter upon a second Respect Life Week in the fall of 1973. . . . I am not suggesting for a moment that we should soft-pedal our opposition to abortion. If anything, I think we should redouble our efforts to sensitize our people to this terrible evil. On the other hand, I am equally convinced that we will simply have to be consistent in the statement of our moral principles if we hope to retain even a shred of credibility. Abortion is admittedly a clear violation of the moral law. But so is the bombing of innocent people in Vietnam. Why not say so, at long last, in quite specific terms?''

In view of his abiding interest in Catholic-Jewish relations and his sympathetic concern for the progress of the state of Israel, it is not surprising that Higgins has devoted many Yardstick columns to Middle Eastern events. More often as not, however, he dealt with specific crises only in relation to wider topics, as he did in writing (June 30, 1967) about Israel's war with the United Arab Republic, which had taken place a few weeks earlier. The column responded to criticism of the Catholic Church in the United States, offered by Rabbis Balfour Brickner and Arthur Hertzberg, for failing to speak out more vigorously on behalf of Israel.

Despite his personal friendship with Brickner and his respect for Hertzberg, Higgins pulled no punches in refuting their argument.

"Reluctantly," he said, "I am compelled to say. . .that their 'what-have-you-done-for-us lately?' criticism of the Catholic Church in the U.S., whether they realize it or not, is a form of ecumenical or interreligious blackmail."

Their criticism, he continued, meant that in order to enter into religious dialogue with the American Jewish community, the American bishops must declare support for the position that Israel's struggle constituted a "religious, not to say a holy war." He added: "I regard this as a form of blackmail pure and simple."

His own credentials were in order, he said—when it came to backing the Israeli position in the war. "I did not, however, regard it as a religious, much less a 'holy' war, and would have felt no obligation to take the side of Israel on 'religious' grounds if I had not been persuaded, on the grounds of justice and international law, that the cause was basically right."

Higgins concluded by observing that he understood the depth of commitment most Jews feel to Israel, no matter where they live. He added that he understood the desire of people like Brickner and Hertzberg to expect him to join with them in supporting Israel's right to exist as a free and independent nation. However, he continued:

"On the other hand, I do not think that they have any right to expect me or anybody else to make a religion out of Israel or to canonize its leaders or its past and present policies. This I simply will not do—period. I say this very bluntly, not to disrupt, but hopefully to advance the cause of Catholic-Jewish relations. In other words, I am firmly persuaded that respectful, but outspoken, honesty is by far the best policy in the field of interreligious affairs."

It was hardly a typical Higgins commentary on Israel. Generally he was supportive and understanding of Israel's particular problems, encouraging in the solutions it proposed. He regularly took on Israel's critics when he saw reason to question their motives, as he did when he challenged Father Daniel Berrigan in January 1974. Before a decidedly pro-Arab audience, Berrigan had accused Israel of criminal imperialism and racism, resulting in charges—both from Jewish and Christian leaders—that the speech was blatantly anti-

Semitic. Higgins said he would take Berrigan at his word if the Jesuit claimed the speech might have been anti-Zionist but not anti-Semitic, but hardly hid his personal reservations: "His speech was an extremely shoddy performance from almost every conceivable point of view and, objectively speaking, came perilously close to being anti-Semitic in tone as well as in content. Closer, in fact, than any recent public statement by an American commentator on the ins-and-outs of the Israeli-Arab conflict. . . . His name is mud in the Jewish community, and for this he has no one but himself to blame."

The column drew flak, as a subsequent Yardstick (February 18, 1974) reported in detail:

"I have received more than the average number of hate letters clobbering me for my remarks about Berrigan's speech, and at the same time viciously attacking Israel. Frankly, these letters tend to confirm my long-standing impression that, in the case of many of Israel's more simplistic and intemperate critics, the line between anti-Zionism and anti-Semitism is so thin as to be almost imperceptible. In all honesty, I must say that with unsolicited friends like the people who have irately rushed to his defense in response to my recent column, Father Berrigan needs no enemies."

A number of Yardstick columns have commented on the Vatican's position in regard to Israel, including one on January 13, 1975, that regretted the failure of the Vatican's then-new Commission on Relations with Judaism to include a reference to Israel in its statement on Catholic-Jewish relations (as noted in the previous chapter).

The following year, Vatican participation in a Catholic-Moslem dialogue at Tripoli took an embarrassing turn when two of the final resolutions that were adopted called Zionism a "racial, aggressive movement foreign to Palestine" and reaffirmed "the national rights of the Palestinian people and their right to return to their homeland, and affirm the Arabism of the city of Jerusalem and the rejection of Judaization, partition and internationalization projects."

It wasn't clear, Higgins said in a column dated February 23, 1976, how the Vatican participants "happened to get trapped into voting for these extremely offensive resolutions," but despite Vatican efforts to set the record straight, the subject was sure to come up at a forthcoming Catholic-Jewish dialogue in Jerusalem. The resolutions, he added, "serve as a reminder that hostility to Israel on the part of all too many Arab leaders, religious and secular alike, is virulent and unrelenting." However, he said, there was hope: "This has been a nerve-wracking year for the Jewish people throughout the world, with the United Nations and UNESCO both having indulged in a type of fanatical anti-Zionism which, from the Jewish point of view and from mine, can hardly be distinguished from anti-Semitism. For this reason, the Vatican's prompt rejection of the anti-Israel resolutions adopted at the Tripoli meeting must have caused a sigh of relief in Jewish circles throughout the world."

Higgins held no brief for those he perceived as out-and-out enemies of Israel: Archbishop Hilarion Capucci, for example, or Yasser Arafat and the Palestine Liberation Organization.

But he applauded all efforts to settle the protracted Middle East crisis by peaceful means, and particularly praised Israel for making concessions, and abiding by its word to keep them, as part of the Camp David accord. Under terms of the accord initiated by President Carter and agreed to by Israeli Prime Minister Menachem Begin and Egyptian President Anwar Sadat, Israel would return to Egyptian control land it had acquired in battle, including the Sinai Desert. Its formal return in 1982 inspired a Higgins column, dated May 17, which referred to the event as "one of the most significant deeds of peace in this century of unremitting warfare."

"It has become fashionable to blame Israel in general and the Begin government in particular for all the woes of the Middle East," Higgins said. "Forgotten is the fact that it has been the Arab nations, not Israel, which have started the conflicts there.

"Forgotten too is that it is the Arab nations and the PLO, not Israel, which have jeopardized the Camp David process by their refusal to recognize and negotiate within its broad, inclusive framework. . . .

"When Israel risked its survival by handing over the Sinai—a huge chunk of strategically vital land, not to mention uncounted millions in investment and oil revenue—in return for a promise, many editorialists used the occasion as an excuse for another round of gratuitous advice on what more Israel should do. Scarcely a word was heard that perhaps it's time for the Arabs too to replace the rhetoric of war with the actions of peace."

The return of the Sinai, Higgins said, "is a statement of the highest form of diplomacy, a risk requiring the noblest sort of moral courage," and should serve as "a model for all of us who claim to hold peace dear." It also shifted the burden of proof of peaceful intentions. He concluded: "It is now up to the other actors in the Middle East drama, the Arab states and the Palestinians, to demonstrate what they are willing to risk for peace."

In recent years Higgins has touched on a number of other international issues in The Yardstick, two of them coming in for special and fairly regular comment: the 1977-1978 Belgrade Conference on Security and Cooperation in Europe, and the 1981-1982 crisis in Poland, particularly as it affected the Solidarity labor union.

The Belgrade meeting, known popularly as the Conference on Human Rights, was one Higgins saw from close up. The chairman of the American delegation was his old friend, Arthur Goldberg, who invited Higgins to serve as an official consultant, an honor he happily accepted. Convened to review the implementation of the 1975 Helsinki Conference, especially those resolutions guaranteeing the exercise of human rights within the signatory nations, the Belgrade Conference had more than its share of critics.

Higgins reported on one possible cause of the criticism in a column dated December 26, 1977, just after the conference recessed for several weeks. "Various ethnic and minority groups which are monitoring the conference may become so disillusioned by the slowness of the Belgrade process they may be tempted to conclude—mistakenly—that it is a sham," he said. "They may become disillusioned by the inability of the conference to produce measurable results of a dramatic nature. But I am optimistic. . . ."

He reflected the scope of the difficulty in maintaining his optimism in another column (January 23, 1978) as the conference resumed: "I would be hesitant to conclude that the Helsinki process will be doomed if the Eastern European nations refuse to come to terms with the letter and the spirit of the Helsinki compact on. . .human rights. To the contrary, I would argue that their violation of the human rights provision of the act makes it all the more necessary to keep the Belgrade process going. I think it would be a serious mistake to give up prematurely, no matter how limited the results. . . . The important thing is to keep the review process going while, at the same time, relentlessly holding the Soviet Union and its satellites accountable for their implementation of the Helsinki Final Act. To give into despair by calling off the Belgrade process prematurely would play right into the hands of the Soviet bloc. We can be certain that the Soviet Union and its satellites would be overjoyed to get out from under the Belgrade review process and to forget about the implementation of the human rights provisions of the Final Act. We cannot afford to accommodate them.''

The conference ended on what was for most participants and observers a discouraging note: faced with a threat of a Soviet veto, it omitted mention of human rights in its final document. The decision to concur with other participants in approving the document had not been an easy one for the American delegation, Higgins said; had the Americans exercised their own veto they would have cut short any future hope to bring about international accord on the rights issue. The delegation acted well, Higgins said in a March 20, 1978 column which praised their diligence and patience:

"There is no reason for the U.S. delegates to be discouraged by the apparently meager results of their tireless work. They have planted a tiny seed, the seed of peace, justice, and human rights. One day, like the mustard seed which the Lord himself used as a simile to describe the growth of his Kingdom, it will spring up and send out great branches so that people now oppressed may find freedom and security in its shade. When that day comes, it will be said of them, as of all who work for peace based on justice and human rights: 'Blessed are the peacemakers, for they shall be called the children of God.' In this imperfect world, no greater tribute can be paid to any man or woman.''

Higgins's interest in Solidarity was personal as well—he was the homilist at the Mass opening the union's 1981 convention in Gdansk—and it was bolstered by his understanding of the paths European unionism had taken during the twentieth century. In 1980, as the crisis between Poland's government and its labor force was beginning to intensify, Higgins used a Yardstick column (September 8) to trace the growth of "so-called unions" destined to disappear into monopolistic organizations controlled by the state. That was what had happened in Poland, he wrote, until the emergence of Solidarity:

"The courageous strikers in Poland have challenged the totalitarian system at its roots. The historic significance of their demand for trade-union autonomy can hardly be exaggerated. . . . The Polish strikers, by their courage, have won the admiration of the entire noncommunist world. They also have started a process which cannot be reversed.''

A year later, he delivered a homily at a concelebrated Mass during Solidarity's convention in Gdansk, pointedly avoiding direct involvement in the dispute between the union and government. He did, however, quote at length from Pope John Paul II's endorsement of labor unions in the encyclical *Laborem Exercens,* and extended "the hand of fellowship and solidarity" on behalf of the Catholic social movement in the United States and in the name of the American labor movement.

(The movement was to have been represented in a more direct way, with Lane Kirkland, AFL-CIO president, scheduled to head a delegation from the organization. However, the Polish authorities denied visas to the group, and it fell to Higgins, attending the convention as a private citizen, to distribute copies of a talk which was to have been delivered by Kirkland.)

The homily Higgins gave looked forward to a U.S. visit by Lech Walesa, Solidarity's leader, but the trip never came off. Three months after Higgins spoke, Poland's communist government declared martial law, formally suppressed Solidarity, and soon after placed Walesa in confinement, holding him for several months. Higgins referred to the tragic series of events in a homily at a Mass in St. Matthew's Cathedral, Washington, on December 12, 1982, offered in support of Solidarity. He paid a special tribute to Walesa:

"Jailed for almost a year under conditions of complete solitude and extreme psychological pressure that would have broken the spirit of a less courageous man and might have tempted him to call it quits, Walesa has kept full faith with Solidarity and, please God, will live to see it reestablished within the not-too-distant future. . . . Upon his release from prison several weeks ago, he said that he had sought an agreement with the Polish regime but not 'on my knees. . . . ' Walesa still believes, as he told the press a month ago, and as he told the Polish government last week, that in the long run there can be no retreat from the Gdansk agreements that led to Solidarity's birth. 'The spirit of the Gdansk agreements,' he said, 'is immortal. It cannot be defeated.' Spoken like the true son of a courageous people.''

Too many Americans, Higgins continued, were complaining

that Solidarity had "gone too far" and left the Polish government no choice but to enforce a crackdown. Happily, he said, that was not the case with the American labor movement, which had continued to give all-out support to Solidarity.

He also called attention to what he referred to as highly selective support for trade unionism on the part of the American press in general and the conservative press in particular, both of which had given Solidarity extremely favorable coverage:

"Their extensive and almost uniformly favorable coverage of Solidarity is highly commendable, of course, but it contrasts sharply with the lukewarm support that many of them have given to the right of workers living under right-wing dictatorships in many parts of the world to enjoy the same rights that the Polish workers are demanding of their own communist government.

"Why this double standard? Why is a violation of workers' rights in communist Poland more reprehensible than a similar violation of workers' rights under a right-wing dictatorship?. . . Hypocrisy may be putting it too strongly. . .(but) Pope John Paul II will have none of this selective indignation. In one of his many public allocutions protesting the suppression of Solidarity, he said very pointedly that 'wherever in the world, in whatever state or system, there has taken place a similar event it ought to provoke a proper reaction dictated by concern for man and respect for his basic rights.' "

One of the points Higgins emphasized in his references to Solidarity, repeated in a Yardstick column December 20, 1982, was the organization's intimate relationship with the Church, a relationship from which both partners seemed to draw strength. It reflected his long-standing belief that the Church must be a presence in the world as well as in the temple, helping to guide mankind in its social, economic, and political deliberations. In few areas is that presence as critical as it is in regard to international issues of justice and peace, and it is in that context that Higgins has periodically called attention to the pastoral role both of the universal Church and the American hierarchy in addressing specific concerns.

After a 1966 seminar in which some participants expressed disappointment that the Vatican Council had not gone further in its treatment of war and peace in the *Pastoral Constitution on the*

Church in the Modern World, Higgins used The Yardstick (May 16) to remind them of the document's purpose. "This particular conciliar document," he said, "is, by definition, a 'pastoral' constitution. Its purpose is not to say the last word on current problems from the point of view of Catholic theology, but rather to call attention to certain practical steps that men of good will can take to limit international conflicts and to build a stable and lasting peace. . . . Faithful to the spirit of Pope John XXIII, the document refrains from sterile criticism of individuals and institutions and concentrates singlemindedly on its pastoral task. . . ."

That does not mean, however, that the Church's moral leadership on issues of war and peace must be restricted to bland generalities, even if the course it proposes is at odds with that of the particular government under which it lives. When the American bishops were criticized for doing just that with their anti-Vietnam war statement of 1971 (as they would be a decade later during deliberations on their war and peace pastoral letter), commentators called it a radical departure from the past. The Catholic hierarchy, it was assumed, had always, out of patriotism, backed the American government on issues of war and peace.

Not so, Higgins pointed out in a column dated February 14, 1972. He cited the period just before and just after the United States' entry into World War II, when isolationist sentiment ran high within the Catholic community and among its leaders.

"For whatever reasons," Higgins wrote, "the position of a large segment of the Catholic population and of the Catholic hierarchy was not one of unquestioning compliance with, but, to the contrary, one of open opposition to President Roosevelt's interventionist policy. No one, of course, knew this better than the president himself, and to say that he was deeply concerned about it would be putting it mildly."

As one illustration, Higgins pointed to the case of Bishop Joseph Hurley—then of the St. Augustine (Florida) diocese and a one-time member of the Vatican diplomatic corps—who delivered a "dramatic" radio address in 1941 calling for U.S. intervention in the war, suggesting that the timing and circumstances be left to Roosevelt's judgment. "To say that the roof fell in on Hurley because of this rather sensational speech would be an understatement," Higgins said. The reaction of American Catholics to the talk was highly unfavorable, and no bishops came forward to defend it.

(But, Higgins noted, "as a young priest studying in Washington at the time, I strongly supported Bishop Hurley.")

The incident, Higgins concluded, "seems to suggest that our current impatience with the American bishops to declare themselves on Vietnam shouldn't lead us into the trap of saying without qualification that American Catholics have always blindly followed the lead of the American government in matters of war and peace. The record will not support such a sweeping statement, at least in the case of World War II."

Finally, Higgins has noted that painstaking patience and perseverance are indispensable qualities for the world's true peacemakers, rather than those who clamor for instant solutions to complex problems. He paid a touching tribute to all who labor in that vein for peace in a column written July 8, 1968, after the United Nations General Assembly had approved a treaty on the non-proliferation of nuclear weapons.

Higgins attended the White House ceremony at which some 50 nations signed the treaty, and noted with satisfaction that seated in a place of honor, near President Johnson and next to Secretary of State Dean Rusk, was William C. Foster, then director of the U.S. Arms Control and Disarmament Agency. Three years earlier, he recalled, he had taken part in a seminar on peace in which Foster gave a progress report on East-West efforts to stem the arms race, a report which, because of the slow pace it projected, drew a lackadaisical response.

Seeing Foster in this new setting, Higgins said, made him realize "that while many other Americans had been hitting the headlines with dramatic public statements calling for instant peace, this man, for three long years, had been closeted, month after dreary month, in a conference room in Geneva, Switzerland, patiently working behind the scenes and completely out of the limelight on the almost infinitely complex details of the treaty." Such men, he said, "deserve the sincere thanks of a world which is sick unto death of war."

As Foster signed the document, Higgins said, "I thought of him with profound esteem, as a man who, for years, has been doing a supreme and largely unheralded work of love for mankind."

He concluded: "Other men, working for some cause in a more spectacular way, will continue to receive the lion's share of publicity. So be it. In my judgment, however, the real heroes of the peace movement are the William Fosters of this world who are willing to devote all of their time and energy and talents to the cause of peace, not in dramatic fits and starts, but around the clock, year after year, with the realistic understanding that while their efforts will not eliminate war in one fell swoop, hopefully they will bring us just a little bit closer, one step at a time, to the cherished goal of international peace.''

CHAPTER TWELVE

A MAN OF THE CHURCH

GEORGE HIGGINS'S CLOSE FRIENDS, TALKING ABOUT HIM, strike remarkably similar chords. They make the same associations: his versatility, his intellect. His sure knowledge of the labor scene, and the breadth of his friendships in it. They outdo each other in describing late nights—early mornings, really—where the socializing and the squabbling and the needling goes on for hour after hour, with Higgins at the center, throwing off sparks. In each account he emerges at breakfast time with perhaps two or three hours' sleep, fresh, relaxed, and anxious for a first look at the morning paper.

Unfailingly, they mention one other thing. Be sure that you recognize his spirituality, his deep and all-abiding love for the Church, they will tell an interviewer. Find out what you can about his prayer life, says one friend; it's a model for the priests who know him.

249

"It's very difficult for me to comment on that," he said when asked about it. "All I've ever tried to do was to keep up a prayer life, and I suppose that's what they're talking about."

The roots of the faith that others admire in Higgins go back to home: to his parents, to the reading his father so carefully fostered, to his early education, and to Father Nawn, the parish priest in LaGrange who befriended young George and made his library available to him.

His personal expression of that faith is a side of Higgins that the public rarely sees even indirectly; he almost never writes about spiritual life in The Yardstick, for example. But it is the same deep spirituality that forms the foundation for his understanding of the social concerns about which he writes, buttressed by the gospel and the social teachings of the Church. Time and again he has pointed to the unique role of the Mass, the Church's central act of worship, in forming socially active Catholics.

In the years just before the Second Vatican Council, when interest in the liturgical movement was at a peak, Higgins was a regular speaker at "liturgy weeks" and other gatherings where he urged an understanding of the social-action function of the Mass. He gently chided liturgists of the day who overlooked the demands of the social gospel, but at the same time expressed regrets that some of those in the social action field were slow to acknowledge the liturgy as the fountainhead of their efforts.

Higgins served, in a real sense, as a bridge between the groups. In talks and in his columns, he pointed to the primacy of the Mass in a democratic society, where people were united not as isolated individuals but as brothers and sisters living and working together for the good of all. In the same way, he explained, those at Mass were present as members of a group, acting, receiving, worshiping together with their fellow Catholics. The sense of fellowship in relation to all that was fostered by such community worship should be carried over into the political order, he said.

At a liturgy week program in Worcester, Mass., in August 1955, he noted that the liturgy will not supply a perfect theory for specific political action. "But," he continued, "it can and should spiritually prepare the Catholics of the United States to take the lead in developing such a theory as one more step forward in mankind's eternal quest for a more perfect community in the political order. The liturgy and more specifically the Mass-liturgy is the great source of those virtues of justice and charity.''

On May 8 and 15, 1961, he developed the theme further in consecutive Yardstick columns, highlighting once again his understanding of the Sacrifice of the Mass:

"Social reform will not be effective unless there is a widespread reform of morals. . . . For Catholics, an indispensable means of effecting this necessary reform of morals is an active and intelligent participation in the liturgy of the Church. It is the Mass that matters most, even in the political order and especially in a democracy."

Given that perception of the role of the Church in forming people's political agenda, it is no surprise that Higgins has devoted much of his writing to reflections on its priests, its people, and its general state of health. Some of his finest reporting on that account appeared in his behind-the-scenes coverage of the 1971 Synod of Bishops, which was one of the most eagerly-awaited and closely followed of the regular convocations of bishops in synod that came about as a result of the Vatican Council.

The 1971 synod had twin topics. One of them was the justice in the world, but it was the second, the ministerial priesthood, which had captured the public imagination. It was a period few Catholics could have imagined a decade earlier. Angry priests were excoriating the Church, impatient priests were demanding fundamental changes in the ministry, disaffected priests were simply giving up. Many other priests were upset and bewildered by it all, and a sizeable portion of the Catholic public was bitterly intolerant of a group it saw as traitorous. All turned to the synod to see how the Church of Rome would deal with what was becoming an increasingly serious problem, for many a scandal: the explosive state of the Catholic priesthood.

To help the bishops in their deliberations, a number of priest-auditors would be present, including two from the United States. The American bishops asked priests to give them two slates of names, one for diocesan clergy, the other for religious priests, from which to make their selections, and Higgins's name headed the list in the first category when the votes were in. (The others were Father Frank

Bonnike, then president of the National Federation of Priests' Councils; Msgr. Bernard Law, who became bishop of Springfield-Cape Girardeau and later archbishop of Boston; Andrew Greeley; and Msgr. Colin MacDonald.) Higgins was duly named, and along with his religious-order counterpart, Passionist Barnabas Ahern, went to the synod, not only to serve as an auditor, but to cover it as well. It turned out to be a first-rate job of analytical reporting.

Columns from October through December 1971 provided a running commentary on the synod's progress, beginning (October 11) with the observation that a four-week synod could hardly be expected to solve what admittedly was the growing crisis of the declining number of priests. "I don't think we would look to the synod for a miracle," he said. "We should have learned from the experience of Vatican II that councils and synods, far from settling problems once and for all, tend to shake things up even more and to generate new problems of their own, at least in the short run. I like to think, of course, that they do this under the inspiration of the Holy Spirit."

He had mixed feelings about the synod's progress once deliberations got under way. Topics other than clerical celibacy were being discussed, he noted with satisfaction (although he was equally satisfied that the bishop-delegates seemed at ease in airing that issue). He worried at first that the bishops didn't fully appreciate the scope of the crisis in the priesthood, but that fear vanished quickly. And early criticism that the bishops were going too slowly faded as well. "I, for one, would like to see them slow down a bit," he said in the October 18 Yardstick. "Listening to Latin speeches for more than five hours a day (with all sorts of extracurricular meetings thrown in for good measure) can get to be a bit of a grind after a while."

The key topics concerning the bishops about the priesthood, apart from the persistent questions on celibacy, were the need for greater diversity of ministries, the relationship between bishops and priests, the involvement of priests in secular occupations, especially party politics, and the granting of more autonomy to regional conferences of bishops. Ecumenism, too, was a related issue, one that Higgins felt had gotten short shrift. There were no Protestant or Orthodox observers present, he noted with regret, despite the positive experience of Vatican II. Floor discussions, he added, rarely considered the experience of other faiths in dealing with ministerial matters.

In his October 25 column, Higgins put to rest rumors that

the role of the priest-auditors such as himself was more symbolic than effective. "The priest auditors are not only permitted but encouraged to speak their peace, with perfect freedom and complete frankness concerning every issue on the synod agenda. In brief, they are being accorded exactly the same right to speak as the synodal members themselves, without regard to ecclesiastical rank. . . . They do not pretend to be able to 'represent' the clergy of their respective countries (much less the clergy of the universal Church) but they are trying to the best of their ability—and with some success, I believe—to convey to the synodal Fathers an accurate reading of the varying points of view of the clergy on all matters under discussion. In addition, they have had countless opportunities to confer, both formally and informally, with individual bishops and groups of bishops. . . ."

On November 1, Higgins paid tribute to a synod speech given by his old friend, Msgr. Pietro Pavan, the rector of Lateran Seminary in Rome and a man Higgins described as "one of the world's leading authorities in the area of Christian social teaching." Impatient with press criticism of the synod's progress on the subject of world justice—criticism he saw in his own daily sampling of eight or ten English, French, and Italian newspapers—Higgins said the critics were confusing the synod with the universal Church. "As I write this column," he said, "I have before me six or eight newspaper clippings which say, in effect, that the Church will lose all credibility if the synod fails to move beyond the realm of principle and get down to particular cases. . . . Everyone agrees that the time has come for the Church to stand up and be counted in the area of world justice and world peace. But what is the Church, or better still, who are the Church?"

That, he continued, was the question addressed so effectively by Msgr. Pavan, whose talk pointed out that while the Church does not have direct competence in the temporal order it still must work for justice in the world. This it does, he continued, by constantly proclaiming the Gospel, by insisting on the demands of justice, by denouncing violations of justice, by education, by organizing programs designed to help the weak and the poor, and by forming the faithful to take part in political action aimed at achieving justice. While the Church does not involve itself directly in politics, Pavan explained, it should inspire the faithful to do so to work for justice, acting apart from Church authority.

Higgins disagreed with critics who saw the talk as an academic exercise. "If the synod were to ignore the central point that Pavan was trying to make," he said, "it could easily succumb to the temptation of trying to make the Church look good by promising the moon, so to speak. For my own part, I think this would be a most 'impractical' thing for the synod to do and would be a sure sign that the theology of Vatican II still hasn't gotten into the bloodstream of the Church."

The following week Higgins combined some revealing personal insights into the extent of the synod workload with less-than-enthusiastic comments on what it seemed to be ready to produce. On the first point, he scarcely contained his glee at the announcement of a three-and-a-half-day weekend as synod deliberations neared their completion. Of the "bone-weary" bishop delegates, he said:

"They (and the 20 priest auditors, present company included) reacted to this unexpected favor from on high with as much giddy excitement as though they were a bunch of restless teenagers who had been locked up in a no-nonsense, nose-to-the-grindstone boarding school for weeks on end and really hadn't expected to be released, even for a breather, until the end of the semester. Most of the bishops took advantage of the long weekend to catch up on their reading, or to do a little sightseeing, or, if the truth must be told, to enjoy a leisurely round of golf at scenic Acqua Santa on the outskirts of the Eternal City."

Significant minorities among the delegates were dissatisfied with the drafts of the two synod documents, he said, and sentiment seemed to be growing for a revision of the ground rules for the synodal process. However, he said (November 8):

"There are a good number of bishops who feel that the synod, as it is presently constituted, will still be inadequate even if its procedures are improved or tightened up. These bishops [and, inferentially, Higgins as well] are persuaded that a merely consultative synod is not an adequate implementation of the theological principle of collegiality. They feel, in other words, that the synod should become a representative assembly through which the college of bishops could exercise their governing responsibility. As of now, the Church Universal is governed by the pope through the Roman Curia. The bishops referred to above think that it would be more in keeping with the New Testament if the Church were governed by the synod, under the leadership of the Holy Father. In that case the Curia would be dependent upon the synod and not upon the Holy Father alone. It will take time for this to happen, but the sooner the better, in this writer's judgment."

Being a participant in the synod might have deepened Higgins's disappointment in the reviews it received in the press. Higgins told Yardstick readers on November 15 that he digested "a baker's dozen of those post-mortem articles" on his way home. "Frankly," he said, "when I finished them, halfway across the Atlantic, I was so depressed that I had to ask the Sabena stewardess to bring me another martini to lift my normally optimistic spirits."

The articles that disturbed Higgins most were those (including *Newsweek's* and *Time's*) which concluded that the synod was not only a disappointment but a total failure. Even worse, he said, was one which charged that the synod was an out-and-out fraud, rigged by the Curia from the start. That was the best argument he had seen, he continued, for admitting the press to future synod sessions—so that "more jaundiced reporters. . .might have tempered their cynicism if they had been permitted to cover the synod from the inside." The "rigged" synod they were describing was not the one he had seen "on an average of five and a half hours a day for a period of approximately five weeks," he added.

"This writer, for one, has had all the cynicism he can take from his friends in the Fourth Estate," he concluded. "The Fourth Estate is not a sacred cow, although, unfortunately, it sometimes gives the impression that it foolishly expects to be treated as such. . . . While I have great respect for newspaper reporters and columnists and really enjoy working with them, I was not greatly impressed (with notable exception) by their coverage of the synod. And if that be treason, my friends in the Fourth Estate will have to make the most of it."

The Higgins reaction was no less scratchy when Father Andrew Greeley produced his own synod assessment, a negative one, to be sure, a few weeks later.

Greeley's own column had criticized both Higgins's evaluation and the synod itself. "Measured by the needs and problems of the Church today," he had said, "there is no way that the synod can be described as anything but a dismal flop." It was sad, he said, to see Msgr. Higgins "defending the indefensible"; he noted that

"the press didn't create the flop, the Fathers of the synod did."
It was the kind of challenge Higgins relishes.

"I must admit that I enjoy a good clean fight as well as the next man," he said on December 20. "Moreover I wouldn't want Father Greeley to get the idea that I am a patsy or a complete pushover and most certainly wouldn't want him to think, for a moment, that I agree with his rather free-wheeling interpretation of my column."

The record would show, Higgins continued, that a number of qualified observers felt that the synod, whatever its imperfections, was anything but a flop. He quoted from a number of them in the liberal or progressive camp, conceding that they were not necessarily right and Greeley wrong. "It simply means," he concluded, "that there is room for honest disagreement among honorable men about the results of the synod. Q.E.D."

Several columns early in 1972 analyzed the synod document on world justice in more detail (but said little of that on the ministry, which reaffirmed the discipline of celibacy and restated traditional ministerial roles). In both cases, Higgins said, the synod took middle-of-the-road positions.

"It stressed," he said, "the right and the duty of the Church, and of the ordained priest, to preach and give witness to justice at every level of society, to denounce violations of justice, to help promote the full development of persons and of nations—and to do all that this involves without fear or favor. But, it also noted that the institutional Church 'is not alone responsible for justice in the world' and has neither the competence nor the responsibility to offer concrete solutions to particular social problems."

The synod pointed to the laity as carrying the primary responsibility for effecting the necessary structural changes that would bring justice to society, and urged priests to keep their distance from partisan politics, Higgins said. Its cautious approach to far-ranging questions had drawn criticism from both conservatives and liberals, he noted with regret.

"My own feeling," he said (January 17, 1972), "is that what the synod said about the social mission of the Church and the specific role of the ordained priest in the field of social reform is reasonably adequate as a statement of general principles but is not and was never intended to be the final word on this matter. The synod—to its credit, in this writer's opinion—deliberately refrained from getting bogged down in particulars. Fully conscious of the fact that social, economic and political conditions vary enormously from one part of the world to the other, the synod made no pretense at being able to come up with a set of definitive formulae or propositions which could automatically be applied across the board, without reference to local need and circumstances. . . .

"It remains, then, for the local churches to take up where the synod left off and to assume their own responsibility in the area of social reform. . . .   There is nothing in the synod document on world justice to prevent the local churches from fulfilling their responsibilities in this regard. Critics of the document notwithstanding, it's a set of forward-looking guidelines aimed at promoting an all-out effort on the part of the entire Church in behalf of social justice."

The synod had taken place in the midst of the turmoil that engulfed the Church in the years immediately following the Second Vatican Council, an ongoing storm that obviously was responsible for much of the criticism directed against the synod Fathers. Higgins used his column and his influence during those years as a mediating force, counseling patience to those for whom the changes in Church life came too slowly, and understanding to those who found the same changes impossible to accept.

"Since rapid change, even in the area of religion, is, whether we like it or not, a fact of life, it makes good sense for Church leaders to try to prepare their people to cope with it as mature Christians instead of wasting their time and energy lamenting the inevitable as men who have lost their nerve, so to speak, and have given up on Providence," he wrote on October 23, 1972. "This is not to say that change for the sake of change is either necessary or desirable, much less that confusion for its own sake is something to be welcomed or even tolerated. It is to say, however, that change—more rapid and more far-reaching than the Church has ever experienced in the past—is most certainly to be expected and very probably would have come to pass if Vatican II had never been convened."

Higgins dealt gently with angry Catholic critics of the Church, those who, he said, had allowed themselves in the wake of the Council "to become obsessed by the past failures and mistakes of the Church."

James Colaianni's 1968 book, *The Catholic Left: The Crisis of Radicalism in the Church* (Chilton), attacked "clericalism" in the Church, but Higgins charged (July 22, 1968) that Colaianni himself was guilty of the same offense. He did this, he said, "not to twit Mr. Colaianni," but "because, rightly or wrongly, I happen to think that the shoe fits the Catholic left very snugly." By clericalism, he continued, he meant "an excessive, not to say obsessive preoccupation with the clerical or hierarchical aspects of the Church." Unquestionably, Higgins said, individual churchmen had made serious errors from time to time in conducting Church affairs. "The point is," he noted, "that Mr. Colaianni just can't seem to get them off his mind and that, instead of telling us what the Catholic Left has done or proposes to do to clean up the intolerable mess that the bishops have allegedly made of things, he prefers to spend the better part of his time talking about the mess itself." He concluded: "Candid criticism of the ecclesiastical establishment is perfectly in order. But, to my way of thinking, there is a vast difference between candid criticism on the one hand and obsessive criticism on the other."

A year later (July 21, 1969) Higgins struck a similar note when he discussed a new book by John O'Connor that he called a "rip-snortin', sock-it-to-'em report on the 'radical split in the American Church' over the issue of freedom and authority." Of *The People Versus Rome* (Random House), Higgins said simply, "It's the angriest book of the year on this or any other subject."

O'Connor had edited two diocesan newspapers (in San Francisco and Wilmington) and was known as an outspoken advocate of lay responsibility and shared authority in the Church. In this book, as Higgins said, he "showed no mercy." Repeating the point he made in discussing the Colaianni book, he added that while "righteous indignation" is understandable, it requires a sense of proportion.

Higgins's reservations were tempered with a measure of encouragement: "While Mr. O'Connor's fiercely aggressive bedside manner will never win him an AMA award as the most compassionate and most patient and most understanding practitioner of the year 1969, and while I personally have the impression that he has yet to master the difficult art of counting to ten before he puts a sentence down on paper, I admire his frankness, his unyielding devotion to the truth as he sees it, and his determination, come what may, to call the shots as he sees them."

O'Connor's most important contribution was his call for openness within the Catholic press, Higgins said. As he concluded the column: "The Church will irreparably damage its own credibility unless and until it recognizes, in fact as well as theory, the need for an informed public opinion in the Church and, to that end, the need for the fullest possible measure of freedom for the Catholic press and the need for greater sensitivity and greater honesty on the part of ecclesiastical authorities in dealing with the secular press as well."

In his column for July 29, 1968 Higgins described his experience of participating in a "think-session" on the changing Church sponsored by a Catholic periodical (identified, for some reason, as "XYZ," a thinly-disguised *National Catholic Reporter*). His specific invitation, he said, was to prepare a paper discussing whether the periodical should remain close to the institutional Church in its editorial comments on Church problems. His answer was clear:

"I think XYZ ought to take the same approach to the institutional Church—i.e., a calmly objective, sophisticated, courteous and even-tempered approach which tries to keep things in focus and in balance and is not too easily 'scandalized' or bored or discouraged, disgusted or angered by the disconcerting but inevitable complexities of life. . . .

"The editors, when they write about the institutional Church, ought to lean over backwards to avoid leaving the impression that they are somehow judging the institutional Church from an intellectual ivory tower as completely uninvolved outsiders who, so to speak, are glad that they are not like the rest of their less perspective and less enlightened fellow Catholics.

"If we really believe that the Church is the People of God, and not a clerical bureaucracy, we shouldn't think exclusively in terms of insiders or outsiders or in terms of 'we' (editors) and 'they' (bishops), for example. I am not suggesting, of course, that 'we' should refrain from criticizing 'them' whenever we deem it necesssary to do so. Quite the contrary. All I am saying is that 'we' should do so—and should give the appearance of doing so—as insiders, if you will, rather than outsiders."

On February 24, 1969 he noted with satisfaction that the National Conference of Catholic Bishops had authorized a $300,000 "no-strings-attached" study of the American Catholic priesthood, saying it marked "a permanent change for the better in the attitude of the American bishops" toward religious sociology. . .and, not coincidentally, in plumbing as skillfully as possible the problems that were troubling American priests.

The Yardstick for September 6, 1971 paid tribute to a book written 21 years earlier by Dominican Father Yves Congar that so disconcertingly (and, as it turned out, accurately) forecast the turmoil of the postconciliar era that it was speedily withdrawn from publication. Higgins called the book "a remarkably foresighted preview of things to come," and said that Congar's old warning about a Church divided into traditional and progressive camps still commanded serious attention.

"In some cases," he said, "the dialogue between so-called traditionalists and so-called progressives in the American Church seems to be degenerating, at least in certain conservative circles, into a kind of theological witch hunt or a new form of heresy hunting which is much too spiteful and far too vindictive in tone and fails to make the necessary distinction between those matters which are essential to the faith and those which are open to free and frank discussion and lend themselves to quite legitimate, not to say wholesome, differences of opinion.

"On the other side of the fence, in the so-called liberal or progressive camp, while theological witch hunting, for the most part, is taboo, fraternal charity is sometimes in short supply. Ridiculing the 'opposition' or judging the other fellow's motives and putting the worst possible interpretation on them is a human enough failing, to be sure. But it is one thing to err in this regard and something else again to pretend that hitting below the belt or going for the jugular vein, so to speak, is a virtue and that the practice of fraternal charity in the liberal-conservative dialogue is a sign of weakness or a lack of commitment to the truth."

Higgins was impressed with a pastoral letter on change in the Church issued by the bishops of Ireland in 1972 to mark the tenth anniversary of the opening of the Second Vatican Council. In a column on October 23 of that year, he explained that its basic premise was that change is a part of human life and that in a time of rapid change the world must expect to pay for the skills it has developed. As with every other institution in society, the Church would be affected.

"This strikes me as being a sound pastoral reaction to the phenomenon of change in the life of the Church," he said. The Council did not generate that change, he noted, setting forth a view he would restate on other occasions; but coincided with it, and gave it a certain validity, impetus, and a pastoral and theological respectability. The change would have taken place with or without the Council, Higgins said; the Council served as a safety valve that probably forestalled a disastrous explosion.

Many Catholics, he said, worry that what happened *was* an explosion, but that was not true of the Council Fathers:

"It might be said that the Council Fathers would have been contradicting their own theology—which, by that time, had already been stated in the Constitution on the Church—if, when they got around to discussing the Church in the modern world, they had suddenly reversed themselves and started wringing their hands at the troublesome thought that the Church might be facing a prolonged period of constant change, confusion, and uncertainty."

He quoted from Jesuit Father Avery Dulles, who had expressed concern in *Beyond Dogma* about the lack of a sufficient sense of history on the part of "committed Christians." For many, he said, that failing had ill-prepared them for the changes of our day, although, "in many sections of the Church there are thrilling signs of a new spirit of hope and community now being born."

"This kind of ecclesiology," concluded Higgins, "makes for realism—but not for pessimism, much less despair, about the confusion and uncertainty that lie in store for the pilgrim People of God, not just for a generation or two but (if we take our theology seriously) until the end of time."

As most priests do, George Higgins draws on other members of the priesthood for his closest friendships. But unlike most other priests, the range of close friends goes far beyond the bounds of a single diocese or religious community.

"I really think that George knows more priests than anyone else in the country," a friend remarked with absolute sincerity. "And I mean he *knows* them; he knows where they are and what they're doing. He'll come across a priest from some out-of-the-way diocese, maybe at O'Hare Airport, and he'll reel off half a dozen names. 'How's Jack O'Malley doing? I heard he was getting a new parish. What about McCarthy? Is he out of the hospital yet?' And on it goes."

The assertion is arguable, by any odds, but the election that sent Higgins to the 1971 synod at least makes a case for those who advance it. In any event, Higgins knows a good deal about priests and about the priesthood.

As closely identified with the labor movement as he has been over the years, he rejected the short-lived notion (which surfaced immediately after the Second Vatican Council) that priests might do well to form a labor union, but enthusiastically endorsed the concept of priests' associations and proudly proclaimed his membership in two of them.

The union idea had been floated in 1966 by Father William DuBay, of Los Angeles, and when a reporter asked George Meany if there'd be room for such an affiliate within the AFL-CIO, he replied, somewhat mischievously, that the matter ought to be referred to the president of the International Brotherhood of Teamsters— at the time, Jimmy Hoffa. But it was no laughing matter to some people within the Teamsters, including the editor of a Teamster publication who not only supported the idea but criticized priests who refused to go along with it.

Higgins argued (in The Yardstick for December 5, 1966) that where a union negotiates, a priests' association structures a dialogue; and where a union would use the strike as a weapon, an association would seek to find a consensus. The divisiveness that a union would tend to encourage would be contrary to the spirit of the Council, he added. Most Catholic trade unionists would voice the same feelings, Higgins said.

"This column is not intended to be critical of Father DuBay as an individual," he said. "He, too, has the right to his own opinion with regard to the organization of clerical unions, but. . .I must respectfully disagree with it."

Although he had not lived in Chicago since his seminary days, Higgins stayed in close touch with Chicago priest friends, and with activities in the archdiocese in general. He was an early member of the Association of Chicago Priests (ACP), formed in 1966 by predominantly younger and more liberal priests eager to implement the newly-proclaimed reforms of Vatican II. The adversary relationship that quickly developed between the ACP and Cardinal John Cody encompassed a variety of problems: authority, personality, a new Church struggling with the old.

Higgins, however, was "proud to be a member," and in a 1967 Yardstick column (May 22) described its second annual convention (which attracted 1,200 voting delegates to the Hilton Hotel) as "history-making" for the program of reform it endorsed: open housing, civil rights measures, pulpit exchanges and family visits to draw white and black neighborhoods closer together, peace studies, better working conditions for Church employees.

"Never before, to the best of this writer's knowledge," Higgins said, "have the priests of a given diocese pledged themselves as members of an association, which is empowered, within limits, to act in their name and on their behalf, to assume responsibility for the implementation of such a far-reaching program of social and economic reform." In so doing, he continued, "they started a new and very significant trend in the field of social action. In effect, if not in so many words, they went on record as saying that vigorous leadership in the field of Catholic social action is the responsibility, in varying degrees, of all the priests of a given diocese and one which cannot be delegated—or, worse than that, relegated—to a handful of specialists."

Higgins was no less pleased to be associated with the National Federation of Priests' Councils (NFPC), and he used several Yardstick columns to defend the organization from its conservative critics—who appeared, in the early Seventies, in increasing number and volume. The 1971 NFPC convention in Baltimore, at which delegates adopted a resolution in favor of optional celibacy for the clergy, not surprisingly attracted heavy flak, including what Higgins called "a declaration of open warfare" from *The Wanderer,* the independent lay weekly published in St. Paul.

On April 26, 1971 Higgins scored the tone of the newspaper's criticism, which he said impugned the loyalty and questioned the orthodoxy of the delegates. Its broadside hit not only at the celibacy resolution, but the full sweep of the NFPC program, which it termed revolutionary. Higgins responded by ticking off the other resolutions, which covered a range of political and socio-economic problems, including farm labor, selective conscientious objection, and the war in Vietnam. A.J. Matt, *The Wanderer's* editor-in-chief, had said the program was assembled by an unrepresentative group of "militant priests" who controlled NFPC and were using the organization as "a tool for revolution," which brought on a spirited Higgins response.

"Mr. Matt and his associates at *The Wanderer* are free to disagree with any or all of these resolutions, but they are more than a little naive if they think they can get away with the elaborate hoax of labeling them as 'revolutionary' in the pejorative sense of that ambiguous, not to say slippery, word. Let me say it again: They know better than to try a thing like that. . . . This isn't the first time they have tried to impose their own ultraconservative social philosophy on the entire Catholic community by the disreputable tactic of shouting 'heresy' or its equivalent at the opposition. This time, however, they can hardly expect to pull it off successfully. The priests of the United States, whom they have called upon to repudiate all of the NFPC socioeconomic resolutions without exception, are much too sophisticated, by and large, to be taken in by this familiar ploy. . . . I strongly suspect that the majority of American clergy will disdainfully ignore *The Wanderer's* importunate and somewhat presumptuous overture and, following the lead of Vatican II in this regard, will opt instead, like the mature and sensible Christians that they are, for the utmost freedom of opinion within the Church on controversial socioeconomic matters.''

A year later (May 8-15, 1972), Higgins again sprang to the defense of the NFPC, this time against an anti-NFPC tract written by Jesuit Father Kenneth Baker, then editor of *The Homiletic and Pastoral Review,* and Father Joel Munzing, a Franciscan stationed in northern New Jersey who wrote for several publications. The six-page tract was distributed through the mail to some 13,000 American priests. Its tone clearly incensed Higgins:

''NFPC has made its share of mistakes and, like every other organization I know anything about, is open to criticism on a number of scores. But Baker and Munzing are not content to criticize the federation objectively. They have deliberately set out to destroy the organization by fair means or foul, and some of the means they employ in their report on the federation's last convention are very foul indeed.''

The criticism that stung Higgins most deeply was the assertion that when certain speakers at the 1972 convention called on NFPC members to become involved in political and social action, ''they were thereby denying the sacramental or so-called cultic side of the priestly ministry and were clearly demonstrating that they 'have little use for the idea that the priestly ministry is a religious and spiritual one.' '' The priests were all well known to Higgins: Frank Bonnike (who later left the active ministry), then the NFPC president; theologian Richard McBrien; San Francisco's Gene Boyle; Bob Kennedy and John Fagan, both of Brooklyn. ''While I might quarrel with some of their rhetoric and might disagree with one or other of them on this or that particular point," Higgins said, "I hold all of them in high esteem as zealous and dedicated priests."

The attack on Boyle was particularly strong. Baker and Munzing referred to his "controversial" civil rights involvements, including support for the Black Panthers, prompting Higgins's comment that they were "stooping pretty low—in fact, all the way into the gutter—to undermine the reputation of a wonderfully zealous priest." He listed some of Boyle's accomplishments and areas of pastoral service, then continued:

"I should think that two priests who, through no fault of their own, of course, but by sheer force of circumstances, have had much less experience than that in the ordinary pastoral ministry would be ashamed to sit in pharasaical judgment on the priestliness of a man who has served as effectively as Father Boyle has in such an extraordinarily wide range of challenging pastoral assignments. To suggest that he is preaching a 'humanistic gospel' and that his voluntary transfer from San Francisco to his new assignment on the NFPC staff serves to prove this ugly accusation is, in this writer's judgment, beneath contempt."

There could be only two reasons, Higgins said, for "putting the shiv into Father Boyle" as Baker and Munzing had: "They don't really think that social action is an integral part of the priestly ministry or. . .they don't agree with Father Boyle's particular approach to social action."

Assuming for argument's sake, he said, that it was the latter reason, Higgins concluded: "They are perfectly free to disagree with Father Boyle's approach to social action, but they are kidding themselves if they think that by shouting heresy they can frighten Boyle or any of the rest of us in the social action movement or reduce us to silence. For my own part, while I might disagree with Father Boyle at times. . . . I happen to agree with the main thrust of his approach to social problems. And if that's not to the liking of Baker and Munzing, I am sorry for their trouble. They will simply have to make the most of it."

Higgins was impatient with priests of that era who used the postconciliar period to vent personal frustrations with the Church—such as Father James Kavanaugh, whose 1967 book, *A Modern Priest Looks at His Outdated Church,* attracted national attention. Unhappy with the tone of the book to begin with, and particularly

disturbed when Kavanaugh came up with inane conclusions after
straying into areas such as Catholic-Jewish relations, Higgins bluntly
dismissed the entire effort: "It's a terrible pity that a man of Father
Kavanaugh's native ability has permitted his pent-up disillusionment
with the institutional Church to trap him into the blind alley of enervating and corroding cynicism."

In the ranks of the American clergy, as noted above, Higgins can
number friends by the hundreds. And, not surprisingly, for a man
with such strong opinions, so precisely and publicly expressed, there
are enemies as well. It is due in part to Higgins's politics, to a
liberalism voiced over the years without fear or favor, as he would
put it. Part of it stems from his labor associations, and part, certainly, from his long-standing identification with Jewish causes and
with the state of Israel. And yet another part is due to the Higgins
personality.

"George loves to put the cat among the pigeons," said Msgr.
John Tracy Ellis, the Church historian, during a conversation about
his friend of many years. "He says there's nothing he likes better
than a good fight, and he means it. He likes to get things going,
to stir things up."

It works well when the man on the other side of the table
can hold his own with Higgins and when he, too, likes nothing better than a good fight, as did Msgr. James McHugh during the 1976
staff house encounters on the Ford-Carter presidential campaign.
On the morning after even the steamiest nighttime debates on the
topic, Higgins and McHugh would share breakfast pleasantries as
if they were friends who hadn't met in years.

It wasn't that pleasant for others who were there, however.

"George could simply terrorize the table," said a friend who
was on the staff at the time. "When he tagged you out, you were
out. When that business with Jim McHugh was going on, there were
priests in the house who'd find any excuse to have dinner someplace
else. They just couldn't stand all the noise and all the tension."

In 1980 the late Bishop Rausch, who, as general secretary,
had finally called a halt to that particular debate, recalled his initial
encounter with Higgins, shortly after he was appointed to the U.S.
Catholic Conference staff:

"Msgr. Art Yzermans was in town, and we gathered in a room

where Art was staying, and George did what he does with new staff people—he puts you through a rough session to find out whether you have backbone or you don't, whether you have smarts or you don't, whether you'll work out or you won't. They went on and on, with any new staff priests, and they usually broke up around dawn. It's a rare case when a new priest on the staff didn't go through a night of being hammered by George.

"There were times that you resented it, but you were forewarned that it was going to happen. It was just a case of when. At about five that morning I went off to bed, feeling that I had really been pounded into the ground. But he made me feel that I had passed the test."

Relishing intellectual combat as much as he does, Higgins finds it difficult, perhaps impossible, to understand why, no matter how intense the debate becomes, it should endanger friendships. Again, it's not always that clear to the other party.

Frequently Higgins will lead off a critical book review or a Yardstick comment with a line that says, one way or another, "It grieves me to say this about So-and-So, because we've been such good friends for so many years, but. . ." and then goes on to point out that the hapless friend has written something that adds up to pure drivel. Higgins regrets it if the "friend" takes offense. But they often do.

He has gone this route with Andrew Greeley on a number of occasions. As recently as January 1983 he led off a Yardstick column: "My fellow-diocesan and good friend, Father Andrew Greeley. . ." and proceeded from that point to castigate Greeley for attacks on the bishops' Justice and Peace staff in particular, and Father Bryan Hehir in particular. Some of the "friendly" comments made by Higgins included observations that Greeley's attack was "embarrassingly unprofessional," written in "purple prose." Said Higgins: "Greeley is an extremely competent empirical sociologist, one of the best in the business, but this kind of undisciplined rhetoric bears as little resemblance to empirical sociology as Sunday-supplement astrology bears to scientific astronomy." And as far as Greeley's suggestion that Hehir be fired was concerned: "There is as little chance of that happening as there is of Greeley's flying to the moon on a handmade paper kite." This, the reader imagines, surely puts friendship to the test.

Another case in point involves Msgr. George A. Kelly, the

New York archdiocesan priest who wrote extensively for many years on family life concerns and who has concentrated more recently on problems in the contemporary Church. Higgins's review of his book, *The Crisis of Authority: Pope John Paul II & the American Bishops,* which appeared in *America* June 5, 1982, noted that the two priests had been friends for more than 40 years, and that he was criticizing the book "reluctantly and with a heavy heart." Then he let loose with both barrels.

Kelly's way of dealing with differing theological opinions, Higgins said, "is not to dialogue with those whom he disagrees with, but compulsively to put the worst possible interpretation on their theological statements, to question their motives, and then imperiously to demand that they be silenced. Kelly has done this before in other publications, but he does it with greater frenzy and with wrathful vengeance in his present book. . .which can only be described as a merciless exercise in *odium theologicum* (theological hatred). . . . It gives me no satisfaction to be crossing swords with a friend of such long standing. But the bishops whom Kelly has charged, as a group, with 'appeasement,' disloyalty to the Holy See, and other assorted crimes, are also friends of mine. So are the two dozen or so theologians, scripture scholars, educators, and publicists whom Kelly has savaged in his new book. And what Kelly does to some of these people you wouldn't do to a dog."

The scathing review drew some critical mail to *America's* editors (including one comment, from New York's Msgr. Francis M. Costello, that must have amused Higgins: It described the review as "an unreliable and spiteful analysis" and the reviewer as sounding like Richard Nixon) and a lengthy response from Kelly himself. In part, he said of Higgins:

"His intemperate, and even vituperative, review of *The Crisis of Authority* in *America* magazine is not altogether out of character. But I am pleased to see him emerge as a defender of bishops since a good part of his priestly life has been spent criticizing, and sometimes opposing, them. The last time we confronted each other was one night in 1965 in the Staff House of what would become the U.S. Catholic Conference, where Father Higgins was declaring with certitude, because he wanted it so, that Paul VI would change Catholic doctrine on contraception. We know how wrong he was then not only on a point of fact but on a point of Catholic doctrine as well."

Another who did not take kindly to a typical Higgins "my-good-friend" critique was Saul Alinsky, who fired off an angry letter to Higgins after a column along those lines appeared. You've shown your true colors, Alinsky said bitterly; how dare you call me your friend?

Father John Hotchkin, director of the bishops' ecumenical and interreligious affairs office, recalls that he and Higgins were checking into a Boston hotel for a convention not long after that when Higgins spied Alinsky standing on the other side of the lobby. "Watch this," he said to Hotchkin. He put down his suitcase, strode across the lobby, and threw his arm around Alinsky's shoulder. "Well," he bellowed, "if it isn't my good friend Saul Alinsky!"

Alinsky exploded, but his anger was short-lived. Before long, he and Higgins were back on excellent terms, which was just the way Higgins wanted it.

Many who failed to share in the enthusiasm Higgins's friends felt for him were not, properly speaking, enemies; they simply had questions. How was Higgins able to operate as freely as he did, they wondered? To whom did he answer? How was it that his own views managed to come out as conference policy? Some of the questions came from within the conference itself—from the more conservative-minded bishops, from others who simply were irritated with specific Higgins positions on issues such as farm labor. During the author's long interview with the late Bishop Rausch, the bishop asked at one point that the tape recorder be turned off briefly. In that interval he said that when he was named general secretary of the conference a prominent prelate—whom he identified, with the proviso that the name not be used—told him the job would be difficult, with a number of challenging assignments. Said Bishop Rausch: "He told me that one of them would be to get rid of George Higgins."

Higgins had no apology to offer for his freedom, for the agenda he set for himself (which, as noted earlier, remained essentially the same through three or four title changes and continues that way in his retirement). Most of all, he had no apologies for what he was able to accomplish in that environment, and he was frank about the circumstances that kept him there. Talking about the satisfaction he derived from his long-running work on farm labor, he told the author: "I'd been here long enough so that nobody was going to tell me what to do or what not to do."

All of these elements were part of the background of the news that sent a shock wave through the Church family in the United States, in Rome, and in other parts of the world on October 13, 1978, when the conference announced that Higgins's department—at that point known as the Office of Special Concerns—would be closed the following year, and that Higgins would be asked to take an early retirement, a few weeks short of his 64th birthday. Budget cuts were responsible for the decision, the conference said. This particular move would save about $45,000. As it turned out, it cost an incalculable amount in terms of the conference's reputation.

The decision had been made by the conference's Committee on Research, Plans and Programs, which included the officers (Archbishop John Quinn of San Francisco, then president; Archbishop John R. Roach of St. Paul-Minneapolis, vice president; Archbishop John J. Maguire, then coadjutor of New York, now retired, the treasurer, and Archbishop Thomas Kelly of Louisville, then a bishop and the conference's general secretary) and the immediate past president, Cardinal Joseph Bernardin of Chicago, at the time archbishop of Cincinnati.

Bishop Kelly's explanatory statement went out on the NC News Service wire Monday, October 16. "The financial problems of the conference, both immediate and long range, have caused the conference to take a close look at all of its activities and to discontinue some of them," he said. "When the conference came to the realization that it could not continue to fund the Office of Special Concerns beyond an additional year, Msgr. Higgins was informed of this well in advance. . . . Everyone at the conference is deeply appreciative of the enormous contributions which this extraordinary priest has made to the life of the Church and the nation and we will continue to remain deeply in his debt. We are confident, however, that his eventual retirement from the conference will not end his contributions to the cause of the labor movement and the many national and international issues which he has so eloquently addressed."

A year and a half later, in an interview early in 1980 with the author, Kelly made substantially the same points. "The retrenchment that we were starting to go through then is very visible to us now," he said. "We knew we were going to have to make cuts, and it seemed as if this were an area where we could start. I regretted that it was so badly misperceived."

Cardinal Bernardin, interviewed in March of 1980 in Cincinnati, agreed.

"Basically it was a question of looking for places where the conference might economize," he said. "I don't think the question of Msgr. Higgins's early retirement would have ever come up if we hadn't been faced with an insufficient amount of money, given all the things that the conference was doing. The committee knew that before too long he would be reaching retirement age, and that we did have a department of social development and world peace. Many of the issues that Msgr. Higgins had traditionally addressed over the years were being addressed by that department."

Not many saw it that way. Those in the labor and social action fields where Higgins's name was best known, and even more so his own associates in the Church, read the move as, at best, a mistake of enormous proportions. "As we would say in the streets of Chicago, it was dumb, just dumb," said Msgr. John Egan. Still others found darker motives in the early retirement decision—as did the veteran conference staff member who labeled the official explanation as "hogwash." They felt that personal differences between Higgins and key members of the hierarchy were behind the move; if pressed for specifics, they generally cited the 1976 presidential campaign, memories of which still simmered.

Reaction came in swift and strong, all of it negative. The late Father John Reedy spoke for many when he referred to the decision in his syndicated Catholic press column as "embarrassing." In Pittsburgh, Msgr. Charles Owen Rice thought over the distressing news and concluded: "It is a case of bureaucratic stupidity and arrogance, also a case of the Church aping the business and government worlds, as it organizes, reorganizes, and re-reorganizes its bureaus and staffs." A bishop who had worked with Higgins shook his head sadly as he discussed the furor with the author two years after it took place. "I'm just amazed that the conference leadership didn't really understand what kind of role George Higgins had been playing for the conference through the years, and that all hell was going to break loose when this announcement was made."

Other voices weighed in. Rabbi Marc Tanenbaum told Kelly

that delegates to a national workshop on Christian-Jewish relations "expressed much concern" about the retirement, and labor newsletter publisher John Herling headlined his report on the incident "astounding stupidity." As far as budget considerations were concerned as the reason for the closing of Higgins's office, Herling said: "Nobody believes such poppycock. Rather they see in this act of severance an incredible abandonment of a most sensitive and creative activity which has become one of the glorious careers of our time. . . . He is the ambassador from his Church to the labor movement and the messenger of good sense and understanding from the labor movement to his Church."

But the most telling comments came from within the Church family.

Father Andrew Greeley—past differences, however serious or superficial, put aside—used two consecutive columns (syndicated in the Catholic press) not only to express his deep affection and respect for Higgins, but his displeasure with the hierarchy as well. In characteristically outspoken language, he said:

"In a staff bureaucracy of amateur bunglers and wide-eyed enthusiasts, Higgins has, since memory runs not to the contrary, shone as a beacon light of professionalism. Now, as he approaches his fortieth anniversary in the priesthood, he is unceremoniously kicked out on Massachusetts Avenue because they don't have the few thousand dollars a year necessary to pay his salary. I would think that if they had to fire everyone else in the building first, they should keep Higgins because of his enormous prestige and influence in Washington and in the labor movement.

"It is a cruel, insensitive, and, worst of all, dumb move. In the world of labor and government, where Higgins is considered a genius, the reaction is one of stunned disbelief. The Church can't be that idiotic, can it? Sad to say, I guess it can. . . .

"The Higgins dismissal involves more than a violation of charity, more than a violation of justice; it is a violation of the solemn obligation of the bishops to provide intelligent leadership for the Church. How can you provide that kind of leadership when you treat the most competent man you've had around for the last century like dirt?"

"George Higgins has always been a loyal servant of the national hierarchy, pushing loyalty so far that it sometimes seemed to me that in the name of loyalty he was defending the indefensible.

Occasionally he and I clashed (privately) on this subject, with my arguing that the ineptitude of the leadership of the national conference did not deserve loyalty. I think they have made my point for me. But I am sure that George, being what and who he is, will not speak a word of criticism.

"Two things must be said to those who have ears to listen:

"1. If you are loyal to the national hierarchy, they'll kick you in the teeth.

"2. If Samuel Stritch or Albert Meyer were alive, the conference wouldn't dare get rid of George Higgins after 34 years of loyal service."

In the unlikely event that his point were lost on anyone, Greeley also dispatched a personal letter to Archbishop Quinn as conference president, offering, as "one priest who is free to say what he thinks without fear of reprisal," his thoughts on the matter: "You and the other men responsible for this stupid action have disgraced and humiliated the Church. You are guilty of an injustice which cries to heaven for vengeance. You all should be ashamed of yourselves. When the history books are written about this era, the Higgins dismissal is the one thing for which you will be remembered above all others. Catholics of the future will think even worse of you than we do today. As a mixture of ineptitude and cruelty your action is hard to match in the last two hundred years of Catholic life in America."

Two other comments carried their message in diverse ways.

In a sensitive and articulate private memorandum to Kelly, Father Bryan Hehir dispassionately presented the case for retaining George Higgins. What had been essentially wrong with the committee's decision, he said, was its classification of Higgins as "simply another staff professional." Higgins, he continued, had "no peer or analogue" on the staff, and because of that singular stature the budgetary reasons given were not credible in the eyes of the general public. He personally believed that no animus toward Higgins was involved in the decision, Hehir said, but what does that say about the USCC vision? He continued:

"John A. Ryan, John Courtney Murray, and George Higgins are the only names presently guaranteed to be in the history of Catholic social thought in the United States. . . . How does quality of this kind become dispensable? The unenviable situation facing the USCC is either to answer that question or suffer the disbelief and suspicion of interested observers who will remain convinced that sinister motives are behind the Higgins decision.''

Hehir proceeded to describe the "reverence" with which international labor delegates had treated Higgins at a meeting which had taken place not long before, and continued:

"The point here is that a subtle but significant difference exists between conventional (even competent) performance of a task and excellence. George Higgins is acknowledged as a person of excellence in the way no other member of the Catholic social action community is. The inevitable incontrovertible result of allowing George Higgins to leave the USCC for any reason other than an act of God is the perception that the conference is willing to exchange excellence for conventional performance. . . . The resources of the USCC are such that it cannot afford to let George Higgins go, either for budgetary reasons now or for retirement policy in 1981. Only death or senility are convincing reasons for George Higgins to leave; happily neither seem now to be threatening.''

In its lead editorial for October 26, 1978, *The Tablet,* the venerable but always lively newspaper of the Brooklyn Diocese, said it another way: "For 34 years they've let George do it; now it looks like someone's trying to do it to George.''

To outward appearances, George Higgins was the calm at the center of the storm.

"I am sleeping well as usual and my appetite, alas, is very good," he wrote to Father Theodore Hesburgh on October 12, 1968. He was responding to an invitation from the Notre Dame president, relayed by Msgr. Egan, to consider a position at the university. "In short," the letter continued, "I am not the least concerned about my personal status. Thanks to good friends like yourself, I feel confident that, come what may, I will be able to lead a useful life in the years, however few or many, that lie ahead.''

Some of his closest friends, however—Bishop Rausch, Bishop McCarthy, Msgr. Frank Lally—maintained that Higgins's calm exterior masked a deep hurt at the time. The next few lines of the letter to Hesburgh might have hinted at just that:

"Needless to add, however, I am greatly concerned about the future of the conference. Nobody, of course, is indispensable. In my own case, I know that perfectly well. On the other hand, I would hate to see the work that I have been doing go down the drain, and, if I were to leave within the next 12 months, I am afraid that might happen for the simple reason that, so far as I can see, nobody would be hired to take my place.''

There were traces of Higgins's deeper feelings, too, in his reflections on that period—and of his relations with the conference in general—in the course of a long interview with the author during the 1980 UAW convention in California.

"Egan and some of the others thought that I was taking this too calmly," he said. "But to me it wasn't a personal thing. I can say that controversy doesn't bother me, personally, and I've never seen any reason why you couldn't have a real good argument and still be good friends. But it just wasn't personal. It's possible, although I don't know this, that some of the people in connection with my case might have gone up to Joe Bernardin and said, 'Well, you got Higgins because he disagreed with you in 'seventy-six, but I don't know. I deliberately never moved a finger on that thing, and I didn't want to know what other people were doing. I just didn't want to get involved.

"I know there were some people who just felt I'd been around too long. I don't know about the staff, but I think it would be true of a good number of the bishops.

"There were two points of view with regard to the staff. I held very strongly, maybe a minority view in the building, that they're making a terrible mistake by having this constant turnover in staff. We've had 110 priests go through that building in the last 12 years—roughly, that is, maybe 110 or 112. Nobody believes that when you give them that figure. I just think that's an impossible way to run a railroad. Some stay for two years, some stay for three years. I don't think they can get enough seniority, experience, call it prestige, in such a short period. It takes a long time to establish yourself in certain areas. For example, I consider it important that the Church have some contact with the UAW. But you don't get that in a three-year staff. I've been at every UAW convention since 1943. That takes a lot of time just sitting it out, sometimes just sitting for a week and listening to the debate. You don't bring a man in for three years and expect him to do that. They tend to think that if you can put somebody in a parish for three years, you can put him in a chancery for three years, or anyplace else—that we're interchangeable, like soldiers.

"One reason they don't want you around too long, and they wouldn't admit this, is that they don't want you to become too independent. Some of the bishops probably regretted they had allowed somebody like me to be in there so long that they couldn't do anything with me. I never defied them as such, but I just don't think it will happen again.

"But it's more important than ever now to be out there representing the Church. All of a sudden everybody is beginning to realize that it's a new ball game, and that's why I intend to keep on what I've been doing, whether they like it or not. I don't need the title of USCC behind me. I am going to continue to go and do what I have done in the past. The great fear I have with the conference is with the budget cuts. They are going to become a sideshow. Take care of the essential ecclesiastical things they have to deal with, but not have enough staff around to freewheel it a bit, and to get out into the big world. . . .

"Many people misunderstood this incident, when they wanted me to leave. I said, and I was being very honest about it, that the conference had been very good to me. They created that job. When I told them I didn't want to be director of the department, they had every reason to say, 'Take your time, but by Christmas you'll have to be out of here.' Instead they said, 'We've created a job for you.' That's what they did, and I'm sure it was Rausch who did it. But I could hardly complain that they were cutting the ground out from under me. They leaned over backwards to accommodate me for ten or fifteen years. This was all a free ride as far as I was concerned.

"I'm disappointed with some of the changes that will take place because of the budget cuts. I think it's the end of our contact with the labor movement, and not only the labor movement, but the other things that are related to it. They don't have anybody who can do it. Farm labor, too. What happens when Cesar Chavez comes to us and says, 'We need some help'? There won't be anybody here on the staff to help.

"But you can be sure there'll never be another freelancer around, and I don't blame them. I understand their position very well. I'd been there for years and years when this happened. They don't want to take the chance of having somebody with that kind of seniority.

"I know a lot of the bishops on a first-name basis, and on a drinking basis, too. And over the years you do a lot of favors for them. They aren't adverse to calling upon you when they want something done, sometimes at some inconvenience. But that's all right; I have a good relationship with them. The one thing I would *not* do for them—and this is the reason some of them would have been happy to see me go, and the reason I was never invited to their meetings—was to play games. I would say what I thought.

"The only time I was ever at a board meeting was a few years ago, when the conference was going to withdraw its support from the farm workers' boycott. I think it was Rausch who said I'd better come in. I told them I completely disagreed with the resolution, that it would be a disaster. I said I'd heard the California bishops say it was a California problem, but that was nonsense. That would be like saying that a strike against General Motors is a Detroit problem, when we're driving GM cars all over the country. If you want to keep California products in California and never sell them anywhere else, I said, then you can call it a California problem. But as things stand now, it's not. It didn't make a damn bit of difference if they liked it or not—and they didn't—but I'd made it clear: you ask me to speak and I'm going to speak. It's up to you to make the decision.

"And to be honest about it, I guess that if I were the general secretary or the conference president, I wouldn't want too many people around who had that kind of seniority."

Higgins himself did nothing to reverse the conference's early-retirement decision. "He was really magnificent," Cardinal Bernardin said. "He was marvelous during this whole time. He wasn't the one putting pressure on us, but I think he was pleased that there were others who were."

Indeed there were others, and their efforts were carefully orchestrated by an inner core of planners that included Bishop McCarthy, Msgr. Egan, and Msgr. Geno Baroni, the onetime USCC urban affairs expert who was assistant secretary for Housing and Urban Development in the Carter administration. All of the plans were coordinated by the late Nevila McCaig, Higgins's secretary, who conducted a kind of battle headquarters in her sixth-floor office at the conference. Higgins, of course, realized that protest efforts were under way, but literally had no idea what they involved.

Archbishop Kelly broke the news about the committee's decision to Higgins on a Sunday morning, and the following day, when

Higgins was attending a meeting in Florida, called Miss McCaig in
to give her the same information. Caught by surprise, she responded
angrily, much more so than had Higgins. ("The man had every right
to fire me," she confessed in an interview in 1980. "I was very blunt
about the whole thing.") At any rate, she began notifying key people of what had taken place, and plans for a protest began to mount
almost immediately.

"There was just no common sense to that decision," Egan
said in an interview. "I knew right away this was going to be a public
thing. I felt that the labor movement would be stunned by it. It would
hurt our Catholic labor relationships. I thought everybody from the
White House down to the farm workers would be affected by this,
and would question it. I felt that if the decision went through it would
be to the detriment of the total social action effort of the Roman
Catholic Church, and that it would affect the bonds of ecumenism
here and across the country. So I called up George and said, 'I'm
coming to Washington. And unless you forbid me to do something,
it sounds like we have to go to war.' "

"We got together for lunch, and George gave me the story,
as much as he knew about it. I told him I thought it should be
reversed, and asked if he'd mind if I started to mobilize our friends.
'Jack, I'm going under a tree,' he said. 'Do whatever you want.'

"The thing really began to develop," said Egan. "What we
did was to divide off organizations, sections of the country, bishops,
archbishops. . .we went to work."

Bishop McCarthy recalled his feelings as well. "One of the
things that generated so much anger," he said, "was the fact that
George had been so loyal to the Church and to the conference. He
could be irascible, but you couldn't get a better company man than
George Higgins when the doors open on Monday morning. Inter-
nally he's their severest critic, but he's been a straight company man
for 40 years, following straight company policy."

McCarthy, Egan, and Baroni held a strategy meeting in
Washington and decided to contact key people across the country
in various church and labor positions, as well as leaders of Jewish
organizations. They would ask bishops and others in the Church to
express their feelings about Higgins directly to conference officials.
For those outside the Church, it was suggested that they take an
approach that would say, in effect: "Look, I don't want to interfere
in your internal affairs, but do you realize how much George Hig-

gins means to our organization, to our interests? Does this decision mean that the Church is backing off its commitment in this area?'' Those questions would be addressed not only to conference officials, but to leaders of influential large-city archdioceses as well.

"Our job was to put out on the wires as quickly as possible what had actually happened," McCarthy said, "and to get somebody to do something about it."

Two years later, Bishop Rausch recalled his own telephone call from Egan. "His voice wasn't one of pleading," he said; "it was more like a command: 'You've got to do something!' Although I must say, I didn't need that command."

Miss McCaig tactfully stayed in the background. She did keep McCarthy, Egan, and Baroni informed about developments in the office (Higgins was away on a retreat in New York at this point), while they kept her posted on their progress. Egan discovered that the campaign was easy to sell.

"When you have a candidate like George Higgins, you're dealing with Mr. Clean," he said with a chuckle. "All you had to do was say, 'This is the situation.' You'd have an archbishop answer simply, 'Jack, what do you want me to do?' Or the head of a labor union would say, 'Just tell me what has to be done.'

"We didn't want overkill, of course. All we wanted was to have George reinstated, without embarrassing the bishops' committee, without embarrassing the administrative board. Everything was done very quietly. And the response was overwhelming. We also tried to keep controls. The bishops weren't snowed under with ten thousand letters. They did get maybe three hundred letters, from three hundred significant people. And that's what was important."

Other friends of Higgins made contributions as well, some of them old Washington comrades. "I read about the incident in *The Washington Post*," said the ADA's Joseph Rauh. "We closed down business in this town for a couple of days to get them to keep George on." Arthur Goldberg was in San Francisco when he heard the news and promptly phoned Archbishop Quinn (using an old friend at the White House switchboard to track down the number) to request an immediate appointment.

"He told me to come at four o'clock, and he was as pleasant as could be," said Goldberg. " 'Archbishop, I have to be very candid with you,' I said. I asked him to forgive me for being presumptuous, but that George was a national asset, not just an asset to the

Church. I told him I thought it was an outrageous thing. I said the reason could only be that the Church disagrees with his lifelong activities. He told me that he hadn't realized the widespread implications I had described, and that he thought the matter should be reviewed. At which point I dropped it. When someone says that, it's enough. The next week I invited the archbishop to have dinner with us, and then he invited us to his place in San Francisco. We've been friends ever since, and I never mentioned George's name after that time."

The protests accomplished what their strategists had hoped.

"There was pressure from many different people," Cardinal Bernardin said. "Some people simply did not accept the reason that had been given. They suspected that some other motive might have been present. And in any case they felt that he had been of such great service that his connection with the conference should not be terminated in this way. Well, you can argue that poor judgment was used in focusing on this office, but I don't think that you can quarrel with the motivation.

"Now, I was a member of this committee, and had gone along with the decision. But once I became aware of the way that it was being interpreted—once I realized that this might be looked upon by the public as something that was very offensive to Msgr. Higgins—then I was one of the first ones on that committee to say that we must back down, withdraw. I went along with it because at the time we were under pressure to trim the budget, and this seemed the logical thing to do. When the uproar occurred I took another look at it. I said, 'I don't think we can do this. If we do it may be interpreted as an effort on our part to disassociate ourselves from what he has stood for.' It seemed to me that we didn't take all the factors into consideration. So we reversed it."

"The committee never wanted to get rid of George at all," Archbishop Kelly said in a separate interview. "And they were sorry to lose his services. But you could see that it was coming, and we knew that we were going to have to make the adjustment sometime. I regretted that it was so badly misperceived."

Bernardin notified Higgins of the committee's change of heart—reaching him by phone in Los Angeles—and the following day, the Saturday before the bishops' annual fall meeting would begin in Washington, informed the administrative board that the proposal had been dropped. The decision staved off a probable debate within the board, and a sure floor fight at the general meeting. (As it was, a committee was formed from administrative board membership to recommend measures that would rein in the committee's power somewhat.)

At the general meeting itself Higgins received a magnificent round of applause from the bishops ("Sitting there in his inimitable way," Rausch recalled, "eyes closed, red as a beet, probably feeling down deep a tremendous sense of satisfaction in the confidence that was shown him"). After an informal "victory dinner" at an Italian restaurant in Washington not long after—with McCarthy, Egan, Baroni, and a few other close friends—the early retirement issue faded into the background. Some might have preferred to keep it alive. For Higgins, it was already mentally filed with the stuff of ancient history.

Two years later it became official. On June 6, 1980 NC News Service carried the announcement that Msgr. George G. Higgins would be retiring on Labor Day, taking a position at Catholic University. The official announcement seemed woefully inadequate to the task:

"Msgr. Higgins has been a long-time supporter of the labor movement and an activist in the civil rights movement in the United States and the human rights movement abroad.

"He was a member of the U.S. delegation which returned St. Stephen's Crown to Hungary and was an adviser to the U.S. delegation to the Belgrade Conference reviewing implementation of the 1975 Helsinki agreement on European security and cooperation and human rights.

"He is chairman of the public review board of the United Auto Workers and a member of the executive committee of the Leadership Conference on Civil Rights.

"A native of Chicago, Msgr. Higgins attended St. Mary of the Lake Seminary in Mundelein, Ill., and was ordained in 1940. He received a doctorate in 1944 from the Catholic University of America, where he taught in the economics department."

Archbishop Kelly added to the official announcement, praising Higgins for his "exceptional service," and for his "unique blend of candor, conviction, and commitment to principle."

A round of farewells followed, a round which had already begun, in fact, with the Goldberg dinner honoring him in January

1980. There, as he did throughout the year, he thanked the bishops for allowing him the freedom to operate as he had during the years with the conference (and, taking his cue from the then-unresolved Iranian crisis, said that "Catholics, without fear or favor, must stand up and be counted, in season and out of season, in defense of Israel's right to exist as a sovereign and independent nation within secure and stable boundaries"). Kelly, on hand to represent the conference, said, "You have kept us up on the mark over the years."

On May 17, speaking at the Catholic University commencement, where he received one of many honorary doctorates, he urged graduates to look beyond conformity as their guideposts to the future: "Though some would prefer to think that unity in the Church and in Church-related institutions means uniformity, and that opposition, of necessity, is synonymous with disloyalty, the study of theology and the study of history, which, unfortunately, seems to be losing ground even in our better universities, suggests that there may be something lacking in their understanding of the nature of the Church and the nature of a Catholic university."

The citation accompanying the honorary doctorate was unusually eloquent. It read, in part:

"Predisposed by his seminary experience in the Archdiocese of Chicago, a young priest pursuing his doctorate during World War II prepared himself to follow in the steps of Monsignor John A. Ryan, Bishop Francis J. Haas, and other pioneers through organizational and journalistic effort based in the secretariat of the American hierarchy. No priest has ever been closer to the American labor movement. Few can have been as well informed or as balanced in judgment. Through his weekly column, 'The Yardstick,' countless numbers of Americans have gained awareness of the relevance of Christian values in a complex industrial society. With admiration for his attainment in his special apostolate, the Catholic University of America confers upon her own loyal son, the Reverend Monsignor George Gilmary Higgins, the degree of doctor of laws, *honoris causa*."

A day later, awarding its own honorary doctorate, King's College in Wilkes-Barre addressed Higgins: "Christ's priest and Newman's gentleman, we recognize in you one whose life has been dedicated as a teacher of social justice, a defender of America's workers and the poor, an advocate of civil and human rights, and a facilitator of Jewish-Christian relations."

Higgins's final Labor Day statement, that venerable and honorable institution that lingered on from the old NCWC days, called for, in the face of crippling budget cuts, a vigorous defense of the needs of the poor.

"Under the pretext or pretense of managing our economy," he said, "social programs are being severely cut back, labor's right to organize is being effectively thwarted in many industries, unemployment has been allowed to rise to intolerable levels, and the poor and the aged are being left to their own devices for survival." The effort to "turn back the clock" on society's concern for the poor raises serious questions about the future, he continued:

"Are we in danger of becoming an increasingly atomized society in which private gain is placed above social and religious values? Will our national and global communities be torn apart by the struggle for limited resources? Will our economic problems be 'solved' at the expense of the poor and the weak both at home and abroad?

"The answer depends on our willingness to place the values of human dignity and equality at the heart of the debate over our nation's future."

As retirements go, if retirement conjures up images of sitting back and taking it easy, this one fails to make the grade. George Higgins, in good health, has been as busy as always: speaking, traveling, consulting, still charting his daily agenda with the help of a morning paper. And mostly, he continues to teach—not in a formal way, for the most part, but through the column, which continues to appear each week, and in the talks he gives on college campuses throughout the country.

He will talk about changes in the world and changes in the Church, often repeating his observation that the Second Vatican Council acted as a "providential safety valve" for changes that would have taken place one way or another. He concedes that the changes are not always easy to deal with, and that as the Church continues to experience the phenomenon of rapid change, its people can become confused and discouraged. He expresses concern that in setting up new structures to cope with the changes in its own life, the Church may become more introverted, less open to the world. And that, he says, would be turning its back on a primary responsibility.

In explaining that, he capsulizes in a paragraph the message he has attempted to spread down through the years:

" As a religious institution, the Church must work for justice, by the constant proclamation of the gospel, by denouncing violations of justice, by education, by forming the faithful to take part in political action aimed at achieving justice, and by organizing programs or projects aimed at helping the poor, the weak, and the oppressed. The Church has an indispensable role to play in supporting the efforts of the poor and the disadvantaged. The Church must become, without fear or favor, the champion of the poor in our society."

INDEX

Gerald M. Costello has been a newspaperman since his graduation from the University of Notre Dame in 1952, working in the daily, weekly, and religious journalism fields. He is the founding editor of two award-winning diocesan weeklies: *The Beacon,* of Paterson, N.J., in 1967, and *Catholic New York,* of the New York Archdiocese, in 1981. His first book, *Mission to Latin America,* published in 1979, describes the successes and failures of Catholic missionaries from the United States working in Latin America. He and his wife, Jane, are the parents of six children.